Twayne's United States Authors Series

EDITOR OF THIS VOLUME

Kenneth Eble

University of Utah

Randolph Bourne

TUSAS 408

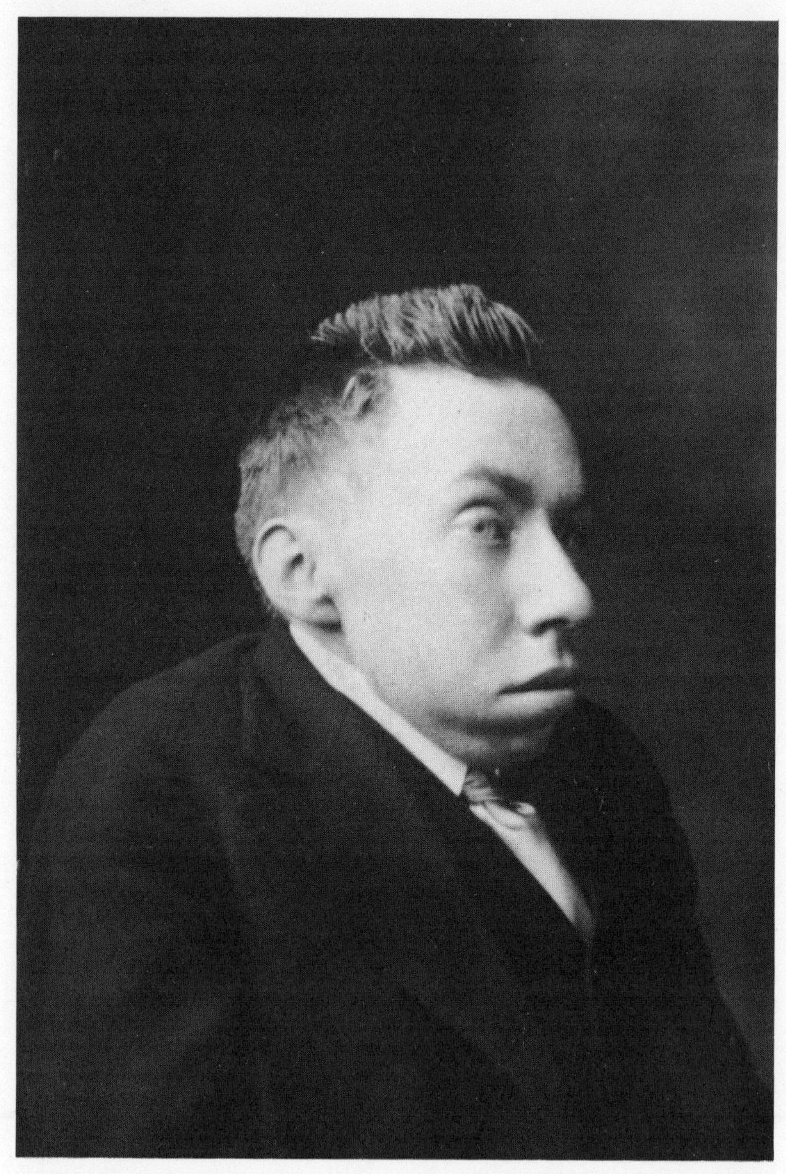

Photo: courtesy of Columbia University

Randolph Bourne

RANDOLPH BOURNE

By JAMES R. VITELLI
Lafayette College

TWAYNE PUBLISHERS
A DIVISION OF G.K. HALL & CO., BOSTON

Published in 1981 by Twayne Publishers
A Division of G.K. Hall & Co.

Printed on permanent/durable acid-free paper and bound
in the United States of America

First Printing

Library of Congress Cataloging in Publication Data

Vitelli, James R 1920–
Randolph Bourne.

(Twayne's United States authors series; TUSAS 408)
Bibliography: p. 175–92
Includes index.
1. Bourne, Randolph Silliman, 1886–1918.
2. Authors, American—20th century—Biography.
PS3503.08Z93 818'.5209 [B] 80-26550
ISBN 0-8057-7337-1

For K.D., Jeff, 'Oise, Steve, and Lil

Contents

About the Author

James R. Vitelli is Chairman of the English Department at Lafayette College in Easton, Pennsylvania, where he initiated and long served as Chairman of the Program in American Civilization. He has a B.A. degree from the College of Wooster in Wooster, Ohio, and an M.A. and Ph.D. in American Civilization from the University of Pennsylvania. He has been a Fulbright lecturer in American Studies at the University of Trieste, Italy, and Visiting Lecturer in American Literature at the University of Bombay, India. He is the author of *Van Wyck Brooks* in the Twayne USA series and of *Van Wyck Brooks: A Reference Guide*, G.K. Hall; in India he edited, with an introduction, *An Amazing Sense*, selected letters and poems of Emily Dickinson; he has written articles and reviews in *Pennsylvania History, Bucknell Review*, *New England Quarterly, The Cabellian*, and elsewhere.

Preface

Randolph Silliman Bourne, self-styled "literary radical," was born on May 30, 1886, in Bloomfield, New Jersey. He died December 23, 1918, in New York City, aged 32, a victim of the influenza epidemic of that postwar year.

A brief life, a tragically shortened career—these are the first romantic ingredients for the making of a myth about a personality. There must be more, of course, for the myth to endure, as the myth of Randolph Bourne has. Something in the personality or the way it has been given form for public recognition must come together with something in the culture which reacts to it: the personality is looked upon and becomes representative, symbolic of cultural need or desire, some reflex of fear or dread. This essay seeks to show what more there is in the writings of Bourne that persistently and recurringly has made him available for rediscovery as a writer, a critic of America, and as a personality who is important to Americans.

Randolph Bourne not only belongs on the list of creative spirits whose lives were rudely ended in the midst of high youthful promise—a John Keats, a Stephen Crane, all the other sung and unsung Lycidases and Adonaises for whom, recalling their youth, we weep. In one sense, he is entitled to head the list as a kind of spokesman for them all. The short life, the career ironically terminated at a moment of great expectations, are all the more susceptible to translation into myth because Bourne made "youth" and all the inchoate desires associated with that stage of growth his major theme and subject. He did so in a way that made for intimate connections with the culture of America. Youth—the word, the concept, the experience, and especially the expression of that experience as a value for Americans—was peculiarly his possession, almost, indeed, his creation.

Youth has also been the peculiar possession of Americans, and again, indeed, almost an American creation, at least in the new meanings and values which the historical experience of Americans has given it in the twentieth century. A self-consciously new and therefore, in the metaphor of personality, "youthful" nation had from the outset prized the virtues and especially the energy conventionally associated with youth. The parent-child metaphor, given currency in the American Revolution against a tyrannical parent, had Americans proudly young. On the metaphorical level, however, the founding of the nation had America leaping swiftly from childhood to adulthood. That might have put a strain on the metaphor. But on the personal level too there was little conscious recognition of any intervening stage or stages in the individual's life cycle. For most early Americans, as Kenneth Kenniston[1] has observed, early life began in infancy, moved quickly into a period of childhood lasting until puberty—occurring much later than it does now—and then they entered some form of apprenticeship for the adult world. Not until after the turn of the twentieth century, in 1904 according to Kenniston, with the publication of G. Stanley Hall's "monumental work" *Adolescence: Its Psychology and Its Relations to Physiology, Anthropology, Sociology, Sex, Crime, Religion, and Education*, was a further "pre-adult stage widely recognized." The ensuing discussion provoked by Hall's book widely popularized "adolescence" until it became a household word and a concept now "unshakably enshrined in our view of human life."

Once Hall had defined "adolescence," as Kenniston further remarks, it became possible to look back in history and find men and women "who had shown the hallmarks of this stage long before it was identified and named." At about the same time, American society was experiencing a major historical transformation, moving from an agrarian to an urban, industrial "age," and onto a world stage with other "adult" nations. Massive waves of new immigrants arrived, leaving "fatherlands" and "motherlands" to become new young Americans. Not surprisingly, therefore, it became possible for Americans to look back upon America's history and, reasserting a metaphor of personality, see an age of innocence in its recent past and address themselves to the present problems of "America's Coming-of-Age."

The coming together on both the personal and the national level of public concerns with growth and development, accompanied and assisted by a rising interest in psychology, seems no coincidence in retrospect. As Kenniston avers, Hall's concept of adolescence reflected "a real change in the human experience, a change intimately tied to the new kind of industrial society that was emerging in America and Europe." On the other hand, it *is* a coincidence, that in the same year, 1904, when Hall released his concept of adolescence upon the public consciousness, Randolph Bourne, just graduated from high school and thwarted by failing family resources from entering Princeton University, underwent, as he later called it, "my transvaluation of values." Thus began the gathering and shaping of impressions that in another decade's time would make him, in Van Wyck Brooks's phrase, "the flying wedge of the younger generation."

Bourne achieved that status by successfully joining the personal and the social concerns of his generation. He prevails as myth because he succeeded in identifying youth with America, more particularly with "the promise of America." The myth of Randolph Bourne is enduring because it is also what Van Wyck Brooks once proposed to call "The America Myth."

Bourne chose what Kenniston has called the "venerable but vague" term "youth" rather than the more clinical sounding "adolescence" as the code word with which he sounded America. As Hall had done with adolescence, Bourne addressed himself to the psychology of youth and explored its relations to all the areas—excepting crime—listed in Hall's lengthy title; but the venerability of "youth" permitted also a long poetic reach into culture and, hence, more myth-making possibilities.

But in remarkable ways Bourne anticipated Kenneth Kenniston's more recent attempt to redefine "youth" in our time as "*a previously unrecognized stage of life*, a stage that intervenes between adolescence and adulthood." Like adolescence when Hall first "discovered" it, youth is not new in any absolute sense, but it is new in that "this stage of life is today being entered not by tiny minorities of unusually creative or unusually disturbed young men and women, but by millions of young people in the advanced nations of the world."[2] Bourne is one of those figures who promoted the historical emergence of Kenniston's "youth," and who has been rediscovered by members of each new younger generation since his own as a personality who had been a youth before them. To a remarkable degree Bourne gave voice to or embodied all the major themes and transformations which Kenniston has proposed in defining an ideal type or model for his concept of youth. Bourne is, to paraphrase Van Wyck Brooks, "youth incarnate." Had he not existed, like Kenniston we'd have had to invent him. In a sense, the myth of Randolph Bourne *is* that invention.

JAMES R. VITELLI

Lafayette College
Easton, Pennsylvania

Acknowledgments

After long years of studied attention to Randolph Bourne, commencing with my associated interest in Van Wyck Brooks during graduate school years in the late 1940s, I have accumulated more debts than I can possibly enumerate with full fidelity and accuracy.

I am most consciously grateful to several generations of Lafayette College students who have repeatedly assured me that Randolph Bourne was still "usable" and "relevant" to them on a personal plane.

I am grateful to the Trustees of Lafayette College for twice granting me leaves of absence: one for a full year on a Humanities Enrichment grant, and again for a half-year sabbatical; on the first I completed most of my research and study, and the second gave me the time to put my several drafts in order.

I am grateful for the kind assistance given me by staff members of the Rare Books and Manuscripts division of the Butler Library of Columbia University, and for permission granted me by Mr. Kenneth A. Lohf, Librarian for Rare Books and Manuscripts, to quote from many of the materials in Columbia's Bourne Collection: from the manuscript of Bourne's student essay, "What Plato Means to Me," from letters of Stanley M. Bligh to Bourne, and several others of Bourne's correspondents.

I am grateful to Mr. Eric Sandeen for his generous aid in several matters of identification in Bourne's letters and for his readily granting me permission to cite and quote from his comprehensive edition of Bourne's letters. The publication of that edition marks Mr. Sandeen as the most meticulous and assiduous of researchers into the story of Randolph Bourne. Mr. Lohf kindly acquiesced to my request that I cite Mr. Sandeen's edition for the convenience and usefulness to others which that permits. Columbia University possesses the originals or the typescripts of most of the letters in Mr. Sandeen's edition, and most of these I inspected first in the Bourne Collection there. For others, I am indebted, as I have been for many years, to Ms. Neda Westlake and others of the staff at the Rare Book Room of the Van Pelt Library at the University of Pennsylvania for their assistance in permitting me access to and use of materials in the Van Wyck Brooks Collection and for some items in the Dreiser Collection.

For innumerable little assists, to me as an unknown visitor, I acknowledge here my indebtedness to staff members of the Library at Bowdoin College where I was privileged to work through a Maine fall, winter, spring, and summer, 1971–1972, and similarly, where I was known, to the staff of the Skillman Library at Lafayette College, especially to Mr. Ronald E. Robbins and Mr. Daniel A. Evans who patiently tracked down and retrieved hard-to-get printed sources for me.

For the work in print by other students of Bourne, my acknowledgment of indebtedness appears elsewhere, but I should like to single out here a work which was a starting point for me, by one of my own generation, Mr. Vincent Broderick's Princeton University senior thesis, "Randolph Bourne" (1941), and John Adam Moreau's thoroughly researched biography, *Randolph Bourne: Legend and Reality* (Washington, D.C.: Public Affairs Press, 1966).

For their patience and skill in the typing of an ever-changing manuscript, including careful correction of my own errors, my thanks to Marilyn Kastenhuber and Arlene Ahles.

Finally, for insights which neither they nor I were fully conscious of at the time, I am grateful to my own sons and daughters, who moved from childhood into youth, during the late 1960s and early 1970s, more precipitously and amid more widespread conflicting currents and countercurrents of cultural change than were ever experienced by Bourne and the generation he spoke for. The experiences were theirs, but something of what I saw and heard and felt has probably entered into the pages that follow.

Chronology

1886 May 30, Randolph Silliman Bourne born in Bloomfield, N.J., first son of Sarah Barrett and Charles R. Bourne.

1890 Suffers from spinal tuberculosis resulting in further physical deformity.

1896 Father leaves household about this time.

1901 Studies English, Latin (4 years), Greek (3 years), German, physics, music, geometry.

1903 June 28, graduates from high school; delivers commencement oration, "Washington's Campaigns in New Jersey." Passes entrance exams to Princeton University, but uncle, Halsey Barrett, lawyer, otherwise supporting the family, refuses to provide college support.

1904 The year of his "transvaluation of values," as he later says. Jobhunting.

1904–1909 Employed by Frederick A. Hoschke, organist, in a home-factory, turning out piano-roll music, and as a piano accompanist in music studios above Carnegie Hall.

1909 Applies to Columbia University, wins a scholarship, and enrolls in September.

1910 January, first published piece in the *Columbia Monthly;* becomes a regular contributor; May editorial announces his election to the editorial board.

1911 Becomes editor of *Columbia Monthly.* "The Two Generations," in the *Atlantic Monthly.*

1912–1913 Receives master's degree from Columbia, with thesis entitled "A Study of the 'Suburbanizing' of a Town [Bloomfield] and the Effects of the Process upon its Social Life."

1913 March, "The Life of Irony," in *Atlantic Monthly* and first book, *Youth and Life*; July 5, sails for Europe,

	having been awarded a fellowship by Columbia, permitting a year's travel.
1913–1914	Travels in Europe.
1914	Returns to United States. Takes up residency with old Columbia friend, Carl Zigrosser, at quarters on 335 E. 31st St., New York. November 7, the first number of the *New Republic* appears with Bourne's first contribution, "In a Schoolroom."
1915	March, goes to Gary, Indiana, for *New Republic* to observe and report on the school experiment there.
1915–1916	Falls in and out of love. Friendship with Zigrosser and other old friends strained; meets Van Wyck Brooks, Floyd Dell, Paul Rosenfeld, James Oppenheim.
1916	January, *The Gary Schools*. November, first number of the *Seven Arts*.
1917	April, first two articles appear in the *Seven Arts*, "The Puritan's Will to Power," and the unsigned supplement "American Independence and the War." *Education and Living*.
1917	Part of summer spent with Van Wyck Brooks at Cos Cob, Connecticut. Bourne's war articles appearing in the *Seven Arts*. October, last issue of the *Seven Arts*.
1918	Writes for *Dial*, now moved from Chicago to New York. Plans marriage.
1918	December 19, Bourne, ill, moves into apartment of Agnes de Lima and Esther Cornell, on 18 W. 8th Street. December 23, dies, victim of the influenza epidemic of that year.

CHAPTER 1

The Forming of the Myth

I The Person and the Life

THE first essential fact about Randolph Bourne that one must confront is the literally physical fact which everyone who ever met him had immediately to see and come to terms with; his physical appearance. He was a hunchback, a dwarf in a twisted frame, and with a face to match, out of balance with a misshapen ear and a mouth permanently askew in grimace—consequences of two early tragedies, a "terribly messy birth," as he described the cause of his facial deformity, and the spinal tuberculosis suffered at the age of four that trapped him forever in a crippled body. Add then to this fact, for those who may never have heard of Bourne, the knowledge that, burdened with this handicap, he nevertheless went on to become a writer, asserting his personality as a powerful spokesman for a whole generation of young men and women. Like those who first met him in person and, recoiling from him, then discovered with surprise and awe something of the vibrant personality behind the grotesque mask, we must acknowledge that we are already in the presence, at least potentially, of a figure of mythical dimensions.

The contradiction between appearance and achievement, the way the initial shock of meeting the grotesque visage is topped, then abrogated or neutralized by the succeeding shock of the discovery of humanity behind the mask, are all too forceful to explain or account for, in the ordinary discourse of reason. We might resort to psychology to explain our ambivalent, conflicting reactions, or to the mythology of ugliness and to the history of the roles assigned by various cultures, including our own, to the dwarf, the hunchback, the physical caricatures of humanity in our midst.

Very few of those people who actually met him, and of whom we have a record of their reactions to his physical presence, responded with unalloyed repulsion. Amy Lowell, herself an obese caricature of a woman, is almost singular in reversing the usual recorded experience. After a first fairly amicable and mutually approving meeting of the two she reportedly concluded that Bourne was a "weakling," and that his deformity showed in his "tortured and twisted mentality" and in everything he wrote. The more typical pattern of response was that of Ellery Sedgwick. The *Atlantic Monthly* editor who assisted in launching Bourne's career initially found Bourne's appearance "without a redeeming feature," and in a tone still shivering with faint disgust many years later he described Bourne's "mouldy brown" face with its skin so tightly drawn over the jaw that his teeth stood out "like fangs." Similarly, Beulah Amidon, one of the young women Bourne fell in love with, in later years could also say, "there was no redeeming feature in his appearance—even his eyes had no magnetism—and his hands were clumsy and undistinguished."[1]

Yet Sedgwick overcame his initial dismay, developed an increasingly warm relationship with Bourne, almost paternal, and hoped for absolution from his original meanness of response; and Beulah Amidon characteristically followed up her blunt description by quickly adding: "And yet when he talked one forgot the misshapen body, the scarred head and face, the awkward gestures." Waldo Frank, a close associate of Bourne's on the *Seven Arts* magazine, looked at Bourne through the personality and saw not undistinguished eyes or clumsy hands but, on the contrary, precisely those features "that brought about the wonder." The hands of Bourne, he said, "were exquisite, gentle, quiet . . . they bespoke his style—the caress of his ruthless understandings. And they flowered from his body with the inevitable irony of all his being. The eyes were penetrant, studious. There was a reticence in them, after the adventure, not before it. You knew from them that Randolph Bourne was wise. . . ." Van Wyck Brooks, closer still as friend, perhaps the most intimate of all on the intellectual plane, recalled his first meeting with "that odd little apparition with his vibrant eyes, his quick, birdlike steps" and saw "a sort of permanent youthfulness on his queer, twisted, appealing face."[2]

The same note was struck again and again by others, as though Bourne's friends were under some kind of shared compulsion to submit testimonials as witnesses to a miraculous conversion. Paul

Rosenfeld, yet another of Bourne's close associates on the *Seven Arts*, reported: "The first time one saw the man, one saw, perhaps, the crippled frame, the poor twisted ear, and shrank involuntarily from them. They were gone the second time; gone never again to obtrude. Only the long sensitive Gothic face remained; the fine musician's hands with their delightful language; the joyous, youthful, certain dance of the mind." Theodore Dreiser in fact called what he experienced a "miracle," the miracle that mind could perform in transforming "as frightening a dwarf as I had ever seen"—on his first encounter with Bourne—into "a tall, strong, powerful man, whose body matched the fine mind that occupied it." Like Sedgwick, Dreiser confessed shame and deep regret at how he had originally recoiled, "affected by some accursed prejudice." For Dreiser, his subsequent meeting with Bourne had been a mystical experience, with "chemism, mysticism, deeps upon deeps of undecipherable life affecting me" as the dwarfed body "completely vanished." In the free verse poem he opened and closed his reminiscent account with, he wrote "That which was crooked/straightened." Finally, to round out this litany of testimonials, James Oppenheim, editor of the *Seven Arts*, in his memorial poem to Bourne, spoke of how "He rose above his body and came among us/Prophetic of the race"—the language of canonization.[3]

These were his friends, of course, many of them writing while still close to their bereavement at his loss. The list could be extended by many more, and for those who recalled Bourne many years after his death, the memory of Bourne's person echoed all the more hauntingly over time's distance as they sought to explain his impact upon themselves, recalling him often in some low or desperate moment in the national life when they wished he could be with them at that hour. Lewis Mumford, a young man in his early twenties when Bourne died and who did not know him at firsthand, wrote in 1930 that Bourne "was precious to us because of what he was rather than because of what he had actually written." Mumford has been quoted or echoed many times since. Lillian Schlissel, no acquaintance of Bourne's but one of the best of the more recent commentators on him, has written that "Bourne was one of those men whose life itself somehow becomes the gesture of his thought." Almost as by apology for making so much of a writer whose output was relatively slight, friends and acquaintances first, then students following their lead, have sought to delineate—to use a key word in Bourne's own writing—the "radiant" personality of the man, to seek and demonstrate his meaning and wherein he is "usable" in his person, in his life story.[4]

The person of Bourne obviously is paradoxical: crooked in appearance, yet in some essence of the personality, straight. Just as obviously, had he not been the grotesque physical creature he was, the appropriate language of paradox could not have been used to pass on this image of his person. He was an ironic contradiction at birth. A life of irony and paradox was the only one open to him. As Dorothy Teall put it, in the inevitable pun on his name, he was "Bourne into Myth."

His life story compounds the irony of his birth. He came of good American stock, as we say, with both maternal and paternal lines traceable to the early seventeenth century in America, with connections in New York and New England. His grandfather Theodore Bourne had been pastor of the Presbyterian church at Sleepy Hollow, New York; and his great-grandfather, George Bourne, an abolitionist and acquaintance of Ralph Waldo Emerson and William Lloyd Garrison. Members of his mother's line of descent, the Barretts, had arrived in America as early as 1628, eventually moving from Cornwall, New York, to New Jersey. From an uncle, Colonel William Silliman, a union officer killed in the Civil War, came Bourne's middle name—one no one has ever dared to pun upon.[5]

It's a familiar pattern, common in the backgrounds of the middle-class families of the latter nineteenth century, inheritors of that moral vision, almost Hebraic, deriving as it does from the Old Testament, which we call puritan. Succeeding to it himself, Bourne would subject that vision to stern analysis, attacking it with almost as much moral fervor as the early puritans possessed, and more than once asserting that to be "a good appreciating pagan" one perhaps had to have been first a puritan, "a bad puritan."

Perhaps it was his father, Charles Bourne, he had in mind. Though Charles Bourne outlived his son, dying in 1924, he had been barely a presence in Bourne's early childhood and even less so thereafter. Bourne later referred to him hardly at all, and then ambiguously, once with shame and sometimes with pity and even affection. For though Charles Bourne had inherited some of the outer graces of his forebears—he was described as handsome—he had apparently none of the inner strengths which enabled others of his generation to translate their ancestors' moral vision into material success. His marriage to Sarah Barrett in 1884 endured through the births of four children: Randolph first in 1886—almost a failure—then a daughter, another son, and another daughter; but shortly after the last, sometime in 1896, Charles and Sarah separated, by mutual consent, but with the enforcing ultimatum from Sarah's brother, Halsey Barrett, a good puritan and successful Newark lawyer, who agreed to support the mother and children if the father would leave and never return. Charles had failed in one job or undertaking after another. He was something of a "gay blade who liked his fun" as one daughter recalled.[6] And the fun apparently included drink. Exile was the traditional fate of bad puritans.

Bourne's biographer John Adam Moreau makes the conventional inference that the absence of a father from the household during Bourne's formative years had an unfavorable influence on him, with hovering protective mother and sisters and grandmother and maiden aunt accounting for a later continuing need for coddling and attention from women. Probably so. But it seems just as likely and more significant that the presence in his awareness of a nearby father in exile—for Charles seems never to have wandered further from home in Bloomfield than to nearby Montclair—and of a failed father at that, of whom one did not speak except with embarrassment or pity, was responsible for Bourne's later animus toward America's "business civilization" and his linking it with puritanism, expressed in the uncle who had issued the decree of banishment. It would seem, too, to account for the almost instant recognition of an identity of interest and purpose between Bourne and his most intimate of male friends, Van Wyck Brooks. Born in the same year, 1886, and in another nearby suburb of Newark and New York—Plainfield, New Jersey, only a little more genteel than Bloomfield, perhaps, in its social and economic aspirations, somewhat richer, but in all else a similarly small, pinched cosmos—Brooks too had had a father who had failed at business, upsetting the normal expectations, and who had been left socially and economically dependent upon his wife's family, becoming an outsider in Plainfield, an embarrassment. Brooks too found the puritanic atmosphere of his early years cloying and oppressive, and the life of business not simply risky, but dangerous, liable to kill, as it did his father. For Bourne, already cursed with an outcast's appearance, the dismissed and failed father was a reinforcing source for the allusions he sometimes made to himself as a would-be prophet, wishing to be an Ezekiel, but destined to end up an Ishmael. The two young men might have met as undergraduates at Princeton, where each appeared headed at about the same time, 1903–1904, had not their respective family fortunes, declining in each instance as a consequence of an inadequate father-provider, altered so as to send each man on a more circuitous route to their meeting. When they did meet and became associates on the *Seven Arts*, their respective contributions to that magazine amounted almost to a collaboration in a joint assault on the twinned mentalities of business enterprise and puritanism, with each writer urging his young contemporaries to reject both in favor of their own more youthful desires.[7]

This Dickensian touch about his father aside, along with his physical handicap (and neither can be put very far aside), other features of Bourne's early years appear relatively normal. The fragment of fictionalized autobiography he left upon his death, a brief chapter covering the earliest years of memory, when his mother moved the family into her mother's house and he started his schooling, gives us some insight into how he may have wished to remember his early years. There is but one reference to a father, who is otherwise not present, which is true enough; but neither is there any reference to a crippled or in any way handicapped "Gilbert," the six or seven year old through whose eyes the sketch is recorded. A mother, grandmother, younger sister and baby brother (a second sister would not have been born yet), an aunt, his mother's sister, "his father's father whom he had once been taken to see," an "Uncle Marcus," in whose church pew they were sometimes privileged to sit—these are all verifiable in fact; as are the details of his grandmother's house, "ridiculous but . . . not despicable," and the yard at its side, stretching out toward pine trees, all sorts of fruit trees, six or seven lines of grape arbors, a vegetable garden in summer, and at the far end a barn, empty of the horse and carriage, but still packed with treasures for a boy to discover. Though here and there the sketch is gently skewed through the ironic lens he had learned to turn upon himself (as, after describing a quarrel with his sister, "Gilbert felt the perversity of Fate, the inexorable aloofness of the gods, the fragility of happiness"), it is for the most part a fondly affectionate reminiscence of the people and places of those days. One is persuaded that most of the sketch is fact, the fiction provided by the thin overlay of irony.

Most readers of Bourne have been so persuaded. A standard way of recounting his life story is to paraphrase or quote from those "autobiographic chapters," the one cited above, and others, changing the fictional name from "Gilbert" or "Miro" back to "[Randolph]." Then one mines the letters for the telling self-descriptive lines Bourne so frequently indulged, adding them to fill out the portrait Bourne has presented of himself in his published writings.[8]

There is ample precedent for this standard tactic, of course, and Bourne's remark to one of his correspondents that "the fact is, each of my essays has expressed an aspect of me" provides further sanction. He promised his correspondent that the then forthcoming *Youth and Life* collection of his essays would have still more of himself, and though the essays might sound like many different personalities, "or like many insincere aspects of one personality . . . they were all thoroughly and almost uncannily autobiographical." Still, it would be incautious not to note also that he had said those aspects of his person were "horribly idealized," and that to another correspondent he confessed, after *Youth and Life* was two years behind him, that it was "a good deal of a fraud if it is taken as *me* [*sic*] instead of what I would like to be or to have been."[9]

We come back to the centrality of irony in his life story: the fact is that the story he told is a species of fiction. The truth lies in the irony.

All lives that follow the dictates of convention and tradition are, to the extent they do, fictions, of course, but insofar as a convention is "a fable agreed upon"[10] the fictional lives are accepted as true. With all who can conform, more or less, and who to all appearances fit and follow the conventions, there is no great strain, no great awareness of disparities. The pangs that mark the stage of adolescence may be the first signs of a felt awareness, rising to differing levels of conscious understanding as adolescence extends into youth.

Hence, the irony in the appearance of Bourne's "relatively normal" early years. His deformity would have necessitated a doubling of the effort to sustain the conventions, to consciously work at the fiction of normality, first on the part of his elders and others close to him, then by himself. The protectiveness of mother and sisters, and by unspoken agreement from others, his teachers for instance, was more influential in assuring the irony in his soul than in simply prolonging in him a desire for coddling. When the fiction was finally exposed the ironist was born and he was ready to make himself into the symbol of youth, one of whose major themes, as Kenneth Kenniston points out, is the recognition "of conflict and disparity between his emerging selfhood and his social order,"[11] between what he senses he is and what the fictions of society said he was.

It would be difficult to say precisely when that moment of recognition came to Bourne, but one can surmise that it probably came during that year of transvaluation of values, shortly after his graduation from high school.

There must have been many times before that when he half divined the truth of his deformity and the world's response to it, and of the fiction he was compelled to live. But it was only afterward that he realized what tortures he had suffered in order to "learn to skate, to climb trees, to play ball, to conform in general to the ways of the world."[12] It was the later youth who learned and argued that "the first duty of self-conscious youth is to dodge the pressures" and to make provision "for silencing the voices that whisper continually at his side, 'Conform!'"[13] The record of the boyhood, on the other hand, has all the appearances of a normal, even eager conformist, happy with his lot.

During 1901—his fifteenth year—he kept a diary, parts of which have been published.[14] Our attention is easily caught by the signs of precocity it reveals, at least as we inevitably measure its notes against those that today's fifteen year olds, even college freshmen, might record. He fondly recorded his purchase and reading of books: Lowell's "Vision of Sir Launfal," some of Whittier's poems, John Fiske's "War of Independence," "Ivanhoe," and Maurice Thompson's best-selling novel of the year before, "Alice of Old Vincennes." The bookishness is expected, even the titles he read; not so a fifteen-year-old critic's finding the style of a novel he read "pompous and forced, and the plot . . . rather improbable" and who pronounced it "decidedly middle-class," or who would express his pleasure in "the nicest combination of words I have ever seen"—Daniel Webster's speech "Liberty and Union," which he memorized for delivery at school.

There is little or no sign of any growing awareness of disparities in his lot. He resents being required by his teacher of German to sit in the front of the classroom in recitation. He hates that, preferring "to see what goes on in front of me," but there is no questioning the teacher's arbitrary command. He records resentment of his Aunt Fan's inspecting his person "right there before some of the Gymnasium girls," unbuttoning his coat, checking his collar, his fingernails, his teeth. But both of these notes would seem quite normal resentments of normal boys, and no especial sign of one self-conscious of his public appearance. He admits to probably not being popular in school, and hence, though nominated for some school-wide position, he expects not to be elected. But that is because he was not well known, he writes, and he is pleased that he *has* been elected class president. The bulk of the diary entries are the commonplace ones of a teenaged lad recording his pride at going to church, "uniting" in holy communion with the rest of his Sunday school class, going to Christian Endeavor, buying his class pin, losing it, collecting stamps, and, far from precocious by today's standards, engaging in the puppy-love rites of St. Valentine's Day.

Most of the information we have beyond the diary is corroborative of the conventional portrait we find in it. Other children apparently flocked to the Bourne "open house," and to the biggest yard in the neighborhood. A sister recalled that Randolph often took the lead in their games, having more imagination than the others. He learned to play the piano very early, a valuable socializing skill that elevated him in the eyes of his peers and drew admiring applause from his elders. He began his schooling somewhat ahead of his classmates, having already learned to read at home, but he ended his high school years with a modest, gentlemanly record of achievement, good enough to make him one of seven graduating scholars selected to deliver commencement orations at the ceremonies in Old First Church where he was a member. Bourne's address, "Washington's Campaigns in New Jersey," was well received.[15] He was a success.

He had even passed the entrance examinations for Princeton University. But that was the last of his early laurels, completing the fiction of his early life; then the reality and the irony set in. "Uncle Marcus"—his mother's brother, Halsey Barrett—still supporting the family, drew the line short of subsidizing a college eduction. Bourne's deep disappointment at having to forego the next step in the agreed upon fable must have marked his first recognition of what he would later write "the deformed man is *always* conscious" of—"that the world does not expect very much from him."[16] Sending *him* to college was thought a futile gesture.

What was expected of the ordinary young man who could not go on to college was that he "settle down," begin to support himself, start his apprenticeship for the adult world. Bourne was so admonished; but he was no ordinary young man.

We know he tried, and in a limited way he succeeded. That is, he went job hunting; and he finally landed some jobs—through sympathetic connections. For a while he was a factory hand in the office of a relative in Morristown, New Jersey. Then the organist of Old First Church hired him to help make perforated music rolls for the then popular mechanical piano players, enabling Bourne to apply one of his skills. He gave piano lessons too, and when the piano roll job ended he worked as an accompanist in studios near New York City's Carnegie Hall. Beyond these bare facts, however, we know less about him in the years 1903–1909, between his high school graduation and his going to Columbia College, than of any of the years before or after. We can be pretty certain, however, that these were the years when one shock after another followed the first shattering of his fictional life as he sought to extend it into an acceptable pattern.

Support himself? Easily said for others. For one like Bourne, deformed, as he later wrote, "the bitterest struggles . . . come when he tackles the business world." Enter into those rites that were preparatory for adulthood, enter into "the world of youth" where it was "one of dances and parties and social evenings and boy-and-girl attachments"? Into the conventions of this world he could not gain admittance as, in his earlier years, through sheer determination and audacity of will, he could convert even the cruel jests of children, brutal acknowledgments of his deformity, into irrelevancy and find himself accepted, the deformity of no apparent importance. *Invited* into this world, yes, "[b]ut it was more as if a ragged urchin had been asked to come and look through the window at the light and warmth of the glittering party; I was truly in the world," he wrote, "but not of the world. Indeed there were times when one would almost prefer conscious cruelty to this silent, unconscious, gentle oblivion."[17]

There was to be much more that went into the making of Randolph Bourne the writer, and the Randolph Bourne who created in himself the myth of youth—the books he read, the studies he undertook at college, his teachers, the men and women he met, the decisive year of travel in Europe, the ideas he pursued, discarded, picked up again, and the sweeping crucial events of his time, the war especially. Nothing else that happened to him, however, could have been so fundamentally important in preparing him to be the ironic spokesman for youth as were the unrecorded experiences of the years of struggle in "the world of youth."

Being "in the world, but not of the world" is the common experience of youth—in greater or lesser degree. It is also the essential stance of the ironist. The experience for Bourne was extremely acute, more absolute than that of most young people, a heightened instance of the general predicament. He learned to convert that predicament into "a positive advantage," he said, and to acquire a lively interest in "the social politics" of the world he was not a part of while preserving his feelings for the world he was in. His ability to articulate the latter, combined with his deft depiction of the social politics youth has perhaps always had to contend with, enabled him to touch responsive chords of feeling and thought in his own and subsequent "younger generations."

When he arrived at Columbia, aged twenty-three, he was once more ahead of most of his classmates, older yes, but with the experience of youth already his he understood their hopes and anxieties in ways most of them were only about to start understanding. In his later characteristic irony, he said that he had solved his own difficulties "only by evading them, by throwing overboard some of my responsibility, and taking the desperate step of entering college on a scholarship."[18] He did no such thing, of course. Desperate he may have been for the intellectual fare and companionship he craved, but in advancing on the one institution in American life where "youth" was accorded some status, some recognition, he was about to assume a heavier responsibility than any he had evaded. College then as now furnished "an ideal environment," as he said, where the things at which he could succeed "really count." Bourne had the "handicapped" in mind here, but successive generations of increasingly numerous young Americans, vaguely feeling themselves inadequate or too "handicapped" to count for much in the bewildering mazes of modern society, have come to cherish their college years for much the same reason.

II *The College Years*

Bourne's public career as a writer effectively began with his

Columbia College years. He was twenty-three years old when he began in September 1909. As has often been remarked, it was a good time to be at Columbia, and with his advantage in years and some kinds of experience over most of his classmates Bourne made the most of it.

A modest small college less than two decades before when it was located in mid-Manhattan, Columbia, now at Morningside Heights, was well on its way to becoming the distinguished modern urban university it is today. Student registration—only 1,768 in 1889—was over 6,000 when Bourne enrolled, and exceeded 9,000 when he left in 1913. A new generation of professors dominated the intellectual climate, making it crackle with new enthusiasms. Men like James Harvey Robinson, John Dewey, and Joel Spingarn, exponents respectively of the "new history," the "new education," and the "new criticism," disturbed the old scholarship and provided opportunities for a clash of ideas. Others, like Charles A. Beard, busy exploring the relationship between American ideals and American economic realities, and William P. Trent, pioneering the study of American literature in the classroom, directed a new and lively attention to contemporary issues in America. Others in literature, like Brander Matthews, John Erskine, and Carl Van Doren, commanded or were about to receive respectful attention to their views. Franz Boas was there, leading the way in the study of anthropology, a newly emerging discipline. The usual collegiate ferment spilled over the campus walls and spread into the larger public arena. Bourne had entered no ivory tower.

Contrary to the impression he gave in his history of the literary radical named "Miro," Bourne thrived in this atmosphere. "Miro," arrived at college, had "expanded his cultural interests on the approved lines," only to find the approved studies fatiguing, Plato beginning to bore him, literary scholarship "dusty," and too many of his instructors content to remain "in the state of reverence which saw all things good that had been immemorially taught."[19] Not so with Bourne in fact.

Arrived at Columbia with the award of a scholarship, Bourne set about earnestly to prove deserving of the award. He early attracted the attention of his teachers and profited from their encouragement. His student papers betray a studious mind engaged with evident delight in "the pure pleasure of thought." Far from finding Plato boring, his essay "What Plato Means to Me" (probably written in his second year for Frederick Woodbridge's courses in the history of philosophy) suggests that Plato may have been, in fact, the model he most sought to emulate. Much of the student paper was later incorporated into the essay "The Life of Irony" published in the *Atlantic Monthly* and then in *Youth and Life*, and it would appear from this and the overt confession in the later essay, that it was his reading of the Socrates of Plato that made him first appreciate irony as "a life, and a life of beauty," that made him understand his own predicament, in short, that "the ironist is born and not made," and that one so endowed was a happy man.

By the time he wrote the story of Miro, Bourne was an accomplished ironist, and he must have privately relished the "delicious contrast" between the Miro who was bored by Plato and the Bourne who had been "delighted" by him. "Delight" and "delightful" sparkle through nearly every paragraph in the ingenuous undergraduate enthusiasm of the first essay. Besides enjoying the Socratic irony, Bourne also delighted, he said, in Plato's concreteness—abstractness, "or so we think in this practical age," being the vice of most philosophers (a vice this practical age often laid on Bourne). He liked Plato's arguing by analogy, though not necessarily his ideas, as he confessed his knowledge of logic was "too elementary and too recent to permit me to say honorably that I follow all the subtleties of his reasoning." As Bourne himself was restive in deciding what to "major" in, settling finally for sociology as permitting him the greatest breadth for the exploring of his many interests—had they been available then, he would have sought out some interdisciplinary major, like American Studies—so he appreciated Plato's wide-ranging over economics and politics, history, the arts, and above all his attention to education, where in Socrates, Bourne wrote, he demonstrates "the need of methods which shall interest and inspire the learner." "Indeed," Bourne observed, "the Dialogues might almost be called a handbook of teaching. And what results Socrates got! That men should seek each other out to talk about philosophy and spend hours and days at it for the pure pleasure of thought! It is delightful to think of it. This practical age has a contempt for mere thought, mere art, or mere literature." All Plato's interests, Bourne concluded, were brought together "into one living tissue of thought": "But through all his work runs his subtle irony, illuminating everything. It is this irony, the appreciation that things are not what they seem, that furnishes him the golden key—and it is the only key in the world, I believe—which can unlock the doors of the world of things and show them AS THEY ARE."[20]

"Excellent!" his instructor wrote on the paper. And in general that was the reaction of most of his teachers, as judged by his grades—nine "A's" and five "B's" his first year—and enough of the same thereafter to get him elected to Phi Beta Kappa, to permit him to complete the undergraduate course in three years, and to earn a fellowship for a fourth year's study for the M.A. Not bad. Still, as Bourne must have come to relish the irony of his triumphs, of being in that ideal environment of college where the things at which he could succeed really counted, his twisting lens of hind sight converted Columbia and its professors into enemies of youth. What he preferred to recall was how he had been moved to rebel.

Outside the classroom, if anything, he succeeded even more brilliantly—for one with his disadvantages—as the world measures success in making friends and influencing people. He very quickly got into the columns of the *Columbia Monthly*, with his first entry, "Some Aspects of Good Talk," in January 1910, followed by two more in March and April of his first year, the one attacking G. K. Chesterton's *Orthodoxy* for making orthodoxy respectable, and the other, "On Hero Making," demurring from the popular mind's tendency to allegorize men rather than systems of thought and ideals. These were judged good enough to enlist him on the editorial staff as a regular contributor and, one year later, to elect him as editor in chief of the *Monthly*. In the same month, May 1911, his first article to reach out beyond Morningside Heights appeared in the prestigious *Atlantic Monthly*. He was a marked man, "a minor celebrity on campus."[21]

His venture into collegiate journalism opened doors for him. He joined undergraduate societies—the Boar's Head Literary Society, The Philolexian Society—and became the dominant member of an informal group calling itself "The Academy," a dozen or so "students of high-brow taste"[22] who gathered once a month, usually in his room, to read and discuss papers on philosophy, socialism, religion, art, and literature.

With many of these fellow students he developed warm and lasting friendships, notably with Arthur Macmahon, with whom he shared a room for a time, and who went on to a distinguished career himself at Columbia, and Carl Zigrosser, who later became curator of fine prints at the Philadelphia Museum. These were his two closest friends. Both young men possessed the handsome charming exteriors denied to Bourne, but their sympathetic sharing of Bourne's lively interests banished any effect of the contrasting appearances between them. There were many others: Dixon Ryan Fox, the future historian, who preceded Bourne as editor of the *Monthly*, admired him and introduced him to the right circles; Joseph Ward Swain, also to become an historian, with whom Bourne later shared some of his European travels; Edward W. Murray, a talented musician who eventually played violin for Eugene Ormandy's Philadelphia Symphony, and who provided the model for Bourne's loving portrait of "Fergus," who breathed "in from the air around him certain large aesthetic and philosophical ideas"—all of them, with many others, providing Bourne a whole gallery of portraits for his idealization of youth.

From beyond Columbia, after his *Atlantic Monthly* articles gave his voice a larger range, still others responded, among them some remarkable young women, like Prudence Winterrowd, whose response to his essay "Youth" provoked a lengthy correspondence. Similar responses from others provided the tonic assurance to Bourne of a kind of constituency "out there" and permitted him in his letters to refine the style and extend the myth he was developing to meet that practical world which never expected much from a hunchback. Friends and friendship became for Bourne a cardinal principle of youth precisely as they had become essential for his own sense of counting for something. Columbia may not have been entirely responsible for the making of his character, as he said privately to Prudence Winterrowd,[23] whom he was trying to persuade to carry out her plans to attend Columbia, but without the encounters it made possible, both inside and outside the classroom, the myth of Randolph Bourne would never have emerged.

His first *Atlantic Monthly* article marks the formal surfacing of that myth. The story of how it happened has often been told. In the February 1911 *Atlantic Monthly* a Cornelia A.P. Comer had written "A Letter to the Rising Generation," one of the expressions of a growing national awareness since the turn of the century that young people constituted something of a "problem."

The assault, for such it was, was heavily moralistic, locating the problem in the younger generation's "softening of fibre" and blaming their attraction to socialism on its appeal to "a weak head, a soft heart, and a desire to shirk." The socialism of the young, Comer quipped, was just an "ism," vague, and of the sort that made young people feel they could achieve salvation "by reading Whitman and G.B.S., or even the mild and uncertain Mr. H. G. Wells . . . ." As has been drearily repeated ever since, Comer also blamed the "newer educational method" for youth's poor spelling, slipshod English, for knowing nothing of the classics or the Bible, and the "vulgarizing" of their tastes on their chosen pleasures, the Sunday supplements, vaudeville, and "moving-picture shows." Chiefly, though, she censured youth for neglecting the upbringing of the soul, for knowing nothing and caring less for conceptions of conduct of earlier times, for abjuring even the words like "fortitude," "duty," and "character."[24]

Frederick Woodbridge brought the article to the attention of his class, suggesting that some one of them might wish to reply, and approaching Bourne in particular. Bourne surprised him by saying that he had already done so, and gave his paper to Woodbridge. Impressed, Woodbridge immediately passed it on to Ellery Sedgwick, and Bourne's reply appeared in the *Atlantic Monthly*'s May issue.

A first reply had already been published in the April 1911 issue, "The Younger Generation: An Apologia," by one Anne Hard. That Sedgwick chose to prolong the discussion through another issue is a measure both of the appeal of Bourne's essay and of the rising interest in the "youth problem." It is instructive to compare the two rebuttals to the Comer attack; the common positions show how much Bourne sensed and shared his generation's views and feelings, and the differences, largely in tone and style, help reveal how Bourne established his leadership in the mounting quarrel with the older guardians of the American scene.

Both essayists offered at the outset "the most obvious retort," as Bourne recognized that the world young people had inherited was, after all, not of their own making. Both agreed on the most important difference, as each saw it, between their own and the generation of their elders: whereas the preceding generation had been concerned, rather, "preoccupied," with personal "ethics" (Hard) or "salvation" (Bourne), with "ideals of individual beauty" (Hard) or individual character (both), the new generation wished for a "socialization of ethics" (Hard), for social salvation, for "not our own characters, but the character of society" (Bourne). Turning her defense into more of an indictment of the preceding generation than did Bourne, Hard summed up this attack on the older generation's own brand of selfishness (of which the younger had been accused) in terms strikingly familiar to our own environmentally conscious younger generations of the past decade or so. The persistence of this concern for America's natural environment as an issue which young people have responded to and rallied around is worth remarking, since it is not usually counted as one of the significant ideals in the cluster of youth's alleged vaporous dreams. The broad charge of irresponsibility so often blanketed over the young is readily turned back by them upon "the system," or "the establishment."

As Anne Hard put it, what was even more menacing to her generation than the disclosures of individual greed or corruption was the revelation, she said, underscoring her outrage, of "the complete lack of *recognition of the public point of view*." She went on:

> Here acres of state land quietly handed over to a steel mill, there a city's lake front given over to a railroad; here a stream—of all the wonderful universe, one would think, most sacred gift of all—poisoned its length, there the very air noxious with unnecessary vapors; forests and mines which should have been the bread of the future children of America made the wine of the women of the Riviera—these are the conditions into which we were born. These are the conditions for which the noble Romans of another generation are responsible.[25]

She concluded, "We resent an individual virtue which exists in the midst of social wrong." Bourne said, with a more deft, stinging choice of language, "We feel social injustice as our fathers felt personal sin."

Taking the inevitable swipes at an older generation's hypocrisy, Hard said of her own that it "is ashamed to be ashamed," preferring frankness and candor in all personal relationships, having, as Bourne said, none of that "repression in our bringing-up . . . that rigid moulding which made our grandfathers what they were." "We have retained from childhood," Bourne stoutly said, "the propensity to see through things, and to tell the truth with startling frankness" —to tell it, a later younger generation would say, "like it is." Both writers took a kind of wry pleasure in contemplating the older generation's likely dismay before a candid younger generation, how "they," said Hard, must "tremble to think how we're going to face" the conditions which they had created, and, Bourne added, evaded, since so much of their activity "seems to consist in glossing over the unpleasant things or hiding the blemishes on the fair face of civilization."

A good one-two punch, with Bourne's blows landing somewhat more firmly on promoting youth's virtues rather than attacking the older generation's sins. Adopting the tactic of conceding a point in order to score his own, he acknowledged that "discipline" had indeed declined, in school, church, even home where only the empty form remained. But, he said, calling up another early American virtue—self-reliance—the result was a rising generation that had "practically brought itself up." "The modern child from the age of ten is almost his own master," he said, making for a helplessness of the modern parent which Bourne declared highly amusing. True too, he said, that the rising generation did not find appealing their secondary education, "that curious fragmentary relic of a vitally humanistic age," since, frankly, they saw no use in it—no "relevance," a later younger generation would say. Having brought themselves up, they judged utility by their own standards, not that of others. And if they appeared more pleasure loving than prior generations, "it is not likely that this is because former generations were less eager for pleasure, but rather because they were more rigidly repressed by parents and custom" ("uptight") and diverted their energies elsewhere, religion for instance—a hint at the puritanism Bourne would scourge at a later time, using the newly current language of psychology. The new youthful society in which boy and girl met as equals, he said, was bound to teach social virtues far better than any taught by moral precepts.

Bourne was at his best, however—and went beyond Hard—in suggesting that it was not a deficiency or slackening of character, or a failure to understand duty and self-sacrifice that distinguished his generation from the older, so much as the changed and changing conditions which he and his contemporaries faced. Though presented in broad and generalized terms, the analysis he offered placed the problem of the younger generation within the larger context of an emerging modern America, and for an undergraduate he showed considerable insight into the changing character of America's economic and industrial life and how those changes affected the role of young Americans.

Although hardly the first to point out some of the changing conditions, he was surely among the first to note that one effect was to prolong for many young people the period of preparation for adult roles and to bring about a change in the value they placed upon those roles. "Our critics," Bourne said, missed the point in accusing the rising generation of going soft. "It is rather that we have the same reserves of ability and effort but that from the complex nature of the economic situation these reserves are not unlocked so early or so automatically as with former generations." Professional training was lengthy nowadays, he pointed out; independent business required big capital for success; "and there is no more West." With the only choice for most young men being between "being swallowed up in the routine of a big corporation" or experiencing the vicissitudes of small business, it was no wonder that many were hesitating, reevaluating those paths to success, and looking for other ways to assume "responsibility." Thrown on its own resources as no other generation had been, "the youth as well as the girl" (for Bourne, "youth" was a masculine noun) wanted to "count for something in life," but not in the conventionalizing ways of the traditional careers in business and the professions. They wanted to preserve their persons, that is, in modern terms, to "find" themselves or "get their heads together."

Bourne concluded on a lecturing note to the older generation, rebuking them for their mistrust and misunderstanding of the young. "We," on the other hand, he said, "believe in ourselves; and this fact, we think, is prophetic for the future. We have an indomitable feeling that we shall attain, or if not, that we shall pave the way for a generation that shall attain."

The combined tones of gentle mockery of the older generation and prophetic affirmation about the young became a distinguishing feature of Bourne's voice. His young audience responded with glee to the first, and felt braced and assured by the latter.

That essay marked the beginning. Over the next two years, while still at Columbia, Bourne published seven more articles in the *Atlantic Monthly,* while also continuing as a regular contributor of essays and reviews to the *Columbia Monthly,* writing an occasional essay or review for other journals and magazines—and completing his master's dissertation, a study of the effects of the suburbanizing process on the social life of a small town—his own Bloomfield, New Jersey. In March 1913, as "The Life of Irony" appeared in the *Atlantic Monthly,* he published his first book, *Youth and Life,* collecting that essay and others from the *Atlantic* and *Columbia Monthly,* along with several new ones. It was a productive pace, and one that never slackened.

Youth and Life secured the myth that had steadily been growing since the first *Atlantic Monthly* entry. There it lies still, available for release when, across the generations, he is heard again, read again, by young people and those who find their own youth reclaimed in his words.

Other acts in his life story remained, but the essential drama lies in the enactment of the myth as the roles he performed in life and in writing became more and more indistinguishably one and the same, fact and symbol interacting. Except, possibly, when we read "The Handicapped," the same miracle that his friends experienced is ours—the deformed hunchback vanishes and we have the fact transformed into the symbolic youth. Even with that essay, when we read it in *Youth and Life* where it is retitled "A Philosophy of Handicap" and as part of the whole mythographic portrait, the deformed lot of Randolph Bourne is universalized into the handicap of the bittersweet experience of being young; it becomes the supportive rationale for the life of irony he advocated as the proper stance for those who would preserve their youthful vision and dodge the pressures to conform.

The ugly face and crippled body did not, of course, in fact disappear. Neither did the agile mind, the avid reader, the acute and sensitive observer of others, the passionate lover of life full of desire to count for something, nor the facile wordsmith. The ironies consequently continued, and Bourne, suffering, stirred each experience into his style until he had fashioned it into an instrument that could sting and inspire.

III *Europe: England*

Bourne capped his Columbia years with the award of the prestigious Richard Watson Gilder traveling fellowship. Even this had its irony. Dreading to repeat the job-hunting experience of his post-high school years, Bourne had hoped that Columbia might see fit to hire him in some academic capacity. But though his teachers and others held him in high regard, there were doubts. The fellowship helped to avoid, or at least to postpone the dilemma, and at the same time gave him the recognition he craved and deserved.

The fellowship permitted him to study political and social conditions through direct observation, either in America or abroad, so Bourne chose to take the classic *wanderjahre* in

Europe. On July 5, 1913, accompanied by his Columbia friend Joseph Ward Swain, who was heading for a year's study at the Sorbonne, Bourne sailed on the *Rochambeau.*

In the "Impressions" he later recorded in his report to the Columbia trustees on his year's work, the crossing itself provoked an almost lyrical account. Paradoxically, in the artificial society of cruise passengers, Bourne made something of a splash as a kind of brilliant entertainer—he actually did perform as a pianist in a benefit concert—and struck up some quick friendships, and in one instance, with "a lovely St. Louis widow,"[26] an intense one. He was sad, he said, when it ended and he and Swain had to fall back on their own resources. The buoyant note of youthful exuberance and happiness with all that he saw carried over through the summer, however, as he and Swain charged through Belgium, Holland, Italy, Switzerland, and then France where, in Paris, they parted.[27]

Now alone, truly on his own resources, without the protective presence of Swain to smooth over the awkward moments, Bourne headed for England and Wales and for a meeting he had long anticipated, on which, when he had started his journey, he said, "my whole year seemed to pivot. . . ."[28] It resulted instead in a curious episode of frustration, embarrassment, and deep disappointment for Bourne, proving pivotal in other ways than he had hoped for, and not just for the year.

The meeting was with one Stanley M. Bligh. Bligh was almost a caricature of the proverbial English country gentleman: a barrister who had never really practiced his profession, dividing his life instead in the managing of his business affairs between London and an inherited country estate in Wales. He had become a kind of amateur psychologist, practicing on his friends and the acquaintances of upper-class circles, and writing books and papers for conferences where the newest theories of social psychology were discussed.

The year before, in August 1912, Bourne had run across the most recent of Bligh's books, *The Desire for Qualities*, and reviewed it for the *Columbia Journal of Philosophy, Psychology, and Scientific Methods.* He had promptly written to Bligh—in part to request permission to use Bligh's phrase, "the dodging of pressures" as a title for an essay—and started a series of lengthy exchanges that lasted until, after mutually high expectations, they met at Bligh's Welsh estate a year later. "Desire" had already become and was to remain a magical word for Bourne, an important one in his lexicography of youth. He would have been attracted by Bligh's title, as to his earlier book, *The Direction of Desire*. It is clear from Bourne's review, and even more so from the ensuing correspondence, that Bourne found Bligh's words instantly applicable to himself and his own desires. Characteristically, of course, he wrote behind the shield of the impersonal pronoun or noun, as in his review, "the student of social sciences," who welcomed a writer like Bligh for breaking ground "towards outlining the bearings of the most modern psychological and sociological science in the moulding of the human personality." The "directive psychology" which Bligh proposed, Bourne said, aimed at "the enrichment of personality," teaching men "by psychological methods to effect an improvement in their own character and in those of others and solve the problem of how their desires may be most profitably directed." Bourne's review ended with a flattering comparison of Bligh and his idol William James—for a similar style that combined scientific validity with personal interest and a firm grip on practical experience.[29]

A curious correspondence followed, full of exchanges of mutual admiration, with Bligh confessing a sense of "mental kinship and affinity" with Bourne such as he had never experienced, and likening his discovery of Bourne to Montaigne's finding his younger friend Etienne de la Boétie, "I think at about my age." Both men wrote with this self-conscious sense of the possible historic importance of their encounter as they shared their ideas on the need for a new science of social psychology.[30]

Perhaps their meeting of minds seemed all the more remarkable to each man as they became more and more aware of the great contrasts in their respective backgrounds, but they avoided any incipient clash by resolutely staying at a high level of impersonal intellectual discourse. As Bourne became somewhat more aggressive, more confident in pressing his own ideas on the older Bligh, the latter modestly retreated somewhat from his first presentation of himself as "something . . . of a pioneer in 'directive' psychology." He conceded, as he described to Bourne how he had started his psychological observation, that his experience had been narrowly limited to only one class of people, "what may be called 'Upper Bohemia,'" he said, that he never knew the "fashionable" class nor "much of the earnest dull kind of people who struggle painfully for a living in what are called in this country the 'middle classes,' little of the student class, and no one at all engaged in sociological work or in writing about psychology. Bourne, he suggested, must have had a wider-ranging experience, and, despite Bourne's criticism of his course work in sociology at Columbia, the amateur Bligh felt Bourne had the advantage of university training denied him.[31] Later still he agreed with Bourne's criticizing him for not making enough allowance for "the constraints of economic and industrial conditions and the blows and shocks of fortune"[32]—such, of course, as Bourne himself had experienced, and such conditions as he was then studying in Bloomfield for his master's essay. And as for Bourne's apparent socialism, well, Bligh knew too little of "general social unrest and political socialism," and "possibly I object to Socialism because making a little money from time to time under the much abused Capitalistic system has been one of the minor amusements of my life."[33] Yes, he agreed, Bourne was a romantic, having much more "fervour and sympathy" and "the reforming spirit" than he possessed.[34]

These mild hints of differences between them were muted, however, by Bligh's genial acceptance of Bourne's criticisms, by their discovery of shared prejudices (that they were both guilty of but preferred "unscholarliness" for their purposes),[35] and even more by the lavish words of praise each laid on the other. Both men published and exchanged a book during the year's correspondence, Bligh's *The Ability to Converse*, in October 1912, and Bourne's *Youth and Life* the following March. Bourne's first *Columbia Monthly* piece, "Some Aspects of Good Talk," quite naturally inclined him to be warmly receptive of Bligh's book when he got it, and Bligh, replying to Bourne's response said "I have never found anyone who wrote as nicely and understandingly about my work. . . . I would so like to have a talk with you. Our minds seem to go together in so many ways."[36]

Just as Bourne had expressed his agreement with Bligh about the importance of good talk in the development of a healthy personality, so Bligh when he received *Youth and Life*, having already read "Youth" in its *Atlantic Monthly* setting, and having encouraged Bourne to put down his thoughts on irony in an article, and agreeing, after Bourne's initial hesitation, that he should include "The Handicapped" in his book, found himself on reading it through in "entire agreement" with all his views, and he reiterated, "You and I seem to think singularly on the same lines." He especially praised Bourne's style—Bourne having wondered whether he was too rhetorical. The "lyrical quality" of the essay "Youth," he said, "very forcibly brought back to me the 'affective tone' of my own Youth." He was certain, he said, that Bourne would have "a very considerable influence as an essayist," just as earlier he had said that Bourne could "occupy a prominent position in the psychological and sociological world."[37]

Where Bourne pressed Bligh to pay more heed to the impact of social forces on personality, to such things as "the traditional Puritan Ethics" (with which Bligh confessed to having had little contact), and to emphasize the importance of "diminishing the fashion which is now so strong in favour of reticence and reserve," Bligh undertook to provide Bourne with information and instruction about "the more or less new lines opened out in psychology by Freud's researches," directing him to articles and books and passing on his own notes from lectures he had heard by Freud.[38]

In the course of the latter effort Bligh touched close the trembling nerve of Bourne's most ardent, and most frustrated, of desires—sex. That Bligh had penetrated Bourne's masking language in some of the questions he raised is evident in Bligh's occasional practice of answering the "more personal parts" of Bourne's letters by hand—whilst generally he dictated his letters for a typist—but most obviously in one striking series of responses to Bourne's questions. It is also evident that Bligh's sensitive insight had not been capable of imagining the full reality.

In the same letter [39] that expressed his sense of mental kinship with Bourne, Bligh responded to some of Bourne's queries about youth and sex, veiled apparently behind some discussion of Stendhal's views. Bligh wrote:

> As regard [*sic*] sexual wish emotions. I think they mostly come to young men in a form which is as you say "unpleasant & exaggerated." I know they did to me. . . . Stendhal's view, if I remember right, is something like your own namely that a certain encouragement (not of course necessarily a true reciprocity) is an essential condition of what he calls "crystallization": that is the focusing of vague sexual imaginations on one particular person. . . . Very little work of a definite kind has been done on the conditions of crystallization and if you are interested in this matter you might do well to take it up. I judge from your letter that you will be likely to have strong personal experiences to go upon.
>
> Now as to the production of "a sense of physical attraction." That is a somewhat delicate matter for I gather from your letters that something stands in the way of your doing this easily. I hope I shall be excused for

saying that persons who do not easily produce "a sense of physical attraction" very generally or some only very rarely, do when once they exercise any attraction, arouse very violent passions.

So far, a tactful reply. In what followed, however, Bligh revealed how far short he had fallen in his imagination of Bourne's particular dilemma: "I knew a man who was very sickly, very puny, undersized, very hunchbacked and generally almost painful to look at. He had ability but it by no means amounted to genius." If Bourne winced in self-recognition here, the anecdote that followed provided little comfort, though some salve, perhaps, in the final tribute to his potential capacity for arousing the passion of mind.

Bligh went on:

He [his hunchbacked acquaintance] inspired a passion in two women which I have rarely seen equalled. We will call the man A & his 2 women B & C. B was in love with him, but had some shrinking from marrying a deformed person. She went abroad to think it over. B & C were close friends. All the parties were poor. Whilst B was away thinking it over, C made violent love to A in defiance of her duty as a friend. A & C married. C has devoted herself to nursing & looking after A. B was for months nearly distraught.

Bligh told "this little anecdote," he said, "because it seems to have a very direct bearing on your own case." He could not have known how direct, nor how prophetic the anecdote would prove; but Bourne must subsequently have recalled it with pained reminiscence, for at least twice in the next few years he found himself enmeshed with two different pairs of women in comparable triangulations.[40] With the latter of these he was, at last, about to marry one of the two women; with the others, he could only draw comfort from Bligh's final counsel: "To judge by your letters you seem to be a person capable of both feeling & arousing very considerable passion of the type that Bourget calls, 'Cerebrale.' That is in some ways the best & highest kind, but it needs a good deal of watching & knowledge to bring to perfection as it depends so largely on the imagination."

Within a few days Bligh followed up this letter with a lengthy continuation of the same subject, but this time dictated over a period of several days and typed, and resumed in the language of high-minded discourse about such new but soon-to-becomejargonish issues as sublimation. Bligh had been reading the newly published *Papers on Psychoanalysis* by Ernest Jones ("a man whom Freud thinks a great deal of, as he himself said to me"). Summarizing his understanding of Jones on "sublimation" and the need to drag a "repressed" idea into full consciousness, even against strong "resistances," Bligh obliquely cautioned Bourne against expecting too much. Yes, Bourne's proposal about the efficacy of "exposure to sublimating stimuli" seemed sound enough in theory, resembling some of Jones' ideas, but, what with the "angst" that might accompany such experience, difficult in application. He went on:

> With regard to your next point about the "companionship of attractive and appealing persons" [a theme Bourne elaborated on in his *Youth and Life* essay, "The Excitement of Friendship," first published in the December, 1912 *Atlantic Monthly*, shortly after his letter to Bligh] I fully agree that this is the best remedy available where it is obtainable, and I also agree with your view about the sublimation or draining away of undesirable wish-emotions in conversation. What I find however is that the remedy, though the best if obtainable, is rarely to be had. Those in need of the ministrations of directive psychology are usually unpopular either from undue sympathy or from some form of eccentricity. They find it difficult to get anyone let alone attractive people to listen to any sort of account of their more objectionable wish-emotions.

He had read that part of Bourne's letter, he said, to "a very clever Scotch-woman who knows a good deal of psychology," and she had not judged Bourne's suggestion a very effective "mode of sublimation," in fact thought "it would be highly antisocial to talk much about one's wish-emotions," however it might help the person talking. This prejudice against listening to accounts of wish-emotions was unfortunate, said Bligh, but "also very widespread." Maybe that was why "art & music are generally recommended as modes of sublimation."

Of course social prejudice was just one of "the external difficulties," Bligh conceded, and perhaps with the rightly sympathetic person one could practice "something equivalent to the original 'talking cure' as originally invented by Breuer and Freud"—if one could also then overcome two further difficulties, the "censure [*sic*]" and the need for "a special psycho-analytical technique" to achieve a return to "early childish memories" for complete sublimation. But like you, he said to Bourne, "I am not aware of any personal trouble," and he offered these opinions only "in case they may be of use to you in studying any persons who may come your way."[41]

With such cleansing tactics of exoneration, Bligh kept the discussion above the plane of the personal and gave Bourne the opportunity to direct his subjective concerns into the appearance of broader, objective, "philosophical" channels. This whole correspondence upon "wish-emotions," emanating, one strongly surmises, from Bourne's deepest longings for love—not for coddling or pampering, but sexual love and fulfillment—illustrates something of the baffling ventriloquist's voice one hears in the *Youth and Life* essays, perhaps what Paul Rosenfeld had in mind when he referred to "the gingerly *Atlantic Monthly* style, with its mincingness of persons perpetually afeard of stepping on eggs."[42] The voice is indubitably Bourne's, intoned in the rapturous diction that resounds through every essay—"desire," "passion," "passion and enthusiasm," the "glory of being young," "radiant," "wistful," and inspired by sex, sexual love, "objectified" in "some charming and appealing girl," but also in "love for ideals," for youth is "swept away by a flood of love" no matter "if it be art, a girl, socialism, religion, the sentiment is the same." And yet these eloquent sounds seem like echoes off the distant wall or circumference of some imagined personality—"Youth," "the youth," "a youth" generally, but even the occasional first-person—and never from the center of a real person speaking his own real private desires.

What we witness in this Bligh-Bourne encounter is less an actual meeting of minds than a kind of charade with each man initially acting out the role flatteringly assigned him by the other, followed by a subtle, gradual reversal. Bourne the original petitioner became instructor to Bligh on the passions of youth; Bligh, responding at first as the older sage to an enthusiastic disciple, became the cautionary counselor, assenting to agreement in thought, but uncomfortable with the applications Bourne pressed for. Both men were enlightened Victorians, but Victorians still. The one sought liberation purely intellectual through a kind of *a priori* play with the ideas and concepts of the new psychology of personality; the other sought to liberate his emotions through a play with language, mixing the poetic abstractions of romantic idealism with the newer abstractions of psychology. Listen, for instance, to Bourne, in an essay newly written for *Youth and Life*,

"Virtues and Seasons of Life," in which he advocates for youth, of all things, temperance, a much esteemed Victorian virtue, but to which he gives a new twist in a way that seems clearly to echo the discussion with Bligh about sublimation, wish-emotions, and the need for candid talk about them:

And besides courage, youth needs temperance. The sins and excesses of hot-blooded youth are a byword; youth would not seem to be youth without its carnality and extravagance. It is fortunate that youth is able to expend that extravagance partly in idealism. Love is always the antidote to sensuality. And we can always, if we set ourselves resolutely to the task, transmute the lower values into higher. This, indeed, is the crucial virtue of youth, and temperance is the seal and evidence of the transmutation. Temperance in things of the flesh is ordained not through sentimental reasons, but on the best of physiological and psychological motives. Temperance is a virtue because of the evil consequences to one's self and others which follow excess of indulgence in appetite.

But this temperance does not mean quite the same thing as the rigid self-control that used to be preached. The new morality has a more positive ideal than the rigid mastery which self-control implies. We are to fix our attention more in giving our good impulses full play than in checking the bad. The theory is that if one is occupied with healthy ideas and activities, there will be no room or time for the expression of the unhealthy ones. Anything that implies an inhibition or struggle to repress is a draining away into a negative channel of energy that might make for positive constructive work in the character. The repressed desires and interests are not killed, but merely checked, and they persist, with unabated vigor, in struggling to get the upper hand again. . . .

In the realm of emotion, the dangers of rigid self-control are particularly evident. There are fashions in emotion as well as in dress, and it seems to have become the fashion in certain circles of youth to inhibit any emotional expression of the sincere or serious. . . . Such self-control dwarfs the spirit; it results only in misunderstandings and a tragic ignorance of life. It is one of the realest of vices of youth, for it is the parent of a host of minor ailments of the soul. . . . Virtue should actually crowd out vice, and temperance is the tool that youth finds ready to its hand. Temperance means the happy harmonizing and coordinating of the expression of one's personality; it means health, candor, sincerity, and wisdom—knowledge of one's self and the sympathetic understanding of comrades.[43]

If it is not altogether clear here how a temperate rather than rigid exercise of self-control will lead to mitigation of bad impulses, the temperance recommended is certainly one to which consenting youths of all ages and all generations can accommodate.

At any rate, it was through such an admixture of Victorian idealism with the new psychology that Bourne and Bligh seem to have found an accommodation. Both men looked forward to their meeting, and when Bourne hinted as early as November 1912 at a possible trip to Europe, Bligh instantly extended Bourne an invitation to visit him at his place in Wales where "we should have a good opportunity to think and talk out the ideas and aims which we seem to have in common."[44] By the following April when Bourne announced the news of his fellowship, Bligh was urging Bourne to plan for at least a fortnight with him, preferably in Wales and before October, but "after then and during all the Winter I am as sure as anybody can be about an unknown matter that I would like to spend as much time with you as you would care . . . to spend with me. In the psychological department I am rather a lonely person and I should welcome with all my heart the presence and conversation of anyone so sympathetic as yourself." Bourne would provide him, he said, with "the academic side" of psychology, while he could introduce Bourne to some "free lance people" and to his "fairly wide set of acquaintances in London, many of them women," who would surely amuse Bourne. Of course, he said, it was possible Bourne might not like him as well as he did his work and letters—but that seemed unlikely. Never had he found any relationship "which in prospect looks more hopeful or more promising."[45]

Small wonder that Bourne looked forward to his visit with Bligh as "pivotal." Less wonder, as one reviews the correspondence and takes note of the sharpening contrasts beneath the surface expressions of mutual admiration, that the meeting crumbled into embarrassed confusion and near anger instead. The planned fortnight's visit rudely ended after only four days.

Whether by well-intended plan or coincidence Bligh greeted Bourne's arrival with a crowd of other visitors at his house, his upper Bohemian friends, "a sophisticated London crowd—novelists, critics, journalists, conservative lawyers, nobles, and businessmen."[46] At first Bourne responded with awe and his customary expressions of delight. Writing after his first day or so there he reported that Bligh was "a very delightful and keen-sighted psychologist of personality, of great intellectual vigor, and I am having a royal time of talk with him." Bligh was drawing up a psychological diagram of his personality, he said, which would be "a most interesting document" when finished, but meanwhile it had already "thrown a flood of light on the contrast between the fabric of his ideas and mine." The politely muffled differences in their preceding correspondence apparently began to boom out more loudly—Bourne's needling of Bligh to acknowledge the impact on personality of social forces, and Bligh's mild defense of his capitalistic amusements became front lines from which each attacked the other.

Again at first, Bourne "delighted" in the clash—the word ripples through his letter of report. Bligh had delivered, in response to Bourne's "preachments of Socialism," a defense "of the most delightful creed of business success to which I ever listened. . . . I became almost converted to this glorious gospel of success." Bligh provided a complete apologia for laissez-faire, individualism, and the justice of the present industrial system. In this, and in their mutual exchanges of "psychological diagnoses"—for Bourne in his way, in a less "scientific manner" than Bligh's diagram, he admitted, was sizing up his host—Bourne saw all the more "the effect of economic security on personality," and was the more "confirmed in my Socialism," wanting to crush "the old ideals . . . all the more completely."[47]

We can only speculate on what happened in the next day or so, reconstructing the sudden puncturing of Bourne's delight from the confused and hurt tones of his letters to his friends in the first days and weeks after Bligh brusquely suggested he leave—offering the thin excuse of needing space for new visitors. Misjudging the appearance of free talk, "where spades are called spades," as he described the social atmosphere to a Columbia friend, Henry Elsasser, yet puzzled by the absence of both "sexual passion and moral indignation," Bourne evidently tried to provide the latter, enjoying the "triumph," as he said, "in coming out with a real shocker."[48] Was it the memory of those shockers, and the reaction to them, that still vibrated in another letter to Elsasser wherein he railed against those theories of sex which ignored the fact, as proved in his own case he said, "that 'this instinctive emotion of mysterious respect' can coexist perfectly in the same mind with the most disturbing and constant erotic emotion and fantasy?" Was it Bligh he had in mind when he said to Elsasser, in what seems like a self-directed rationalization, that an older person forgets that young people are not, like himself, well integrated, intellectual, and capable therefore of keeping distinct their erotic feelings and their fantasies, but rather are "unstable, slightly neurasthenic, amateurs, whom the shame and mystery of sex inflame, but who would often be perfectly capable . . . of working the whole subject . . . into their personality and acquiring a conscious control of it. . ."? Was it the prudishness he had uncovered beneath the facade of free talk that made him scornfully decry "this Puritanical policy of repression [that] brings everybody up to an idea of the complete divorce of the spiritual and the physical"?[49] (To his mother Bourne had written that Bligh reminded him of his Uncle Halsey—that good puritan— "and all the dominating people who put it over me in the past.")[50] Bourne's "shockers," whatever they were, issued no doubt in caustic ironies, and coming from an already shocking apparition, were too much. He left, and sought refuge in London in a round of externalities—museums, lecture halls, and political rallies.

By late January 1914, with the intervening months in London between him and the Wales experience, and from the more compatible surroundings of Paris, he could write that he had "almost forgotten the existence of S. M. Bligh."[51] But the remark itself, a seemingly casual nonsequitur at the end of a letter, suggests how much the memory still pained him. Dragging himself up out of the depths of his depression, he had turned more and more of his inner anguish against those expressions—institutional and cultural—which reminded him of Bligh and his friends. English social, political, and intellectual life he damned in letter after letter to his friends. The "sickening British unctuousness" made him wish Montcalm had triumphed at Quebec and won the rest of America so that "we had become tied up with French civilization instead of getting all our ideas from England." One good thing, however, he said, resulted from his English experience: his radicalism had been immensely strengthened, and he was heartened to have found "girls and youths here who are going through the same crises that some of us are in America. . . ." The "cleavage between the generations" as he observed it in England was dramatic.[52] Venting his spleen against the English, he thus returned to his warfare with "the older generation," wherever he found it, and to "youth," now being discovered as an international constituency. Revolt and change he professed to find everywhere in the air. He began accumulating concrete examples to fill out the grand generalizations that swept through *Youth and Life*.

In London, swinging to another extreme in English society from that represented by Bligh, he met the Fabian socialists, Beatrice and Sidney Webb, and attended working-class rallies where the rhetoric of socialist ideas seemed to him closer to the realities of the British industrial order. He attended meetings of suffragists, learning that the grievances of women were in many ways like those of the worker—both were among the exploited. He attended a lecture by George Bernard Shaw, whose works he had read and swallowed whole, savoring every morsel of his wit, and was not disappointed when he saw and heard him in person. G.K. Chesterton's public lecture did not change his opinion from his earlier judgment in his review of *Orthodoxy,* and he found the man himself, by contrast to the distinguished figure of Shaw, repulsive, gluttonous in his bulk. He finally met Havelock Ellis, whose studies of the psychology of sex Bligh had recommended to him, but Ellis proved a disappointment, evading Bourne's questions "as if he was afraid his answers would offend me."[53] But a high point was an evening spent with a genial H. G. Wells and a group of young Indian students and other intellectuals. It was reassuring to have had some of his expectations fulfilled, some one of his idols not prone to crumble.

IV *Young Intellectuals Abroad: Brooks and Bourne*

The most significant of his London meetings for his immediate future, however, was a long day of walking, talking, and dining with his younger countryman, Walter Lippmann. As with Bourne, Lippmann's first book, *A Preface to Politics*, had appeared that year, 1913, and he too was a marked man among the rising generation. *(Drift and Mastery,* Lippmann's next book appeared the following year, and Bourne called it "great . . . a book one would have given one's soul to have written.")[54] Possibly they talked of Lippmann's plans for the new weekly of ideas he and some friends were considering—the *New Republic* as it became.

Possibly, too, Bourne first heard from Lippmann about another young compatriot of theirs who had been getting some recognition—Van Wyck Brooks, also in England that year, and whom Lippmann had first met earlier that summer in a London bookshop. Curiously, the paths of Bourne and Brooks still did not cross, though each young writer's pilgrimage in Europe had similar motives, taking them to some of the same places, observing the same events, even seeking out the same people. Brooks met H.G. Wells (about whom he had just written a book), introduced to him by Lippmann; and also G.K. Chesterton, to whose "whale's bulk" he reacted very much as did Bourne. He met the Fabian socialists and was similarly impressed; and, teaching that year at the Workers' Educational Association, like Bourne he admired the working men and women he met, who were conversant with ideas, and who cared for literature in and for itself, "for the sole purpose of enriching their minds."[55]

When the two men finally did meet back in America, they discovered how much they had actually shared in that critical prewar year abroad and, more importantly, how their impressions, though separately recorded, harmonized. Their pilgrimages to Europe had followed parallel lines, though Brooks had a slight edge in time and experience on Bourne. He had first fallen in love with Europe through its art galleries and museums when as a young boy he had lived in Europe for a year with his family, touring Germany, France, Italy, and England. Like Bourne he had finished his undergraduate course in only three years (also elected to Phi Beta Kappa), and then he too had capped his collegiate studies with the next year abroad, in England, where he completed and published his first book, *The Wine of the Puritans* (1908). Inspired by, and in part modeled after G. Lowes Dickinson's *A Modern Symposium*—a book Bourne had also admired, even adopting the pseudonym "G. Lowes" for one of his undergraduate essays—this ambitious "Study of Present-Day America," cast in the form of a dialogue between two young Americans in Italy, might pass for a transcript of the actual talks which Brooks subsequently had with Bourne. The assessment of guilt against the puritans; the diatribes against American materialism but also the "*impossible*, idealists!—utterly scorning the real and the useful and the practical"; the high value placed upon youthful impulse and feelings, while deploring the divorce of feeling from intellect everywhere in American life and how that accounted for the failure of the American personality—all these issues and themes and more were becoming the rhetorical possessions of the prewar younger generation of Americans. Brooks and Bourne were in agreement on them before they met, each having whet his desires for America on the contrasting experiences of Europe.

Each young man experienced a sense of his inadequacy as an American before the appearance in Europe of an intellectual and social ferment that betokened a newly emerging order of free youthful spirits bent on creating a new society, like a work of art. It would be a society whose function—to permit the full expression of human personality—would be matched by its forms, as both young men found in the socialist vision of Kropotkin and the religious vision of Tolstoy; as Bourne found promised in the militant feminist movement in England; as both men saw in the working class movement; a society in which, each argued, scientific principles would serve ideals, the practical being what was the ideal. Such a practical ideal Bourne saw expressed in the communal art and townplanning on the continent, and both men found it illuminated by the example of H. G. Wells. Brooks, too, saw in Wells the model Americans needed: Wells had demonstrated, he said, that "theory divorced from practice is a mode of charlatanism," and he had carried one step further the revelation of socialism that society was "a colossal machine" in which all men were members by endowing society with "a personality," making it "a matter for art and a basis for religion."[56] How to release "the spiritual" in every man? Translate it, said Bourne, translate the word "spiritual" into that of the new religion of the young, the "social." Then everything became clear, "the social movement with all its manifestations—feminism, socialism, social religion, internationalism, etc.—slowly linking the chain of social consciousness, and thus transforming the individual persons, the individual groups, lifting them to a higher level, giving them a more abundant sense of sympathy and unanimity."[57]

Of course there were barriers to the achievement of this new community, "barriers of class, codes, institutions," as Bourne put it in his now habitual mode, which he shared with Brooks, of attributing a private anguish to some obstinacy in the world youth had inherited. Knowing how the world looked upon idealists, and not wanting to be impossible idealists themselves, yet desiring the ideal, caused anguish for both men.

When Bourne met the hardheaded gospel of success preached by Bligh, he protested the "perverse fate" which had imposed on him "a philosophy so cross-grained, so desperately impractical as mine of scorn for institutions, combined with a belief in their reform, —of scorn of exploitation combined with a need of the wherewithal to live, —of a fanatical belief in mass-movements and mass ideals, combined with a sensitiveness to unique and distinctive personality."[58]

Brooks was also disturbed and worried that his own vague yearnings for the ideal might end in a futile quest for the unobtainable, or worse, cripple his artistic ambitions as he faced also the necessity of contending with "the machinery of living," for he had a young wife and infant son besides, needing the wherewithal to live. *The Malady of the Ideal,* written the year before but published in England in 1913, in a small and little noticed edition, had been one attempt to remove the barriers standing in the way of his own artistic development. Projecting his anguish upon the subjects of his study, three representative nineteenth-century French writesr—Etienne de Sénancour, the author of *Obermann,* Maurice de Guérin, and Henri Amiel—he located the common source of their "malady," as revealed by their incomplete personalities and by the withering and fragmentation of their work, in the obstacles of the social order they had each inherited, such as the demands of patriotism, of a Calvinistic inheritance, of literary tradition itself. Hitting the same note as Bourne did again and again, Brooks wrote: "The spiritual nature of the individual will never be perfectly free until the collective nature is submerged in an all-embracing routine."[59] Defining a point of view for himself, Brooks became committed thereafter to a form of literary criticism that attended to the personality of the writer, equating literary form with the integrated personality, the whole person, whole because at one with a universal order of things. It was what he desired for himself; in order to achieve his own salvation he studied how other artists had been thwarted, using criticism to wear away life's obstacles by exposing them to the light of analysis. It was the scientific approach, he alleged, the approach of psychology, promising a cure if men could but see what stood in the way of healthy fulfillment.

Just as Bourne had confessed his desire to be a prophet, a prophet of youth, so Brooks was preparing himself in that year for a similar role. He published *The Malady of the Ideal*, but also completed the manuscripts for three other books, each to be published within the year of his return to America, 1914–1915. Besides the book on Wells, the study of a whole artist who involved himself in worldly affairs without submitting to their pressures, and who yet sought to make the real conform with an ideal vision—socialism—Brooks had first written another study of the incomplete artist, *John Addington Symonds*, in another attempt to diagram "scientifically" some of the repressions he suffered (chiefly puritanism). But it was the third of his projects in this ambitious year which was destined to bring him and Bourne together in the common attempt to purge America of its puritanic inheritance and to prophesy "America's Coming-of-Age," the title Brooks finally gave his book.

The final and most important effect on both men of their experiences that same year in Europe was to direct their thoughts and emotions back to America, to ways of clearing the social order there of impediments to the fulfilled personality, to a search for an American tradition that would help and not block or distract that fulfillment, and to encourage—lecture, as Bourne promised—their contemporaries to express their youthful desires.

A common error of crediting Bourne as a direct influence on the writing of *America's Coming-of-Age*, though indeed an error, is understandable. In the very year Brooks was putting it all together, Bourne was saying many of the same things in his correspondence to his friends, thinking the same thoughts, expressing the same feelings—even in minor ways sharing some of Brooks's references, as in the echo of Brooks's attack on Gerald Stanley Lee's then current book, *Inspired Millionaires*, with a characteristically caustic remark on "our uninspired millionaires . . . paying millions for some Italian painting of the 15th century, or presenting priceless sets of armor to some museum" rather than honoring American genius. But there are more significantly striking correspondences. The pronouncement about America's split mentality so memorably explained by Brooks in those catchwords "highbrow" and "lowbrow," derived as it may have been from George Santayana's earlier description of those two mentalities, one all aggressive enterprise, the other all genteel tradition, was already a commonplace with Bourne, as it became thereafter for others of his generation. The literary judgments both men arrived at that year were remarkably alike and connected to the same feelings. Bourne spent as much time in Europe pursuing his literary interests as he did in observing the social and political scene—in France, to the neglect of "sociology" he confessed. Literature for him was a primary source for the understanding and deciphering of personality. (He had urged Bligh, for instance, to use fiction and drama, autobiography and letters as a source of material for psychological inquiry.) And though he read widely the works of contemporary writers in England and France in his efforts to understand those national personalities, he also read and reread American writers, sorting out his critical assessments of his own country's literature, looking for the truly "indigenous" American personality.[60]

He carried "America" with him, as betrayed in a notable slip of the pen in a letter written from Paris: "only . . . *here*," he said, could Emerson, Thoreau, Whitman, and William James "have been written." He had started out on his journey, in fact, with Henry James's *The American*, reading it on the *Rochambeau*, and, reading more of him in London—*The Princess Casamassima*, for instance—added Henry James to his list as, surprisingly, "perhaps the most thoroughly American, with that wonderful sensitiveness to the spiritual differences between ourselves and the Older World, and the subtle misunderstandings that follow our contact with it [like his Bligh encounter?]." *The Princess Casamassima* was "a superb novel with wonderful radicals in it"; no doubt Bourne saw himself in that novel's protagonist, Hyacinth Robinson, whose radicalism was as romantically misty and without ideology as Bourne's at that point.[61]

Bourne had prepared for Europe in the spring before his departure by reading Whitman, stimulated by his sensuality and his "serene democratic wisdom." Reading Horace Traubel on Whitman, Bourne found encouragement, he said, in learning that Whitman had never been sure of himself, "that is of the permanency of his message. . . ." He wondered if there was not something, some spirit that made a person like Whitman, like himself perhaps, someone "with the gift of articulation say more than he is, speak clearly and authoritatively what he but dimly strives to reach. . . ." In London he made the delicious discovery of a handsome *de luxe* edition of *Leaves of Grass*, with full page illustrations "in lurid colors, of naked people with their arms around each other," and he facetiously proposed suggesting to the publisher an expurgated edition, "being the pictures that are to be expurgated."[62]

In France, his pains from his English experience were soothed by reading "the newest schools of French literature—some of them showing and acknowledging the strongest influence of Whitman," the "unanimistes" as one group called themselves; "a sort of Gallicized Whitman," Bourne labeled them. At a soiree arranged for him at the Sorbonne with some forty French students of

English, he held forth on his favorite subject, the ideals of youth in France and America, but also offered an exposition of Whitman's poetry, an easy transition for him.[63]

The "great spiritual relief" which Paris provided Bourne after the suffocating atmosphere of London came in large part from this discovery of a shared reverence for Whitman. He responded more to the erotic Whitman than Brooks did, but the private route he traveled through his "doubly endowed" desire led him to the same Whitman Brooks revealed as the hero of "The America Myth," as one who spoke for and to youth: the Whitman who provided, Brooks wrote in his fable for Yankees, "the rudiments of a middle tradition," bringing together theory and practice, in whom "the hitherto incompatible extremes of the American temperament were fused," who precipitated the "American character," casting all its separate elements into a crucible from which they emerged "harmonious and molten, in a fresh democratic ideal, which is based upon the whole personality."

Every strong personal impulse, every cooperating and unifying impulse, everything that enriches the social background, everything that enriches the individual, everything that impels and clarifies in the modern world owes something to Whitman. And especially of those American writers who have written preeminently for young men—and which has not?—Whitman alone . . . has pitched his tone to the real spring of action in them.[64]

Yes, Bourne could have written that, the Bourne who wrote preeminently for youth, and who knew something of the desire that coiled the spring of action in young men. And even as Brooks was probably formulating his iconoclastic chapter on "Our Poets" in *America's Coming-of-Age,* extending Whitman's challenge to "the abnormal dignity of American letters," Bourne was exploding with similar sarcasm at the same group of canonized saints. "Why can't we get patriotic and recognize our great men?" he asked, alluding to Emerson, Thoreau, Whitman, and the two Jameses:

[These] express the American genius and those ideals of adventurous democracy that we are beginning to lose, partly through having filled our heads with admiration of English rubbish, and partly through having formed a stupid canon of our own with Poe and Cooper and lifeless Hawthorne and bourgeois Longfellow and silly Lowell . . . What a great man Holmes would have been if he had had better company than Boston wits and genteel society! . . . There was nothing American about any of these except the Indians of Cooper and the Salem of Hawthorne. None of them but might have been written, like Washington Irving, in England.[65]

Brooks and Bourne did not meet in fact until sometime in the fall of 1915, probably in New York City; but clearly they had already approached each other in their thoughts and feelings about America as both reacted in the same way to what Bourne called "our cultural humility before the civilizations of Europe." They returned from the experience abroad, each of them, to campaign for what Bourne unabashedly called "cultural chauvinism," the most harmless of patriotisms, he said, but "absolutely necessary for a true life of civilization."[66]

V *France*

As his letters and his report on his fellowship abroad to Columbia's trustees make abundantly clear, it was the civilization of the French which he most admired. His single most striking impression of Europe, he reported, "was the extraordinary toughness and homogeneity of the cultural fabric" in the countries he visited. But this impression derived more from his experience in France than anywhere else. The "fatuous cheerfulness" that reigned everywhere in England betrayed to him there an unimaginative people, "well schooled against personal reactions." Discussion there was marked by "incorrigible intellectual frivolity. . . . You found your tone either monstrously prophetic, as of a young Jeremiah sitting at the board, or else unpleasantly cynical. Irony does not seem to be known in England." For one committed to a life of irony, that was damnation enough. But there was worse. Without remarking the contradiction to his impression of Europe's culturally homogeneous nations, he said the English "national mind seemed to have made a sort of permanent derangement of intellect from emotion." The caricatured visage of Bligh still seems to rise from these lines that report his impression of a literary and intellectual life "hobbyized" by leisurely country gentlemen for whom ideas were taken as sports while their real interests lay elsewhere.[67]

By sharp contrast, he reported, in France "I soon felt an intellectual vivacity, a sincerity and candor, a tendency to think emotions and feel ideas, that integrated again the spiritual world as I knew it. . . ."[68] The contrast did not "wipe out" his annoyances with England, however, as he reported, so much as add to the strength of the vinegar he dashed on "Anglo-Saxondom" and puritanism thereafter. And one surmises that the "spiritual world" alluded to was in fact his emotional world, the world of sensation and physical desire, that recovered some measure of wholeness after the shattering rebuffs and, as it had turned out, the women who had not amused him either in Wales or in London. Desire, his personal conflicting physical and spiritual desire; Whitman and comradeship; and women—women in their social roles in England, France, and America, and particular women, women with personality, one of whom he constantly hoped would prove to be the right sympathetic person to release him from his entrapment in a physical and moralistic cage—these are among the recurring and intertwining subjects of the most personal of his letters, the ones that confess more of what was happening *to* him, apart from all else he observed of what was happening around him in Europe. On these subjects the irony is turned back upon himself. There are poignant passages too of the male perplexities that have accompanied "consciousness raising" about sex roles in our own day. But as all his letters were also exercises for the essays he was preparing to write or was actually writing, an idealizing movement sets into his prose. The self-conscious prophet of youth, confirmed in his radicalism, tasting and liking the bitter sweetness of how people reacted to him, is settling into his assumed role.

The "transvaluation of values" begun some ten years before was about complete. So he said to one of his women correspondents, Mary Messer, shortly after he had arrived in France. But he still suffered doubts as to whether he could now actually become the leader of a league of youth, find the right platform or forum for preaching his ideas and values, and achieve fame and joy in his work. He became all the more consciously sensitive to the irony of his lot; yearning for the comradeship that Whitman's poems heralded, he persuaded himself that the key to all his interwoven problems was love, and its deprivation "the one impediment to blossoming."[69]

About the comradeship of men and women, I have a few such wonderful woman friends that I begin to think that perfect play of idea and appreciation is making an ideal real,—when up springs eternal, insatiable desire, the realization of which, inhibited in me, sets the old problem recurring poignantly, and makes me wonder whether Shaw's preface to "Getting Married" is not the profoundest and wisest word on the matter ever written. It is a subject to make one's thoughts, indeed, go round and round without satisfaction, and particularly when one is a man, and a man cruelly blasted by the powers that brought him into the world, in a way that makes him both impossible to be desired and yet—cruel irony that wise Montaigne knew about—doubly endowed with desire. Give him then an extreme fastidiousness of idealism, and you have a soul that should satisfy the most ironical of the gods. Encase that soul, which is myself, in Puritan morality, and you produce a refined species of spiritual torture, which is relieved only by the demands, appeals, fortunately strong, of philosophy and music, and heaven-sent irony which softens and heals the wounds. But, to complete the job, make him poor and deny him the thorough satisfaction of the higher appeals, deny him steady work and thus make easy the sway of desire, and you force all his self-impelled action, all his thinking and constructive work, to be done in hampering struggle with this unrealized desire, which yet—another irony—colors all his appreciations, motivates his love of personality, and fills his life with a sort of smouldering beauty. This is a complete, if perhaps too dark picture. But like many things in life, both it and the other side are true.[70]

There is something at once embarrassing and wistfully appealing in this passage and similar plaintive and complaining notes about himself in other letters—chiefly those to his women correspondents, rarely if ever to his male friends. "Poignant," we may wish to say of it, except that Bourne has embarrassingly anticipated us and provided the label himself, as he has also denied us an original appreciation of the ironies. And it is not too dark a picture, except as we strip it of its formal dressings—the literary allusions to Shaw, to "wise Montaigne"; the highlighting effect of abstractions like "desire," "ideal" and "idealism," the "soul," the "higher appeals," and "smouldering beauty"; the pleasing balanced phrasing of mounting paradoxes ("and particularly when one is a man, and a man cruelly blasted"; "impossible to be desired and yet . . . doubly endowed with desire"; "But . . . make him poor and deny him . . . deny him . . . and you force all . . . all . . . which yet . . . colors . . . motivates . . . and fills. . . ."). The form that contains the picture thus makes it glow with romantic lighting that pushes back the darkness. Only knowing him, reviewing the physical content, his ugly, misshapened appearance, as most of his correspondents could, is it really *too* dark a picture;

possibly, to some of his correspondents, like the women who sensed an appeal directly to them, not dark enough.

Of course it is an ironic portrait, resting upon contradictions, a calculated mixture of the dark and the light. Some of the contradictions lay outside the portrait: he was not, after all, without comradeship and loyal friends; in any absolute sense he was not poor; and though he might still feel that Columbia had "denied" him an appointment, one he still hankered for, he was at the moment enjoying its award of a fairly posh fellowship, and the *Atlantic Monthly* was accepting and publishing several of his essays. These expressions are romantic indulgences, part of a then fashionable pursuit of the life of poverty, like Van Wyck Brooks's choice to travel steerage on his first solo year abroad.

But the striking feature of the irony here as in nearly all Bourne's portraits of youth—the self-portraits like this one and in other letters, the sketch of Miro, the portraits of other "symbolic" youths, the generalized youth in so many of his essays—is the consciousness of the irony. It *is* calculated. Kenneth Kenniston speaks of the kind of process that seems to be unfolding here as characteristic of one of the stages of youth. It involves, he writes, "a new level of consciousness—consciousness of consciousness, awareness of awareness, and a breaking-away of the phenomenological 'I' from the contents of consciousness." The "I" in Bourne's letters and essays often has an uncanny kind of detachment from his subject when that subject is himself, himself as youth. In more conventional literary terms we recognize this as "aesthetic distance," yet it resembles the breaking away that Kenniston remarks, one which "permits phenomenological games, intellectual tricks"—the kind of magic Bourne performed in translating himself from "freak" into "beautiful person" (as members of the young generation of the 1960s could insist on, to the bewilderment of their elders). This stance accounts for the appealing feature of Bourne's style and tone, what enabled his young contemporaries, and others since, to find themselves revealed in his writings. "He had studied his chosen minority [that is, youth] with such instinctive care," Van Wyck Brooks said, "that everything he wrote came as a personal message," and his young readers found in them "a sort of corpus, a text full of secret ciphers, and packed with meaning between the lines, of all the most intimate questions and difficulties and turns of thought and feeling that make up the soul of young America."[71]

Kenniston provides further suggestive insight into why Bourne was able to get this kind of recognition from and identification with his young readers when he observes how this breaking-away of the phenomenological ego provides "a cognitive underpinning for many of the characteristics and special disturbances of youth, for example, youth's hyper awareness of inner processes, the focus upon states of consciousness as objects to be controlled and altered, and the frightening disappearance of the phenomenological ego in an endless regress of awarenesses of awarenesses." To others who experience, or recall the experience of such "transformations of youth"—as Kenniston describes them—Bourne is decipherable. His writings contain such transformations, studied, as Brooks said, with "instinctive care." Brought into sharp, almost painful focus by his own crippled state, Bourne's instincts were those of youth generally. Hence the appeal to him and his generation of psychology as a science promising a way of controlling and releasing personality, of William James's pragmatism and the relativism of its world, of Dewey's instrumentalism for its promise of altering society. These were among the awakening influences on the younger generation of the 1910s, but similar responses to similar forces continue to characterize the moral and intellectual passage of youth toward adulthood, making Bourne still accessible as a spokesman for those making the same passage.

The oracular voice of the *Youth and Life* essays, speaking homilies that still can charm us into acquiescence (like the final sentence of the passage quoted above) could not alone have sustained Bourne's leadership as spokesman. The idealizing tendency that works in each of them is what appeals, but also what makes them vulnerable to criticism: the clinching concrete detail too often is simply not there. The experiences in Europe, however, prepared Bourne to consolidate his role. On the one hand they made him more acutely aware of his own awareness, of the process and strength of his desires—and of the pain of their frustration; but on the other, the obligation of the fellowship itself, reenforcing his need to resolve the self-society tensions he suffered, committed him to "sociology," to seek understanding of himself and youth in the larger context of social and historical forces. His observations were brought into the service of his generalizing habit, and he remained, always, the participant-observer on whom the impressions were recorded, from whom the generalizations were made. His "sociology" was poetic rather than scientific, buttressed with personal sensory data, as it were, rather than with an array of verifiable, objective facts. Nevertheless, his insights were often prophetic, anticipating what others who followed him would verify.

The movement from his personal center of consciousness to a social center is illustrated in the same letter to Mary Messer quoted from above. It is a smooth transition, but in a few lines he has leaped from an apparently highly personal lament onto a plane of sociological speculation about America's future as a civilization:

> So much of the cruelty of human relations seems to me to spring from the unequal endowment of desire and appreciation in men and women, and this arises largely from the inequalities of position and social milieu. That is why my socialism is so democratic and communistic—utterly unlike the English Socialism—and why the feminist movement is so inspiring, for it is going, I hope, to assert the feminine point of view,—the more personal, social, emotional attitude towards things, and so often the crudities of this hard, hierarchical, over-organized, anarchic—in the sense of split-up into uncomprehending groups—civilization which masculine domination has created in Anglo-Saxondom.

The "I" is still in charge here, but the assertive "I" of the preceding paragraph is replaced by the speculative, translating the personal dilemma he has just discussed into that of human relations generally, his own cruel plight now become the cruelty in all relations between the sexes. He found it significant that the feminist movement in France was weak, with little of the strident militancy he had witnessed in England. It was because, he said, women were taken seriously in France; even though without rights, they were "citoyennes" and accepted as an integral part of civilization. In England they were largely superfluous; in America they "occupy a highly artificial position, adored and despised at once." He wondered whether we could overthrow "the evil tentacles of English civilization in America and work the feminine into our spirit and life . . . the personal, the non-official, the spirit that Tolstoi preaches in *Resurrection* and Shaw in his best plays. . . ." In France Bourne learned to identify his desires with "the feminine," and to mate that term with his hitherto lonely masculine noun, "youth."

He learned that in France, but not so much from the French as from his own emotional needs. He had made those confident comparisons within a few days of his arrival in Paris, before he had

had time enough to accumulate many observations, but time enough to prepare for the impressions he desired. He found little thereafter to alter those first recorded convictions about the superiority of the feminine and the French, often repeating the same sentiments in almost identical phrasing in letters written months later.

He remained in Paris until after spring had fully arrived, in late April 1914. During that time he busied himself in a routine that became "general policy" for him during the rest of his stay in Europe—"running down the various social institutions, churches, courts, schools, political meetings, etc. in order to get, at least, a taste of French society in operation." This much he reported to Columbia's trustees; but he did not tell them how he had spent most of his last month in Paris. He reserved that for a sketch he wrote and published a year later, "Mon Amie," about the young nineteen-year-old French woman who had responded to the note he had left at the Sorbonne asking for an exchange of conversation. She was real enough, a Madeleine or an Yvonne, perhaps both, but she became, under his pen, another projection of the ideal of youth, in a small way satisfying the longing he had brought with him to Paris.

When she talked, he wrote, "she seemed too palpably a symbol of luminous youth, a flaming militant of the younger generation," and he expressed amazement at the good fortune of his having crossed the seas to find "my own enthusiasms and ideals vibrating with so intense a glow" in her. All the "enthusiasms and ideals" he had already attributed to youth are there, each haloed by a glowing adjective: the "wistful seriousness" of her face; her "malicious irony," "charming frankness," and "blazing candor"; her "brimming idealism," and especially "the sensual delight which she took in thinking, the way her ideas were all warmly felt and her feelings luminously expressed." Withal, she was mostly, not *a* feminist, but simply, "feminist." Did he fall in love with her? Probably yes, but probably also, as he disarmingly confessed in his sketch, not so much with her as with "the eternal youth of France that she was." The feminine and youth joined.[72]

VI *The Coming of War*

After Paris Bourne joined his friend Arthur Macmahon in Naples, and together they toured Italy, Switzerland, Germany, and—finally and swiftly—the Scandinavian countries. Swiftly, because a

European war had started in August. Caught in Berlin as Austria declared war on Serbia, Bourne witnessed the depressing sight of enthusiastic crowds of youths singing their nationalistic desires—for war. He had to cancel his plans to attend a socialist congress in Vienna and he and Macmahon hastily retreated before the war's swift advance, going to Sweden and Denmark, and taking a ship's passage home from Oslo. "The heavens had fallen." War became the crowning irony for this irony-clad youth.

"Every war is ironic," as Paul Fussell has reminded us, "because every war is worse than expected."[73] But the Great War, he added, was more ironic than any war before or since because it proved such a shocking, horrible reversal of the preceding century's prevailing faith in the idea of progress. Subsequent life in the twentieth century has made even the name "Great War" ironically obsolete, retaining, as it suggests, a trace of that lingering melioristic faith that, if there had been none before so "great," there could surely not be another greater war after it. But we settle now for "World War I," having had "World War II" and several continuations, while we await "World War III" which may be the war to end wars by ending everything. The ironies of war have become the characteristic ironies of our century. The "Great War" is distinctive, as Fussell demonstrates, for having generated so many of the familiar ironies we now live with, so commonplace as to have lost their sting, requiring a reforging of irony as an instrument, as in the hands of some of our black humorists.

In the pre-Orwellian world of the early years of our century, however, the Great War was ironic not only in proving to be horrendously worse than expected: it had been so widely unexpected in the first place. Enlightenment had progressed so far, public faith had it, that wars were no longer possible—not, at least, between the enlightened nations of the world, those, that is, of Europe, of "Western civilization."

Bourne was no exception in being blinded to the war's coming by his own progressive faith. His European correspondence betrays little or no awareness of the approaching cataclysm, despite his commitment to observing the political scene. He had seen or read about a good deal of strife within each country he visited: the Irish rebellion and a series of strikes while he was in England; the general strike he got caught in while in Rome, which for a while seemed to him the beginning of a revolution; and everywhere evidence of military preparation. But what impressed him about the last was the "persistent hostility" to compulsory service in England, and the "unyielding opposition" in France to a similar new military service law, culminating in parliamentary elections in April which he saw as "a clear national expression of reluctance at the increased military expenditures"; and the general strike in Italy seemed to him "a direct popular uprising against war and militarism."[74]

These observations, however, were recorded after the war had come, incorporated in his report, when he was underscoring his own innocence "of the impending horror." Then, in retrospect, he confessed how little his mind had been able to grasp or imagine the fact that the uniformed soldiers he had seen sprinkled on the sidewalks, and the wagon trains and other signs of armaments in the streets were anything but "frozen symbols" of power, menacing and grim, but only expressions in the language of the day whereby nations boasted their strength and prestige. In light of the event "of the world-war" (how quickly that all-embracing label got applied to "the event") his ramblings and interests in those thirteen months preceding it appeared like "the toddlings of an innocent child about the edge of a volcano's crater."[75]

The report is a remarkable document not only for what it reveals of Bourne's own estimate of what he had learned in those thirteen months, but also for the way it voices a special irony released by the Great War at its unexpected onset. Many in England and on the Continent experienced the same "hideous embarrassment," as Fussell aptly describes it. In illustration Fussell quotes Henry James, writing the day after the British enter the war: "The plunge of civilization into this abyss of blood and darkness . . . is a thing that so gives away the whole long age during which we have supposed the world to be, with whatever abatement, gradually bettering, that to have to take it all now for what the treacherous years were all the while really making for and *meaning* is too tragic for any words."[76]

Bourne could not have had the same extent of emotional investment in those treacherous years that James had, of course; indeed he had, or thought he had, renounced his allegiance to many of the values of the preceding older generation. Nevertheless his immediate feeling was similar to James's, a kind of agonized embarrassment at having been duped. Writing from shipboard as he prepared to leave Europe behind him, he said to Alyse Gregory: "The wheels of the clock have so completely stopped in Europe and this civilization that I have been admiring so much seems so palpably about to be torn to shreds that I do not even want to think about Europe until the war is over and life is running again."[77]

He did have to think about Europe as he composed his report, and there he expressed that special irony, appropriately named in a phrase of Gibbon's that Fussell makes use of, "the abridgment of hope." The main body of the report—excepting the caustic comments on the English—is an almost exuberant listing of the virtues of the several national civilizations he had observed, rising to a final high tribute to those of the Scandinavian countries where he had sensed "the most advanced civilization, yet without sophistication, a luminous modern intelligence that selected and controlled and did not allow itself to be overwhelmed by the chaos of twentieth-century possibility." But the opening of the report is about the war, and the closing of the report is about the war, making all in between go sour. Introducing his report he notes that the year he was in Europe may mark the "end of an era"—in self-conscious quotes. All that he is reporting upon—the development of democratic tendencies, social reforms, international understanding, the striking material development in Germany and Italy evidenced in the rebuilding of cities and other "vast communal projects"—have been "snapped off like threads, perhaps never to be pieced together again." He had been innocent of impending disaster, but so were others in "this year of last breathless hush before the explosion." The final pages of the report are about his last two weeks in "the distressed and anxious northern countries." "Nothing but war," there, with mobilizing youths on the country roads of Denmark, in the streets of Stockholm, "even the Norwegians drilling against none knew what possible attack." A final moving interview with a Swedish socialist leader revealed the depths of shock felt at "the wreck of socialist and humanitarian hopes. . . ." The effect of thus enclosing his report between the dark quotation marks of the war is an ironic undercutting or canceling out of the report's validity. History had, as it were, embarrassed him, embarrassed all of Europe.

As with everything about Bourne, there is still another ironic twisting of hope and despair occurring during the breathless pause between the end of the year in Europe and the resumption of his life and ambitions in America. Unlike James and unlike that socialist leader in Sweden, Bourne was still young and he was going home to a land not yet at war and whose likely involvement, indeed, seemed as remote and preposterous as the explosion of it in Europe had been. Though his ready use of the term "world war" and the repeated metaphor in his letters about the clock of the *World* having stopped belied that faith, Bourne and America could still draw on that faith's reserves. "Bracing" himself against the war, as he said, he resolved to use his energy "not in despair or recrimination, but only in an attempt to understand." Paradoxically, for Bourne and many other young Americans, like Brooks and Lippmann, the war in Europe gave America its great opportunity to advance the cause of civilization. In the effort to do that Bourne returned to America with resurgent hope, determined to "sting people into new ideals and tastes."[78]

The genteel ironist of *Youth and Life* had been tempered and hardened in Europe, his innocence seered by the erupting volcano of war. As the fires of Europe's war burned closer to America, his ironic voice rose to a steely pitch against the threatened abridgment of young America's desire.

CHAPTER 2

Youth and Life

A man's "spiritual fabric" is almost completely woven by the time he is into his twenties, according to Bourne. True or not, his own ideas and ideals had been pretty well formulated by the time, aged twenty-eight, he left Europe and returned to America to start living beyond youth. Those ideas and ideals may not have been so radical as he supposed, or at least as he declared them to be, but the way he had formed and expressed them, and the ways in which he proceeded to apply them made him seem radical to others of his generation. They too thought of themselves, self-consciously and proudly, as rebellious and revolutionary. They may not have been very radical either, as some historians of the Progressive era have suggested, but that is how, partly under Bourne's guidance, they perceived themselves. It may be worth-while at this point, therefore, to attempt a summary of the ideas and ideals which made up the spiritual biography of his generation that Bourne gave to them in his *Youth and Life*.

First and foremost was his concept of youth. Nearly all else that he addressed himself to is suffused with that ideal and the special burden of meanings he poured into it. It is an all-embracing term, virtually equated with the second word in his book's title, "life." He defined it and used it in such a way as to take it beyond meaning merely a stage of personal growth; it was for him a state of being, a state of consciousness of being alive. Hence it followed that a life truly lived was the life of perpetual youth, a life that preserved the initial consciousness of the wonder of life that is first fully experienced in youth. Thoroughly romantic, it is Bourne's equivalent to the nineteenth-century concept of the "self," only more perilously poised, having no absolute existence, only a relative one defined by time and how it appears to those no longer young. "Youth," he said, "seems curiously fragile. Perhaps it is because all beauty has something of the precarious and fleeting about it." Youth is a state of heightened awareness of life. Life's "wistfulness and haunting pathos" is especially real only to youth, for "it feels the rush of time past it," and is haunted by the sense of change, not simply "the feeling of past change," the false wistfulness of middle and old age, but also "by the presentiment of future change."

Under Bourne's use of it, the concept of youth has a way of melting and merging with other concepts: life, reality, change—all positive values, of course. Or it takes on positive coloration by being contrasted with its opposition—middle age, old age, the older generation. The concept of the generation is a necessary corollary to that of youth, but these are not defined by chronological gaps between them any more than youth is defined by age—though twenty-five is the magic symbolic age used by Bourne in these essays. The "older generation" consists of those who are running the world with damaged ideals, or ideals become dogma, fixed by tradition, by dead tradition. Hence if youth and the younger generation equal life, reality, change, truth, idealism, then that which is dead, fanciful or unreal, static or immovable, false and sentimental, is the older generation. Once one has gotten the clue to this Manichaean world the rest can be an amusing little game: youth is to democracy as the older generation is to_______? Or, "In this conflict between youth and its elders,_______is the incarnation of reason pitted against the rigidity of tradition."[1]

This may not be altogether fair to Bourne's portrait of youth, risking a reduction of it to caricature. But caricature and the idealized sketch have in common a simplicity of content, even an oversimplification, and depend for their effectiveness on manner and style; the line between them may very well be a brush stroke turned up instead of down. What I wish to emphasize here is that Bourne's achievement was one of style: his brush strokes are consistently up, and the idealized youth that emerges from his book is a charming, forceful, and persuasive champion for the young in heart of all ages, and this achievement is less a triumph of argument by idea than of persuasion by rhetorical skill.

Bourne's most effective rhetorical device, what makes for the oversimplified division of his world between the forces of good and the forces of evil, when reduced to outline, is the balanced, parallel construction. What happens in the sentence is matched by what happens in the paragraph, most often constructed on the principle of comparison and contrast; and similarly, from essay to essay, there is balance and matching and overlapping, the book, like each essay, developing in Emersonian fashion in a spiraling rather than linear progression. One effect, already remarked upon, is that of one concept almost imperceptibly becoming identified with another, less through direct comparison or connection than through a repeated common rhetorical locution. The interconnectedness of all things, the organic universe Bourne valued so highly, is thus intimately manifest in his style and expresses that principle of growth and of awareness which is at the heart of his concept of youth.

It is time for an example from an early page in the essay "Youth":

> The ideas of the young are the living, the potential ideas; those of the old, the dying, or the already dead. This is why it behooves youth to be not less radical, but even more radical, than it would naturally be. It must be not simply contemporaneous, but a generation ahead of the times, so that when it comes into control of the world, it will be precisely right and coincident with the conditions of the world as it finds them. If the youth of today could really achieve this miracle, they would have found the secret of "perpetual youth."[2]

The Manichaean contrast is evident here as is the rhetorical parallelism governing each sentence. The full implications of youth's identity with the radical and radicalism will be expounded by Bourne at greater length in two later essays, "For Radicals" and "The Mystic Turned Radical." In the latter, where Maeterlinck is used by Bourne as "the best of modern mystics," we learn that it was Maeterlinck from whom Bourne learned that "an excess of radicalism is essential to the equilibrium of life." Society's habit, Maeterlinck had said, is always to think in terms less reasonable than are required. We learn that "with the instinct of the true radical, the poet [Maeterlinck] had gone to the root of the social attitude." But this radical who is a poet is also youth. In the first essay the birth of youth was described as follows:

> Youth has suddenly become conscious of life. It has eaten of the tree of knowledge of good and evil.
>
> As the world breaks in on a boy with its crashing thunder, he has a feeling of expansion, of sudden wisdom and sudden care. The atoms of things seem to be disintegrating around him. Then come the tearings and

the grindings and the wrenchings, and in that conflict the radical or the poet is made.[3]

Youth is thus made into the true radical and poet by his titanic struggle with the world's conditions (but also, for the achievement of perpetual youth, he must struggle with "inner spiritual ones"). Still later (in "The Life of Irony") we will learn that what makes the youth into a radical and a poet is also what accounts for his being an ironist born (not made) and whose passion for comprehension is what in turn makes youth as an ironist "a person who counts in the world."

As the "incarnation of reason" youth actually adopts "the scientific attitude," that is, a remorseful questioning of all that is old, and a daring willingness to experiment. And as with radicalism, Bourne argued in "The Adventure of Life," not less but more was needed: "Not less science but more science do we need in order that we may more and more get into our control the forces and properties of nature, and guide them for our benefit." Whether more radicalism or more science, more irony or more mysticism or more poetry, they are needed for "control," for insuring youth's "command" of the world when its turn comes. This recurring exhortation makes *Youth and Life* a kind of manual of power, a series of rhetorical calisthenics proposed as preparation for the assumption of power. They are exercises for the individual but designed to insure a social and collective end. They are proposals for the development of personality, for only "the most glowing personality" is assured of influence, of exercising power. The rationale for this lies, of course, in youth's consciousness of being alive: "We are alive, and we have a right to interpret the world as living; we are persons, and we have the right to interpret the world in terms of personality." This is, moreover, a religious consciousness—a good transcendental awareness, as it turns out—the sense that there is "the humble fragment of a divine personality" in youth's own. And so we come full circle from youth to the mysterious core of life itself which is contained in the personality that is youth.

"Desire," as we have seen, is a crucial word in Bourne's world. Hardly an idea, not quite susceptible to being an ideal, it points rather to a fact of experience, something Bourne felt acutely and attributed to all youth. It is part of the paradoxical figure of Bourne's youth that he can be that supreme ironist, cool, detached, scientific, capable of getting outside himself, and also very much possessed by all sorts of desires and passions that sway him almost beyond control. Bourne's radical youth sought to capitalize upon the strength of youth's desires, releasing them from the restraints imposed on them by social custom and tradition, and directing them to noble fulfilling ends. At bottom, as I have suggested is evidenced in Bourne's correspondence, especially that with Bligh, Bourne recognized youth's desire as a sexual force. Sex is given explicit recognition in *Youth and Life* as one of youth's "supremest and most poignant of adventures," the other being death, "the one the gateway into life, the other out of it."[4] But it is implicitly present behind the masking defenses of an abstract language, a language that throbs with feeling. On the one hand Bourne's diction makes intense the felt wishes and hopes Bourne attributes to the young; on the other, his figurative language emphasizes the frustrating constraints and inhibitions working against the fulfilling expression of youthful personality. Often he takes off on metaphors of battle: "To get command of these arch-enemies [sex and death] is an endeavor worthy of the moral heroes of today. We can get control, it seems, of the rest of our souls but these always lie in wait to torment and harass us."[5] Youth thinks of itself only as the "master of things," never as a mere "soldier in the ranks," but as the leader, "leading the cohorts to victory . . . bringing in some long-awaited change by a brilliant *coup d'etat* or writing and speaking words of fire that win a million hearts at a stroke."[6] (Bourne's youthful warrior often turns out to be that poet whose weapons are words, as with the ironist, too, whose armor is almost impregnable against "the shafts of fortune and blows of friends or enemies" for "he knows how to parry each thrust and prepare for every emergency.")[7] The "enemy" or the barriers, the obstructions, provoke in youth an "intolerant rage" or a "passionate despair" as youth "collides" with them, against the "inertia" of older men, and the "moral hedges" that surround life; or as he struggles to throw off the "weight" of dead tradition, or the "fetters" of a puritan code. When it is not battle that youth is waging, he is contending against some poison, sickness, or festering sores for which "youth is the drastic antiseptic." Yet running throughout this world of conflict or plague is a persistent thread of exuberant hope sparkling with youth's desire, which is also "passion" or "enthusiasm" or both at once, generally "turbulent," or burning in youth's "furnace" or "crucible."[8]

And there is little doubt about youth's eventual triumph. "It is the glory of the present age that in it one can be young," Bourne trumpeted. "Our times give no check to the radical tendencies of youth. On the contrary, they give the directest stimulation. A muddle of a world and a wide outlook combine to inspire us to the bravest of radicalisms. Great issues have been born in the last century, and are now loose in the world. There is a radical philosophy that illuminates our environment, gives us terms in which to express what we see, and coordinates our otherwise aimless reactions." Precisely what the "great issues" were he did not say, presuming his audience would know them, of course—which is another reason why succeeding generations have been able to fill in the blanks with their own notions of the "great issues." Pragmatism is presumably the radical philosophy he alludes to, but nowhere in *Youth and Life* is there any mention of William James as, indeed, there is a paucity of direct reference to any proper names to illuminate the issues which youth is going to bring to some triumphant culmination.

Broadly, very broadly, his words sweep up all the melioristic spirit of the early Progressive era and place youth on the crest of its still moving wave. "The great social movement of yesterday and today and tomorrow has hit us of the younger generation hard." This sentence, opening his essay "For Radicals," leaps beyond history as does much that immediately follows: "Many of us were early converted to a belief in the possibilities of a regenerated social order, and to a passionate desire to do something in aid of that regeneration. The appeal is not only to our sympathy for the weak and exploited, but also to our delight in a healthy, free, social life, to an artistic longing for a society where the treasures of civilization may be open to all, and to our desire for an environment where we ourselves will be able to exercise our capacities, and exert the untrammeled influences which we believe might be ours and our fellows'." All this had for "the disinterested and serious youth of to-day" the powerful attraction of "a practicable ideal." It was this marriage of the ideal with the efficient that made youth "gloriously hopeful" for the future, and this hope "is the lever of progress,—one might say, the only lever of progress."[9]

More than any other feature of the book, this optimistic faith in youth's victory, linked as here with the idea of progress and that in turn dependent upon the marriage of the ideal and the practical, made Bourne appear far less radical than his other words declared his youth to be. As Henry May has pointed out, a belief in progress was one of three main articles in the dominant American faith, and not simply the nineteenth century's belief in an inevitable evolutionary improvement, but in one that men could shape, as Bourne argued that it was youth's special mission to do. Moreover, the average American considered himself, like Bourne's youth, an idealist, but also like Bourne's youth, a "practical idealist," a phrase, May says, that most Americans happily subscribed to, finding it sanctioned by no less an authority than Harvard's philosopher Josiah Royce—one of Bourne's idols at this stage, and whose name he sometimes included in his pantheon of the American geniuses who spoke the ideals of adventurous democracy.[10]

Though Bourne spoke as if his youth were the only practical idealist on the horizon, there were in fact many in his American audience who identified themselves with him, including many in that older generation Bourne was inclined to dismiss with contempt. Indeed, there was some truth in the charge leveled at him by one of his older critics (in rebuttal to an *Atlantic Monthly* essay that appeared after *Youth and Life*) that in his enumeration of tasks the younger generation had to fulfill Bourne cited lessons the older generation had already taught. His book, moreover, was well received, generally praised, and in conservative organs at that—the *Dial* reviewer, for instance, welcoming the arrival of an essayist "who can deal with the larger themes with something like finality" (and noting, too, the paradox of his using "so reflective a form of literary art" as the essay to express the turbulent energies of youth).[11]

With some justification, therefore, historians like Louis Filler have concluded that much of Bourne's radical thinking in this book was only a "facade of idealism"; the abstract nature of his rebellion made him "stimulating," perhaps, but nevertheless "acceptable to the calm-browed reader of the *Atlantic Monthly*."[12] Still, *Youth and Life*, and not just Bourne's subsequent radical postures, as toward the war, for instance, established him in the eyes of his contemporaries as a radical spokesman, and it is still capable of stirring young readers into making radicalism their cause. The facade is deceptive, or a facade at all only if behind it we expect to find specific issues of time and place—and there are none, or few so specific as to have a particular historical identity.

The issue is only one, the big one of life itself, of life in America. *Youth and Life* is therefore little dated by its content. But it was and remains a truly radical book, and some genuinely explosive challenges were imbedded in the cottony abstractions of its language, needing only the events of history, in Bourne's own time and since, to set young readers aglow with a sense of radical defiance of their elders.

To begin with, though his apparent endorsement of the idea of progress posed no challenge to one of the three received doctrines of nineteenth-century America, Bourne's thoroughgoing moral relativism did challenge another. May speaks of it as first in importance and in its widespread acceptance: "the reality, certainty, and eternity of moral values," and the corollary belief in the applicability of moral judgments in all areas of expression and behavior, in art and literature as well as in politics and social conduct. Most Americans, as May said, agreed that right and wrong were most important categories, that all good citizens knew one from the other and would act properly given a choice between them. "Whatever challenged this set of assumptions," according to May, "was genuinely revolutionary."[13]

To be sure, there had been a moment during Bourne's undergraduate years when he betrayed a still lingering allegiance to the demon of the absolute. In a *Columbia Monthly* review of Professor Joel Spingarn's published lecture, *The New Criticism*, he had attacked Spingarn's Crocean views because they ruled out "all that savors of the ethical," and denied the "humanistic" vitality of the art of the past. Bourne had expressed his preference instead for "the sane and healthy message" of Harvard's Professor Irving Babbitt. (In appreciation, Babbitt wrote to Bourne that he was encouraged "to see younger men . . . take up and continue what seems to me the good fight.")[14] But it was not long after this that Bourne began to revise his understanding of Spingarn's views and to shift toward a position that would eventually have him joining in the attack on the humanism of Babbitt and Paul Elmer More and their disciple, Stuart Sherman. *Youth and Life* amply anticipates that attack in its persistent sniping at the dogmas of the past and at puritanic codes of morality. What had intervened in the meantime was Bourne's growing interest in psychology, on the one hand, with its attention to the unconscious aspects of men's behavior, and on the other hand his interest in social and economic issues, like those of women's rights and the rights of workers, both of which groups seemed denied justice under old notions of right and wrong.

He became suspicious of the "Sane and healthy message" of Irving Babbitt with its stress on rationality. "It is good to be reasonable," he wrote in *Youth and Life*, "but too much rationality puts the soul at odds with life." "The old rigid morality," he said, had "riveted the moral life to logic" and "neglected the fundamental fact of our irrationality." In a passage that May might have cited in support of his own description of that moral faith Bourne went on: "It believed that if we only knew what was good we would do it. It was therefore satisfied with telling us what was good, and expecting us automatically to do it. But . . . we are creatures of instincts and impulses that we do not set going. And education has never taught us more than very imperfectly how to train these impulses in accordance with our worthy desires."[15]

Elsewhere in *Youth and Life* he wrote that "social morality" was not something to be taught, to be inculcated in children, for instance—as he had said in his critique of Spingarn that "the common sense of the centuries" testified to—but rather something that could only be built up by each individual "out of a vast store of experience." A child could not get "the relish of right and wrong until he has tasted life, and . . . [t]hat taste comes only with youth," and youth, as we have seen, is a relative stage of consciousness. Yet it was only with youth Bourne asserted, "that the moral life begins, the true relish of right and wrong," and, moreover, this "must be a relish of social right and wrong as well as individual."[16]

If it was genuinely revolutionary simply to question the old assumptions, it was more so to make youth virtually the creator of moral life, forged moreover out of youth's desires, or, as he put it, out of the hot "crucible of passion and enthusiasm" and tested in "the furnace of youth's poignant reactions to the world of possibilities and ideals that has been suddenly opened up to it." A hot metaphor appropriately conveyed a hot idea. And to insure its enthusiastic reception by those he had in mind, Bourne limited this moral life to the elite among youths. Not those victimized by the old morality; they would suffer from the "imposed priggishness," would have their vision of the whole life permanently distorted, or would be stupidly "oblivious of the spiritual wonders on every side." But for those who had somehow escaped? Bourne's rhetoric persuaded them of the virtues of being revolutionary:

> Only those who have been allowed to grow freely like young plants, with the sun and air above their heads, will get the full beauty and benefit of youth. Only those whose eyes have been kept wide open ceaselessly learning the facts of the material and practical world will truly appreciate the values of the moral world, and be able to acquire virtue. Only with this fund of practical knowledge will the youth be able to balance and contrast and compare the bits of his experience, see them in the light of their total meaning, and learn to prefer rightly one bit to another.[17]

Bourne's moral relativism, with its emphasis as here upon the practical, was a feature of his pragmatism, of course, that revolutionary philosophy so inspiring to others of his generation. He was quite consistent in extending it to every other reach of life. In so doing he sounded the really revolutionary note in his book, one that challenged his own apparent commitment to the reigning faith in progress and which anticipated the ironic abridgment of hope he contended with in his final years.

May speaks of "the hinge" which joined the belief in eternal morality with the belief in progress as "the central and most vulnerable point in the American credo of the early twentieth century."[18] In the essay "Seeing, We See Not" Bourne betrayed the fragile nature of his own commitment to progress, raising the questions that would shortly unhinge those joined faiths for himself and others of his generation. This essay, paradoxically, is the most quiet, meditative one in the collection, and it casts a subtle shadow of doubt over the optimism of the rest of the book. Moreover, though Bourne did not confront directly and challenge the third article in the standard American credo, as May enumerates them—the belief in culture—until after his return from Europe with a new sense of a national culture, there is also the faint hint that the hinge which joined a belief in culture to the other faiths was also weak.

The essay is a meditation on historical relativism, taking off with an allusion to Maeterlinck again—one of *Youth and Life*'s favorite touchstones. It expresses a position that Bourne's Columbia teacher, Charles A. Beard, would champion at a later time. It also anticipated his friend Van Wyck Brooks who would seize the same notion and, forging a new hinge, would connect it to the new ideas of culture and argue the need for "creating a usable past."

"History is peculiarly the creation of the present," Bourne wrote, agreeing with Maeterlinck that it was mere superstition to suppose anything about the past was irrevocable. "On the contrary, we are constantly rearranging it, revising it, remaking it." It is only the past we do make, he said, and tradition was nothing more than the "artistic creation of a whole people or race." But this perception led to the depressing thought that we had less to do with making the present than we supposed, and that we could not see what was distinctive or imperishable in our own time. In a series of observations and questions Bourne then pointed out the transitory and possibly deceptive nature of the signs of progress, the doubts that after centuries of man's being "in transition" some kind of "crystallization" or absolute achievement had occurred. "We are weeding out our culture, and casting aside the classical literature that was the breeding ground for the old ideas," he said—a positive achievement for Bourne—but he had misgivings about the little that was taking its place. He was looking for a "robust and vital" grasping of life, but to him most of modern literature, art, and music seemed feverish, morbid, and only a restless groping so far. Was the socialistic state coming into being? Was religion doomed, or simply being transformed? "Will our age actually be distinctive as the era of the Dawn of Peace, or will the baby institution of arbitration disappear before a crude and terrible reality? Are we progressing, or shall we seem to have sown the seeds of world decay in this age of ours, and at a great crisis in history let slip another opportunity to carry mankind to a higher social level?"[19]

In this meditation on time he expressed youth's special sense for the rush of time, for the haunting feeling of past change, but also for the "presentiment of future change." Are we progressing? It was a radical question then, in the 1910s, with all the public emphasis upon progress; but it remains a radical question, always putting the older generation on the defensive as responsible for the past and the present, and making for apprehension about future possibilities to which the young are committed and determined to control when the future arrives.

The special radicalism of youth contained in *Youth and Life* cannot be fully assessed in some historical context alone. Even more than Lippmann's *Drift and Mastery,* which Bourne wished he had written, and with which *Youth and Life* corresponds in so many ways—the common antipathy to absolutes and stasis, to puritanism; the shared faith that science or the scientific attitude could serve desire intelligently, and that control or mastery of progress could be achieved; all these common positions expressed in comparable prophetic tones and with a similar quality of abstraction, even the self-conscious labeling of them all by Lippmann as "the rebel program"—it transcends its contemporary aims. What historical significance it possesses lies in its announcing and containing, almost for the first time, that "new" stage of life called youth; but it provides in its style, tone, and point of view not so much an historical as a mythical model for dissenting youth. *Youth and Life*, unlike *Drift and Mastery* and unlike another "manifesto" of the younger generation of the 1910s, *America's Coming-of-Age*, both of which more consciously issued a call for action in a particular historical moment, is a kind of fiction going on outside of time, the idealized autobiography of a character called "youth."

"The world is in need of true autobiographies," Bourne said in his book, and he argued that "the best autobiographies are still the masters of fiction, those wizards of imaginative sympathy, who create souls and then write their spiritual history, as those souls themselves, were they alive, could perhaps never write them."[20] Bourne may not have exactly created youth, but his imaginative sympathy, sharpened by his unique condition, enabled him to write its spiritual history in advance of the "psychohistorical" analyses we have of youth now, which seem simply, but uncannily, to confirm his insights.

Kenneth Kenniston's compressed, "schematic" summary of the themes of youth—*his* ideal type or model—for instance, is a virtual abstract of the themes in *Youth and Life*. Greatly simplifed, Kenniston's major themes of youth are these: the central conscious issue during youth is the *tension between self and society*, characterized by youth's pervasive *ambivalence* toward both self and society, involving a "characteristic stance" toward both self and society in an effort to reconcile them, a stance Kenniston calls "the *wary probe*" but which resembles Bourne's "life of irony"; phenomenologically, youth is a time of alternating *estrangement and omnipotentiality*, leading to another characteristic, the *refusal of socialization*, Bourne's "dodging of pressures," and a paradoxical relationship to history, often involving an attempt to reject history but in its own way (by creating a more "usable" or relevant past, for instance); there occurs in youth the emergence of *youth-specific identities*, inherently temporary, but involving a deep commitment for whatever the duration to the positive advantages of simply being youthful; another special issue during youth is "the enormous value" placed upon change, with the consequent abhorrence of stasis, often part of a heightened *valuation of development* itself (Bourne's life as adventure and experiment); *fear of death*, as in all stages, takes a special form in youth for which it is simply the cessation of all vitality, the end of all movement, progress, and promise ("Death I do not understand at all. . . . [It is] a perpetual warning of how much there is to be known and one in the way of human progress and development")[21]; this in turn affects the youthful view of adulthood (Bourne's older generation) which is equated with stasis and death; and the desire for perpetual youth proceeds therefore from an assumption that to "grow up" is to cease to be alive. Finally, youths tend to band together into *youthful countercultures*, for youth is a time when solidarity with other youths is important (Bourne's making friendship so important for his youth, his tendency to think of youth as "in league," or in his collective notion of "young America").[22]

There is more in *Youth and Life* and the rest of Bourne's story than just this outline of his themes. He did more than observe and record and report. He created a spokesman; his voice spoke the words of youth, in the tones and accents of the young practical idealist.

CHAPTER 3

The New Republic *and The Education of Young America*

IF all wars are ironic, they are also inherently dramatic. The outbreak of the Great War in Europe in 1914 led to a dramatic cultural situation in America, bringing to the surface latent tensions between abstraction and sensation, between the reality Americans were committed to and the reality they were experiencing. Such tensions had long been present in American culture, throughout most of the nineteenth century, in fact. Ralph Waldo Emerson had first dragged them out into the open, as it were, back in the 1830s, and the geniuses of Henry David Thoreau, Nathaniel Hawthorne, Herman Melville, Walt Whitman, and some others, each in his way, had been challenged to reconcile them in their art. Such a cultural tension makes for what Allen Tate once described as "the perfect literary situation," transpiring, he said, in a society where "culture is not self-contained and sufficient," and where "the spiritual community is breaking up,"[1] where, I might add, the commitment to what experience ought to be seems moving further and further from what experience is. It is a situation made for the ironist.

These cultural tensions had surfaced in the dramatic clash of the Civil War which, after the manner of wars, reduced or oversimplified them to stark opposites of right and wrong. In the years and decades that followed, while in fact the breakup of the spiritual community Americans gave allegiance to continued, even accelerated under forces that brought about sharp cleavages between regions, classes, and new immigrant additions, belief in that community with its sense of mission was reasserted all the more vigorously. A kind of national conspiracy set in to abolish the fact of division and disjunction and to establish as the reigning reality an American success story. The discerning of facts amid appearances and the reconciling of them in art became something of a rarity, the private pursuit of an Emily Dickinson, for instance, or of another born ironist like Henry Adams; or it took the inverted route of humor, as with Mark Twain, or the convoluted analyses of Henry James who quite consciously subjected the tensions between innocense and experience to his scrutiny over the whole range of irony from comic to tragic. For a brief while in the 1890s irony seemed about to break out all over as a number of writers appeared who were capable of capitalizing on a perfect literary situation—Hamlin Garland, Stephen Crane, Frank Norris, even a William Dean Howells exploring the contradictory hazards of new fortunes and using the ironic form of a utopian novel.

Perhaps it was war again which had caused the tensions between American aspirations and American achievements to surface, imaginatively contained in Crane's war novel, *The Red Badge of Courage*, in actuality as the decade and the century closed amid the military sounds of war with Spain. Perhaps too it was war—in this instance a neat, brief, apparently heroic war—and its reductionist effect which once again had modulated those tensions into apparent accord as the triple-headed faith in progress, morality, and culture seemed all the more certified by an American victory. In any event, though subdued, the tensions between hope and despair over the promise of the American mission still throbbed just beneath the surface of American life, and Bourne and others of his generation were responding anew to the tautness between them. It is not surprising that as they sought in their turn to effect some reconciliation of their desires with the facts of their experience and observations, they too became ironists and rediscovered, or discovered for the first time, their kinship with some of their predecessors, revising the American canon and giving new status to an Emily Dickinson and Stephen Crane, reversing the popular estimates of Mark Twain and Henry James, hailing *The Education of Henry Adams* when it finally went public in 1918, and, in time, rescuing Herman Melville from near oblivion.

Two metaphors (and their variants) of those years just before America got swept into the Great War contain between them the cultural tensions which Bourne's irony played upon. One spoke the shocking effect of the Great War on the progressive idea, commonly expressed as Bourne had put it: the wheels of the clock of the world had stopped. The other spoke not of cessation, of endings, but of new beginnings, or renaissance: "The fiddles are tuning as it were all over America." The remark was that of John Butler Yeats, father of the poet William Butler Yeats, and who in his seventieth year had settled in New York City; it was recorded and given currency by Van Wyck Brooks in *America's Coming-of-Age* as coming from "the best, the *youngest* . . . of all good Americans."[2]

The ironic distance between the two metaphors existing side by side at the same time is evident enough in the flat denotative contrasts of stop and start. A subtler tension between them results from connotative differences, for they are different kinds of metaphors. The clock metaphor is mechanical and implies some sense of linear development, of forward movement in time—stopped in this instance. Though Bourne used it in connection with the concept of civilization, whose "advance" of course moved in concert with advancing time, it was war, the ultimate political gesture among nations, which had brought things to a halt. In the context of the event itself, therefore, the metaphor reverberates with implications of political failure; democratic "tendencies," a political measure of a civilization's advance, were what the war had brought to a halt. The metaphor is appropriate for politics. Yeats' metaphor is aesthetic, deriving from the realm of art. It speaks of preparation, but not for some consequent linear development toward some mechanical resolution; rather it implies a pending culmination in the complex order of art, requiring orchestration of diverse parts. The metaphor is appropriate for culture.

Much of the energy of young American critics in the 1910s, Bourne in particular, would be spent in attempts to resolve the tensions between the claims of politics on the one hand and those of culture on the other—or, in some instances, to keep them distinct from one another. Their efforts not only divided them from the older generation but also made for division among themselves. Bourne was almost alone in persisting and insisting to the end—that is, through America's own participation in the Great War—on their intertwining claims. With the juxtaposition of those two metaphors, to paraphrase Lionel Trilling writing in a somewhat different but related context, Bourne had arrived at the dark and bloody crossroads where culture and politics meet.[3]

The extreme contrast of moods expressed in those metaphors also imparted to the prewar years, 1912–1917, a special kind of sorrowful joy not matched before or since in the American experience. The alternations between surges of hope and then of despair were rapid as events inspired first one, then the other. It was a difficult time for youth, a stage acutely sensitive to both moods and peculiarly prone to lapse or rise swiftly from one to the other. Bourne exulted in the experience, however, but with the special painful joy of the ironist. "A life such as the life of irony, lived fully and joyously, cannot be peaceful," he had written, nor could it even be "happy, in the sense of calm content and satisfaction." But it might be wise, it might be fruitful, and in any event the ironist's "ironical interpretation of the world is his life, and this world is his nourishment."[4]

There was plenty to nourish Bourne's life of irony, both in his private world and in the cultural scene in America to which he returned in early September 1914. Along with the moments of private anguish and doubts and the awkward embarrassments during his year in Europe, he had had his moments of triumph, of feeling vindicated in his radical vision of possibilities for America. Along with his despair at the crashing desperate finale of his year in Europe he returned to America with his personal ambitions soaring on the secure certainty of a steady job, one that promised him just the sort of forum he had hoped for—as a regular contributor to the newly founded *New Republic*, at a guaranteed 1,000 dollars a year. And as an outer sign of his determination to count for something, to display his new worldliness, to translate his handicap, he wore a long, flowing student cape brought home from France. He cut a strange but apparently appealing figure as he settled into the bohemian life of Greenwich Village where there was rich nourishment for both abstraction and sensation.

His personal ambitions joined with those of many another young American feeling the excitement of rebellion. The Atlantic's broad expanse deceptively buffered them against the spread of the war's despair. The war was deplorable, but distant, a horrible spectacle to be watched from afar while America seized the opportunity to fulfill its own promise. Rather quickly the war was reduced in dramatic terms to a titanic conflict between civilization and barbarism, though which side represented which got confused by the conflicting loyalties among Americans—until the mix of events, Allied propaganda, and the deeper allegiances of history advanced the claims of the Allies as the defenders of civilization. Only an ironist would appreciate the irony of a barbaric war, of any war, being fought for civilized causes. But such is war, ironically.

Bourne saw this early and saw it late, but it remained a minority view, increasingly so the later it got. In 1914, however, and for a brief few years thereafter, he was in the comforting presence of many like-minded young intellectuals and artists. A youth movement in behalf of America and spurred on rather than depressed by the war in Europe had already taken off.

The *New Republic*'s founding was but one sign among many of an American cultural renaissance. Some of the first signals had come from the hitherto barren cultural wastes of the American midwest, with Chicago providing the center. Harriet Monroe's *Poetry: A Magazine of Verse* had commenced in October 1912. Though it may have begun "almost as pure reaction against the neglect of the poet"[5] and in response to no other glimmering lights of idealism, it shortly became a leading beacon lighting up the whole scene of joyous rebellion, focusing attention upon new talents but also upon the very idea of "the modern" and upon the idea of renaissance. Its motto from Whitman, "To have great poets there must be great audiences too," was also the conviction of the likes of Bourne, Brooks, and the founders of the *New Republic*, Herbert Croly and Walter Lippmann, that the whole cultural fabric needed rethreading, that people needed stirring up, stung into new awareness. (Brooks too recalled Whitman's plea and would say, over and over again, citing Matthew Arnold as his authority, that it was the business of criticism "to make a situation of which the creative power can profitably avail itself.") *Poetry* may have had a midwestern flavor, especially after its "discoveries" of Vachel Lindsay, Edgar Lee Masters, and Carl Sandburg, but the early liaison Harriet Monroe established with Ezra Pound in London also gave the magazine an international reach that conveyed the news of a new flowering everywhere.

In the same year, in fact only weeks after *Poetry*'s first issue, an anthology of verse called *The Lyric Year* was published, undistinguished except for Edna St. Vincent Millay's "Renascence" which released the very word, and worth noting because of the ensuing controversy over the failure to give that precocious effort a prize. Both facts contributed to a public consciousness of youthful rebellions. Millay would further contribute to a joining of the idea of youth with that of the feminine as she became one of the liveliest figures in the youthful culture of Greenwich Village.

As the decade wore on, Pound's countering of *Poetry's* midwestern accent was complemented by a backtracking to the east of many young midwestern rebels like Floyd Dell, Francis Hackett, and others. Their experience of growing up in the midwest became an issue in their rebellion, and writers like Masters, Sherwood Anderson, and Theodore Dreiser, all midwesterners, came along to confirm them in their belief that mid-America was the symbolic center of puritanic America, thwarting youthful desire, fiercely enforcing the Ten Commandments—as Dreiser asserted[6]—and through repression and furtive concealment rendering American lives grotesque. The countering pole attracting these midwestern refugees was in the east, in New York City, in Greenwich Village, with lines of force flowing in from European rebels and challengers to nineteenth-century faiths, like Freud, Wells and Shaw, Marx, Nietzsche and Tolstoy.

Nietzsche represented to Bourne "the splendid liberation from alien codes, the smashing of inequalities and cowardice," while Tolstoy, he said, stood for "the positive interweaving of understanding and love."[7] Both strands were woven into the ironic texture of his own thought and feeling, but it was the Nietzschean emphasis on liberation that shined through most of all.

The early followers of a creed do not prove it, as Nietzsche himself quipped, but young intellectuals like Bourne, for all their commitment to idealism and democracy, found themselves intoxicated by Nietzsche's iconoclastic assault on nineteenth-century morality and they salted their language with Nietzschean aphorisms and phrases (Bourne's use of "transvaluation of values," for instance, and "will-to-power" along with the Nietzschean flavor of disdain for "the herd" as in the essay "The Dodging of Pressures" which echoes Nietzsche as much if not more than it does Thoreau).

In 1914 H.L. Mencken, a young authority on Nietzsche (he had published a popular account of *The Philosophy of Friedrich Nietzsche* in 1908 when he was twenty-eight) became coeditor with George Jean Nathan of *The Smart Set*, "A Magazine for Minds That Are Not Primitive," which over the next several years spread further the gospel according to Nietzsche as applied to the American scene. In time it became indistinguishable from the gospel according to Mencken and added a lively raucous note to youth's rebellion against puritanism and for art. In time, ironically, Bourne would take issue with Mencken for not focusing his attack, "as Nietzsche made it," on the moralism of "our general middle-class civilization" itself rather than on its symptoms. Bourne committed the ironic effrontery of calling Mencken himself a moralist.[8] But for a while they joined in the same crusade for cultural liberation, employing similarly steely rhetorical weapons, though Mencken's were tempered more by laughing brimstone than were Bourne's chillier ironies.

Another magazine with an abrasive sense of humor and, as it boasted in its masthead, "no respect for the respectable," was *The Masses*, emanating from Greenwich Village itself. (*The Smart Set*, originally a New York City based magazine, after 1914 was largely brewed in Baltimore, Mencken's hometown.) In late August 1912, Max Eastman, a recent Columbia graduate student—an ABD we would say today—who had studied with John Dewey, found himself, not yet thirty, elected editor, with no pay, of this cooperatively owned socialist magazine. Like Bourne, Brooks, Croly, Lippmann, and other young rebels of this generation, Eastman too came from a middle-class background. Both his parents, in fact, as he liked to point out, had been Congregational ministers. Eastman gathered around him on the staff of *The Masses* other young self-proclaimed socialists, like John Reed, Harvard, class of 1910, notorious reporter of the Paterson strike of 1913 (he was himself arrested with many of the strikers) and chief organizer of the famous Strike Pageant held in Madison Square Garden; who with his later reports on the Mexican revolt of Pancho Villa and then the war in eastern Europe became the most romantically dashing war correspondent of his generation; who would help in organizing the first Communist party in the United States, and who, after witnessing and reporting at firsthand the Russian revolution would die an untimely death, there in Russia, with honorable burial in the Kremlin itself, destined to make him share martyrdom with Bourne. And then there was Floyd Dell, rebel from the midwest, who joined Eastman as his "superbly gifted associate editor."[9]

In words that Bourne might have written, and would certainly have endorsed, Dell later recalled how he and his *Masses* colleagues had been set afire by the liberating gods of Europe—Shaw, Wells, Roland—but also by Whitman's celebration of the individual, by

Emerson's "burning advice . . . to be uncompromising, [by] the invective of Thoreau upon the spirit of conformity—a veritable arsenal of swordlike thoughts with which to fit youth for its first struggles with whatever tyrannies of traditional society it might meet." Karl Marx too, of course, could have, should have been added to the list of "liberating gods" from Europe, but the native sources Dell listed seem closer to the spirit of the prewar *Masses*. For all the seriousness with which the magazine tackled social issues, exposed the defects of capitalism, and planted itself firmly on the side of the working class, it was the *manner* with which Eastman, for instance, seized "so joyfully upon Marx's idea of progress through class struggle" more than any Marxist idea itself which gave *The Masses* its distinctive voice among Greenwich Village rebels.[10]

More stinging too, and also more indelibly preserving the magazine's special humorous tone and stance in its critique of American society was its stark black-and-white cartoon art, given almost as much space as the printed word. The regular cover drawings and the others inside with their one-line captions gave notoriety to the Ash-Can School of artists—Art Young, John Sloan, Boardman Robinson, Stuart Davis, and George Bellows, to name only some of the more enduring artists among the sixty or so who contributed to *The Masses*. The contributors called themselves socialists, but they were individualists, each and all, and some of them, like Sloan, one of the artists and aspiring writers (Van Wyck Brooks among the latter) who had gathered around J.B. Yeats where he held forth at Petitpas', a pensione on West 29th Street, had been in the forefront of a rebellion in the arts for some time. They were among the fiddlers Yeats saw tuning up. Art and politics came together in *The Masses*, but art was essentially in charge.

Bourne would join with Max Eastman and others in signing manifestoes against the war and even contribute a piece or two to *The Masses* and another to its successor, *The Liberator*. That is the way it was among the young men returning westward from Europe or moving eastward from the Midwest during that "protected little historic moment of peace and progress"[11] before America went to war. They met in the Village, established their own magazines or revamped old ones, met to talk politics and art, to experiment in free love and free verse, and to write for one another's magazines. *The Masses* may have been to the left, as we loosely suggest differences in radical positions, *The Smart Set* on the right, and the *New Republic* somewhere in between (while wanting to appear leaning leftward), but they all were to the left of the older generation, and that is what counted, what brought the young together.

Back from Europe, Bourne enjoyed reunion with old friends and commenced the making of many new ones. He started out sharing an apartment in a model tenement on 31st Street with his old Columbia friend, Carl Zigrosser, who was continuing his study of art. He resumed a friendship with Beulah Amidon, a Barnard student he had met the year before, and with her friend Dorothy Teall they formed a frequent threesome. He fell in love with Beulah, and though he knew it was old-fashioned or out-of-fashion among his Village friends, he wanted to marry her. More serious than his mockery betrayed, he suggested to Dorothy that she get Beulah to offer to marry *him*. He suffered the inevitable rebuff. Bounding back from that blow, he fell in love again with another "free spirit" in the Village, again desperately, and again suffered catastrophic rejection, leaving him with the ironic pangs of resentment and yearning. These were soothed by his meeting yet another pair of vivacious young women, Esther Cornell, a Bryn Mawr graduate and aspiring actress, and Agnes de Lima, a Vassar graduate committed to social work and educational reform, a subject Bourne was becoming expert on: another threesome, with others sometimes joining them. In the summer of 1916 he shared an artist's residence in nearby New Jersey with Cornell, de Lima, and Frances Anderson of the *New Republic*'s staff, later on *The Masses*, all of them commuting to the City while Bourne devoted himself to his writing. And of course he fell in love again—with Esther Cornell.[12]

Emotionally he remained a youth, trying to reconcile the conflicting demands of sexual longings with the social realities of the day, also full of conflict and contradictions. Intellectually he continued as a student, frequenting The New York Public Library, exchanging ideas with new friends among his colleagues on the *New Republic*, writing his essays—his efforts to stir his readers to desire as mightily as he did. "Contradictions and anomalies, the fiercest radicalisms, the most dogged conservatisms, irrepressible gayety, bitter melancholy,"[13] as he had described the time of youth, marked both his private and public worlds, the turbulence in one reenforcing that in the other. And though he might have wished to address larger cultural issues, particularly those having to do with the state of the arts in America, the particular area assigned him by the *New Republic*—education—committed him to continuing preoccupation with the issue of youth.

Prompted by recommendations from both Charles A. Beard and Ellery Sedgwick, Herbert Croly had first written to Bourne while the latter was still in Europe, inviting him to join the *New Republic*, describing it as "a new journal of political, social, economic and literary criticism" that would be "radical without being socialistic and . . . pragmatic rather than doctrinaire" — bound to invite a warm response from Bourne, as it did. In the ensuing correspondence between the two men, they exchanged opinions and discovered broad areas of agreement. Croly probed Bourne to ascertain where he might fit into the staff he was recruiting, and Bourne offered his point of view on the whole spectrum of issues the *New Republic* aimed to cover. By September, with Bourne back in Bloomfield, Croly still spoke broadly of the kind of criticism "we" on the *New Republic* wanted—one with "a certain amount of conscious patriotism," a positive emphasis that would try to discover and develop "the beginning of sound work wherever they [*sic*] appear in this country." In the criticism of the fine arts "we have already decided," he said, to adopt the attitude Bourne had expressed, that the only way to proceed "in the present chaos of artistic standards and practices . . . [was] on the basis of social standards." Such notes may have raised Bourne's hopes, but when Croly also asked to see copies of Bourne's work, *Youth and Life* and an article he had written on "Individuality in Education," he was inevitably cast as the *New Republic's* specialists on education and youth.[14]

No two listings of Bourne's total contributions to the *New Republic* agree, since his articles and reviews were either signed with various combinations of his initials, or over pseudonyms ("Juvenis," "Max Coe"), and many more simply left unsigned, some no doubt not yet identified as his. Yet it seems safe to say that between the magazine's first issue in October 1914, until a month or two before his death in December 1918, Bourne may have contributed well over a hundred essays and reviews, and nearly half of these, more or less (depending upon the total count) had to do with some aspect or issue of education. These in turn are among the ones easily identifiable as his, and most, but not all, were brought together in the only two books after *Youth and Life* published in his lifetime.

The first of these, *The Gary Schools*, published early in 1916, was the result of a specific assignment which had sent him to Gary, Indiana, to study and report upon an experiment there in educating "the whole child." Three schools under the direction of one William Wirt, and supported by the U.S. Steel Corporation's attempt to make Gary a model community for its workers, were actively pursuing John Dewey's ideal of the "embryonic community life" for children. Wirt's success in Gary had brought him national attention, and even as Bourne's reporting appeared Wirt was engaged in a similar effort to remodel some of the public schools in New York City and provoking considerable debate and controversy. It was a hot local issue as well as a national issue. Bourne's pieces placed him well out front among advocates of the Gary plan as the most promising application of the educational philosophy of John Dewey.

Bourne reprinted some of the *Gary Schools* essays along with other *New Republic* pieces in the second book, *Education and Living*, a collection with a broader sweep ranging up through issues connected with college and university. Published in the critical month of April 1917—critical for the country, formally declared at war that month, and for Bourne whose career took a decisive turn with the appearance of his first essay in the *Seven Arts*, most brilliant but short-lived of the new magazines of the younger generation—it is the more important of the two books in any assessment of his developing role as a spokesman for his generation.

The book's title, taken from its lead-off essay, neatly parallels that of *Youth and Life* and is as suggestively all-inclusive; but the shift from "Youth" to "Education" and from "Life" to "Living" is consonant with Bourne's emphasis now on process rather than a state of being. *Youth and Life* had been written largely from his own subjective awareness of what he desired, projected through an idealization of what life should be; youth, that state of awareness, became synonymous with life. His *New Republic* assignment drove him to study the social processes which might best bring that youth into being. Education, the social process becoming dominant if not yet displacing those of church and family, necessarily became synonymous with living—again as an ideal. The point of view of his essays was, as Bourne confessed, "the product of an enthusiasm for the educational philosophy of John Dewey,"[15] but it was also indubitably his own, expressing his own experiences and desires. His modest disclaimer that he offered only "glimpses and paraphrases" of the new tendencies in schools and colleges, and but a paraphrase of Dewey's philosophy, slights the contribution he made, not only to the popularizing of Dewey's theories but also to the resurgent romantic faith of his generation that youth could transform the world.

The essays are uneven in merit, but less so than many a comparable collection of pieces written to meet regular weekly deadlines. The reprinted Gary school pieces are the least remarkable now, the reason for their inclusion—"because of the usefulness of a concrete example to hang wandering theory to"—being the reason they are now dated, albeit historically curious. There is much throughout that one reads today with a sense of déjà vu, since the intervening years have seen much that was experimental or revolutionary in education in 1915 become the norm, with ensuing reactions setting off new waves of experiments. Bourne's criticism of "the old school," of "the wasted years" between primary and high school, of unimaginative teachers, of the educational bureaucracy, of the low intellectual caliber of American undergraduates; his rehearsal of the arguments for and against vocationalism in school and college, his criticism of university trustees, private or public, who act for vested interests rather than for the public welfare—all these may sound familiar. But of course, after making due allowance for the fact of today's new school becoming tomorrow's old school, if the arguments sound familiar that familiarity testifies to Bourne's continuing relevancy and to issues that still are with us. A modern industrial democracy undertaking the responsibility of mass education, as Bourne saw sooner and better than most observers, constantly risks sacrificing or infringing upon its commitment to individualism in order to provide for its social and technological needs. Recognizing the necessity of striking some kind of balance between these two aims, Bourne used his rhetorical skill to enforce the first as primary, reserving his ironic thrusts for those tendencies in educational theory and practice which threatened to stultify the growth of personality—still, and always, his main concern. He had a vision of "community"—a frequently recurring word in these essays, always with positive connotations, often preceded by "joyous"—but it was a community made of free growing, ever spontaneously expanding individual spirits which he envisioned as the ideal.

The rhetoric, the style again, is what is still compelling, still fresh, and blessedly free of the jargon that characterizes most discussions of educational theory. He had his own vocabulary, of course, those code words that he stitched onto the banners of the rebellious younger generation. On the joyous side, the positive notes the *New Republic* wanted to hit—and most of the essays are upbeat, confidently declaring the new education as the wave of the future—he promotes desire, impulse, the natural, the organic, the scientific, and the democratic. Children are not "empty vessels to be filled by knowledge" but they are "pushing wills and desires and curiosities . . . living growing things" (6); the whole object of education in school and college should be "the discovery of what one likes and wants, the control and direction of desire" (61). Schoolmen forget, he writes, that "we are only accidentally intellectual, that our other impulses are far more imperious." He defines discipline as "willed skill," "willed and focused interest," what one wants to be able to do rather than—the ironic stiletto—"the ability to do painful things," the latter a "curious notion," possible of course only "to minds soaked in a Puritan tradition" (13, 168). The Wirt school he admired is "a constantly growing organism" (141) with work, study, and play in the school intimately related to realities in the world beyond; the "old education" is static, rigid, with its emphasis on "unrelated classics" and "unapplied mathematics" (17).

Wholeheartedly endorsing Dewey's "learning through doing," Bourne proved a strong advocate of vocational education, still a relative novelty outside a half-dozen or so major cities but assured eventual nationwide adoption by the passage in 1916 of the Smith-Hughes bill providing federal aid to states on a matching basis for vocational training in high schools. But Bourne warned against the control of such schools falling either into the hands of conservative professional educators or the more narrowly self-interested hands of employers' associations, for each, he feared, would simply preserve "the old antithesis between the cultural and the utilitarian" (178, 182). Between two contending plans being tested in New York City he urged adoption of the Gary plan since, organizing the school itself as a community, it viewed the world outside the school "not as a collection of trades but as a community, a network of occupations and interests, of interweaving services, intellectual, administrative, manual" (185).

"To decide what kind of a school we want," Bourne wrote in the essay "The Democratic School," "is almost to decide what kind of a society we want" (147). The kind of society Bourne wanted was that "joyous community" he so often alluded to, a web, a network, a woven fabric—to use his own recurring metaphors—made up of the diverse and infinitely varied strands of personality. Hence his Democratic School was one that would accommodate to the "sociological reality" of "the heterogeneous distribution of capacities" among children (here, perhaps, he echoed the jargon of some of his sources). Hence he inveighed against educators who, conceding this diversity, would still insist on uniform standards, uniform discipline, in order to preserve the highest degree of like-mindedness (149). Hence he quarreled with the old education—in private secondary schools and in colleges—as "a class education," functioning to preserve a tradition of leisure and cultured wealth.

On this latter theme of class education, one that provided the resisting background in nearly every essay, Bourne was really tilting with his favorite foe, the older generation, the exemplars of that old mentality in America which Santayana had labeled the genteel tradition and which Bourne and his contemporaries called puritanism. Behind any defense of the old education and its valuation of discipline and knowledge over his own preferred standards of interest and efficiency, Bourne saw a puritan and a ready target for his irony.

One such was a young Edith Hamilton, the future classical scholar of the Greek way, who had replied in the *New Republic* with a defense of the old education, for the young women at schools like Bryn Mawr where Hamilton was then teaching. "Her argument against a change in education," Bourne wrote in replying in turn,[16] "seems to be based on the idea that change would be prejudicial to the life which she accepts as worthiest for those fortunate classes with which she is best acquainted." Since life will make no demands upon "the sheltered, economically endowed leisure" in store for her students, they had no need for "the illusory discipline" which the modern school offered—in teaching the domestic sciences, for instance—but would need the external standards provided by the traditional curriculum, "impersonal, cultural, laborious," as Bourne paraphrased her argument, to teach them, he said, "the joy of work by the doing of things because they are hard." Bourne went on:

> At first sight nothing could be more ironic than this gospel of strenuous effort preached in the name of a sheltered class. Why should a girl be disciplined, trained to do things "*because* they are hard," for a life which becomes "easier and easier," unless her teachers wish to provide her with some kind of moral and intellectual justification for her social role? The "old" education combines uselessness and effort, and it is just this combination which would maintain leisure-class functions and yet leave the individual morally justified. The uselessness makes you exclusive and the effort satisfies your moral sense (166–67).

In "The Puritan's Will-to-Power," published a few months after this reply to Hamilton, he expanded on this notion in arguing that it was precisely the process by which the puritan asserted his power and derived satisfaction out of it by "the turning of his self-abasement into purposes of self-regard."

He hit similar notes in "The Cult of the Best," one of the best essays in *Education and Living*, attacking art education and artistic appreciation in America generally as really "almost a branch of moral education." Zealous pursuit of the Arnoldian ideal, labeled in the earlier, companion piece to this essay, "Our Cultural Humility," as the "tyranny of the best" and "the virus of the best," made for an "unpleasantly undemocratic" conception of culture. Educating people in this way, Bourne charged, educated only those whose tastes ran to the classics, making for "hypocrites or 'lowbrows,' with culture reserved only for a few. All the rest of us are left without guides, without encouragement, and tainted with original sin" (52).

The last three essays in *Education and Living*, addressed to issues in college and university education, also struck at persisting puritanic attitudes. The Scott Nearing case, wherein the University of Pennsylvania trustees had dismissed Nearing for his radical views, prompted Bourne to ask "Who Owns the Universities?" and to answer that the time has passed when a "determined autocracy," as he characterized university trustees, should control a modern college or university. With the passing of control "from the ghostly to the moneyed element," from the days when most trustees and practically all instructors were ministers of the Gospel to the present when trustees were men of affairs and professors were committed to scientific and sociological inquiry, the issues were no longer those of private property but of public welfare. "It is wholly undesirable that trustees should be detained [*sic*] only by 'merciful consideration' from discharging professors whom they find uncongenial or who they feel are spreading unsound doctrine." Professors should organize, Bourne concluded, to assert their rights and achieve some security of office.[17]

In "The Undergraduate" he returned to the subject he had spoken to with more optimism in *Youth and Life*, when he was still close to his own Columbia experience. In the earlier essay, "The College: An Inner View," he had dwelled on the hopeful signs of a changing spirit becoming democratic, scientific, critical, and enthusiastic, but in this later essay he accused colleges of still failing to bridge the gulf between their professed intellectual aims and the "sporting philosophy" of their students, a philosophy stemming from "the good old Anglo-Saxon conviction that life is essentially a game whose significance lies in terms of winning or losing." College administrations, yielding to these sporting attitudes, had turned the college course into a "sort of race," in a "quasi-athletic setting," with "intricate system[s] of points and courses and examinations" as part of the elaborate rules of the game. He pleaded for a college life "less like that of an undergraduate country club, and more of an intellectual workshop where men and women in the fire of their youth, with conflicts and idealisms, questions and ambitions and desire for expression, come to serve an apprenticeship under the masters of the time" (288).

This was the apostle of youth still, arguing with all the ardent, abstract language of *Youth and Life*, getting in his little ironic asides (as in his characterizing the departments of literary scholarship—"perhaps as pure an anachronism as we have in the intellectual world to-day"—a lingering prejudice from his Columbia days), attacking a system which did not educate youth for active intellectual involvement in the life of the moment. The colleges were still medieval in their methods, he said, as seen in the continuing reliance on the lecture system, as if "nothing has happened since Abelard spoke in Paris to twelfth-century bookless men" (232). Cultural studies should be turned into power, even as the technical schools made ideas and processes immediately effective.

All this is familiar, now, since nearly every younger generation after Bourne's has questioned anew the relevance of "cultural studies" to an ever increasingly technological age. But Bourne was among the first to do so, providing the rhetoric and singling out the targets—autocratic trustees defending vested interests, puritanic administrators with rigid, "irrelevant" requirements, medieval professors with outmoded methods, passive (apathetic) students, the twin evils of a class education (elitism) and "the sporting philosophy" (athleticism and jocks). And all these, for Bourne, were the legacy of the older generation, of a puritanic, genteel tradition, standing in the way of youth's expression of its desires and youth's assertion of its power.

At bottom, Bourne's education pieces for the *New Republic* were as much about power and control, about politics in the larger sense, as had been his *Youth and Life* essays. Power for youth, for young men and women in fact to control their own destinies, and for the principle of youth in the abstract as the reigning one in life, was what he consistently argued for. The very recurrence of the words "power" and "control" is one testimony of this aim, but even more is his reaching out in nearly every "education" article for some large "sociological, administrative or psychological truth" about American culture generally. Here, in this tendency, he betrayed almost an impatience with "the facts" of education, with which he tried to ballast his articles, as he shaped his essays to convey his bright vision of youth's ascendency over the formidable forces of the older generation. In general too, though he often qualified his attacks on the old education in deference to his emphasis upon the new tendencies—the new "self-consciousness" which he so prized and sought to make others share in the same degree—he patterned his essays on the same Manichaean division as those of *Youth and Life*, with the new education all bathed in light and the old in darkness.

CHAPTER 4

Sketches and Cartoons

UNDERSTANDABLY, Bourne became restless with his assignment as the education expert for the *New Republic*. He came more and more to disparage his contributions to that progressive aim of the magazine, as hinted in the apologetic prefatory note to *Education and Living*. Not only was there the drudgery, as he saw it, of almost daily visits to The New York Public Library in order to keep up with the latest developments—alleviated somewhat by the subsidized visit to Gary early in 1915, his first trip west of Pittsburgh—the subject itself confined him, limiting him in many ways to rehearsing the experience he had already given expression to in *Youth and Life*. He could stretch those limits or leap beyond them, since education was a philosophy of life for him, as he said; but he could not confront and deal directly with the larger themes of culture, of art, and politics and how they needed to join to give coherent shape to American civilization and fulfill its promise. The education assignment limited him to the role of observer and commentator, whereas he wanted to be a participant, the active intellectual immersed in and assisting in the creation of culture. He wanted to be an artist.

He would advance other reasons for his growing dissatisfaction with and eventual sense of utter and complete alienation from the *New Republic*. Though he sat in on editorial policy meetings he felt his voice carried little weight. He still respected and admired Lippmann and appreciated Croly's supportive position on the necessity of cultural nationalism, but their liberalism came to seem to him priggish and timid, middle-aged, more prone to drift with events than to seek mastery over them, and with none of the youthful audacity he preferred. Half of the pieces he submitted, he complained, never saw the light. And then came the decisive issue of the magazine's policy toward the war: by the end of 1915 it had abandoned all pretense at neutrality and become openly hostile toward Germany.[1] But beneath all these complaints, underlying even the furious assault he leveled at *New Republic* liberals when its editors proudly boasted that they had prepared the way for American intervention, was his anguished dismay at his own failure to become the kind of writer he wanted to be—one who counted for something in the world, the best of autobiographers, a master of fiction.

This expressed desire, first so phrased in "The Adventure of Life," continued to surface any number of times in his correspondence with his friends, especially women friends with whom he was more inclined to unburden his innermost desires, and with one like Alyse Gregory whose intense activity as a writer and feminist he both envied and admired. Often self-deprecatory about his passive role and referring to himself, for instance, as "only a feeble little artist," he was clearly searching for the right form in which to shape the subject that interested him most—himself. Autobiography, even such as *Youth and Life*, the confessional, personal essay, he felt was not appreciated or allowed by the literary tastes of the day, yet nothing fascinated him more than the subject of personality, his own especially. He suffered, he complained, from "this indigestion of myself," and wished for a way to write himself out, not "daintily" or "Atlantically" but "more truthfully and widely."[2]

He was not destined in the short time left him to ever fulfill this ambition in a satisfying way, but the solution he sought was clearly in the writing of fiction. Commitment to the life of irony dictated the posture he must assume—simultaneously inside and outside his subject. He needed, as in due course he came to recognize,[3] personal symbols for his intellectual desires and frustrations, symbols that could dramatize and externalize, compress and give order to the chaos of experience. They were all around him, for him to select and choose from, among the personalities he met and the places he associated with them. Friends were important to him, for in and through them he saw aspects of his own personality revealed. Subjecting them to his keen analytical scrutiny—making often for eventual strains with even the closest of his friends, almost always with lesser acquaintances—he was really engaging in self-analysis. Enemies, or those he made out to be his enemies, were no less important as symbols to him, for in them he located the thwarting of his desires. They represented, usually, some burden from a past time, as heavy a legacy as his physical handicap. Places were also important sources for his personal symbols: Bloomfield for small-town, Calvinistic America and the American midwest; Europe generally for its national cultures, with their individual homogeneity and equally their diversity from one another; England for Anglo-Saxondom, and France, his place of fondest memory, the symbolic setting for much that he yearned for in America (where youth was appreciated and performed a meaningful role, where thought and feeling harmonized, where intellectuals took an active part in affairs of state); and Greenwich Village and Dublin, New Hampshire, (where he spent one near-idyllic summer in August and September 1915) as approaches to his ideal community of intellectuals and artists.

To Elizabeth Sheply Sergeant, who eventually secured him the invitation to Dublin, he wrote of his need to check his own drift, to "feel really in command of one's soul"—mastery of himself. The practical solution to getting away from New York for a while was also his artistic solution: "Place," he said, "would help, but it would have to be people too," the right sort, and then in the metaphorical language he so often used, "and then some smashing victory, which just to think of would give me a feeling of power."[4]

Doubts assailed him constantly—that he was too much the critic for one who wanted to create, that "the reformer got such a terrific start in my youth over the artist that I'm afraid the latter is handicapped for life"—and he wished for the nerve to write a book, for the leisure to turn to "a novel with which I coquette." He wanted to "literize" his experience—like the one with Bligh (which, however, proved too painful to ever get reduced to any form).[5]

He never achieved a single smashing victory in any one work, the book he yearned to complete. Yet the fictional impulse did take shape in a series of literary portraits, single and collective characterizations of the two poles of personality between which his own swayed in dramatic conflict—the positive personality of youth, on the one hand, and the negating personality of the older generation with its restricting legacies from the past, on the other.

Each portrait is an experiment in a fictional frame, generally narrated in the first person (several were originally published over the pseudonym "Max Coe"). They are fragments looked at singly, but gathered together they provide a semblance of a coherent whole, preserving more unity than is apparent in the wide-ranging collection of his total writings.

Van Wyck Brooks singled out six of these portraits for inclusion in the posthumous *History of a Literary Radical* (1920) along with "Fragment of a Novel" (first published in the *Dial* as "An Autobiographic Chapter"), and even dared suggest that in these Bourne was "already doing the work of the novelist he might well have become." Brooks might have noted that "My friend Miro," the subject of the leading piece, "History of a Literary Radical," though another autobiographic chapter, was also distanced by the fictional disguise, as was the piece "Ernest: or Parent for a Day" (whose baby-sitting narrator is perhaps Bourne's most charming of his several self-portraits). There are others I would include among these fictional experiments in biography and autobiography: uncollected pieces like "The Architect" (*New Republic*, January 1, 1916, by "Juvenis") and "Making One's Contribution" (*New Republic*, August 26, 1916, by "Max Coe") about "my friend Thomas"; "In a Schoolroom," collected in *Education and Living*; and "Below the Battle," a *Seven Arts* piece included with other war articles in *Untimely Papers* (1919), a posthumous collection edited by James Oppenheim. Both of the latter are presented through a fictionalized first person who is as much a part of the portraiture as the teacher and students he observes in the first, and the war-resisting friend he seeks to understand in the latter. If one adds to these the collective portraits in studies like "The Puritan's Will-to-Power," the only *Seven Arts* essay Brooks included in his selection, and "This Older Generation" (also picked by Brooks), and the obviously composed analytical sketches of his friends scattered through his letters, especially that of Dorothy Teall in his letters to Alyse Gregory, we have a sizable gallery of characters, "sketched from life" we must say of most of them, but symbolic projections nonetheless of the way Bourne imagined the world of personalities he inhabited.[6]

They fall roughly into three groups: portraits of youth, of young men and women, including the narrator; those of particular representatives of the older generation; and the collective portraits of the latter. (Though he continued to use "the younger generation" or "the young intelligentsia" as a collective presence too, his presentation of youth in the abstract was largely behind him in *Youth and Life*.) Each portrait is washed with ironic colors, the hallmarks of his style, ranging from the lightly, gently applied tones in his sketches of the young, to the heavier satiric strokes on his portraits of the older generation.

"Mon Amie" (already discussed) was one of the first of these to be published, accorded him the most satisfaction with warm responses from several of his readers, and was the first of several efforts to delineate types of the new woman, or, to use the contemporary term, the emancipated woman, each in turn exemplars of youth. For all his decrying the tendency of others to categorize or type personalities, Bourne's portraits were all offered as emblems, often explicitly, as "Mon Amie" was called "a symbol of luminous youth, a flaming militant of the younger generation." Each portrait as a whole is of a distinctive personality, with distinguishing differences as national cultural representatives—as "Mon Amie" is put forward as so essentially French, and "Karen," a young Swedish immigrant, and "Sophronisba" (drawn from Elizabeth S. Sergeant), the descendant of a long line of New England puritans. But these differences do not distinguish them so much from each other as from "the older generation," and the remarkable similarity of their responses to their cultural and social backgrounds brings them together under the common emblem of youth.

Though Mon Amie's "sensual delight . . . in thinking" is admiringly recorded by her narrator as a French trait, she is joined by Karen who "did not think, she felt—in slow, sensuous outlines," and by Sophronisba whose "intellectual clarity" combined with a "zestfulness" that belied her puritan background. This joining of feeling with thinking was the virtue Bourne commonly attributed to youth (reenforced perhaps in Mon Amie by her cultural origins), the product of reaction to its past by youth in America, but identical in expression of youthful personality. In the "most remarkable girl of 16," then a sophomore at Barnard, Dorothy Teall, Bourne saw another of the same type, intellectually pugnacious, but always taut with emotion, making him feel in conversation with her, as he told Alyse Gregory,[7] "as if I was just about to touch the raw, sensitive flesh of a soul of youth. . . ." And as he saw Teall (with his conspiring assistance) in rebellion against her family—"solidly built and with an intellectual heritage of dictionary makers"—so Sophronisba was one who had had to exorcise a demon New England conscience (though in her serious talk there lingered still "the slight interested bitter tang of the old Puritan poison"). Delighting in Teall's contentiousness with her straitlaced family, he phrased it in a favorite paradox, concluding his sketch of Sophronisba with his thought that "the most delightful bohemians are those who have been New England Puritans first," as he would end his analysis of "The Puritan's Will-to-Power" with a similar refrain: "Perhaps no one can be really a good appreciating pagan who has not once been a bad puritan." Karen, who "loathed ideas," had struggled to emancipate herself from "the somber irrascibility of that northern land from which she came," from the bitterness of a recent immigrant journey; she despised housework and office drudgery, and like the others was determined to make the world in her own image. Karen was at Bourne's magic age of twenty-five, "and I guessed," the narrator wrote, "that she would always be twenty-five"—eternally youthful. Sophronisba he knew, the narrator records, when she was mellow in her years, perhaps forty, "but she is probably much younger than she was at eleven." At whatever actual age, even a remarkable sixteen, these women were Bourne's emblems of youth, youthful in their persons.

Each of them was "feminist," of course, become synonymous with youth. Mon Amie is "mostly" feminist, ardently committed to the "uncomplicated and happy march of the Frenchwomen, already [the Francophile narrator confidently notes] so practically emancipated, toward a definite social recognition of that liberation." Sophronisba "naturally is feminist to the core" and "a symbol of triumphant spinsterhood . . . an unmarried woman who knows she would make a wretched wife and does not seem to mind." Karen has her "fling of feminism," becomes secretary to a suffrage leader, makes herself "hideous in mannish skirts and waists," feels the "woes of women," and sees everywhere "the devilish hand of the exploiting male."

Possibly the portrait of Karen derives in part from the otherwise unidentified young woman[8] who is the subject of an episode Bourne recounted with characteristic self-directed irony in a letter to Alyse Gregory, from whom he often solicited solace or confirmation of his own reactions to women. The experience, he said, was "deeply typical":

We were a little party at the delightful apartment of a girl who has some sort of office suffrage job. We were alternating a little music on her baby grand, and talk, and were just sinking into that evening comfort about the glowing fire, preparing to be ruminative and delightful when at ten o'clock we were smartly turned out, graciously but finally, on the ground that this was her closing hour, for she had to be at work at 9 the next morning. When you realize that she is usually grumbling about her wage-slavery and envying the untrammeled ones, her incapacity to extract enjoyment from the slow Debussy-accompanied passage of time before a grate-fire, stealing pleasure in the very face of encroaching night, is almost inexplicable. The thing is a personal outrage from which I shall not soon recover. I can only ascribe it to some profound incorrigible perversity of woman. It becomes more malign when you realize that the girl pretends to be not only anti-man but anti-woman too. The vivacity of her defenders convinces me that she is not alone, that we are in the helpless grip of an inexplicable feminine philosophy of life, a sort of spiritual callousness which almost gives point to the claims of my German friends that women have no souls. Can you throw any light on this disaster which has so shaken my faith in womankind? It will be a long time before I take up again the threads of intuitive understanding which I have deluded myself into feeling. I shall watch the clock for the striking of that mechanical hour; when the executioner arrives to end the conversation, I shall click my heels and depart in the middle of a sentence to the scaffold. I shall recognize myself as a filler-in of certain tightly-compressed moments, a stop-gap between 8:30 and 10 P.M., a sort of dull vaudeville act. Is it possible that women regard all men with whom they are not in love as mere more or less interesting vaudeville acts?[9]

Some of the above is surely echoed in the story of Karen, secretary of a suffrage leader, yet despising office drudgery, interested in men but "more as co-actors in a personal drama of her own devising than as lovers or even as men," for whom men existed "only as they brought a touch of ceremonial into their personal relations" and of whom the narrator says, perhaps recalling Bourne's night of promise before the glowing fire: "However glowing and mysterious she might look as she lay before the fire in her room, so that to an impatient friend nothing might seem more important than to catch her up warmly in his arms, he would have been an audacious brigand who violated the atmosphere." In fact Bourne proved incapable of such audacity, only exploding later in ironic expostulation at woman's incorrigible perversity, and in fiction at Karen's "inscrutable" being, leaving trails of "mystery and desire" over which the narrator stumbles and bungles, constantly undergoing at her hands "a course of discipline . . . for my ungovernable temper or my various repellant 'tones.' . . ."

The narrator's own feelings toward these several feminist types come through with a curious ambivalence; it is not easy to distinguish between the ironies directed at his subjects and the types they represent, and those that are aimed at himself, the sensitive masculine ego trying to understand "what women want." On the latter point, irony being the double-edged knife it is, we cannot for certainty conclude that the narrator is truly expressive of Bourne's own sense of masculine perplexity, or whether he is intended, instead, as a kind of parody of a type of masculine ego whose patience with the cause of the feminist is being sorely tried.

The narrator is evidently admiring of these young women, overall, but not so much for their "feminine" traits as for those ingredients of personality which Bourne minted in his medallion of youth—their fusion of thought with feeling, their "blazing candor" (identical phrasing for both Sophronisba and Mon Amie), their deep concern for social issues coupled with the importance they give to personal relations; and if he confesses near adoration, as with Mon Amie, it is for "the eternal youth of France that she was"—for their being representatives of youth. His pronouncing each of them "feminist" is not without its touch of accolade. Yet, as he explores their various feminist postures, especially their attitudes toward men, a note of impatience creeps into the portraits, even, with Karen, a touch of malice. Karen's fling had been largely with feminists "whose feminism had done little more for their emotional life than to make them acutely conscious of the cloven hoof of the male." In her reconstituted life, after her fling, Karen had become self-appointed guardian over her women friends, especially those already married, "eternal vigilance [being] the price of their salvation from masculine tyranny." She brooded over them, "inscrutable, vigilant, a true vestal virgin on the sacred hearth of woman." Since she could not crowd men into her Jamesian world, she solved her problem "by obliterating them," obviously to the narrator's chagrin and distress. Similarly, Sophronisba's discoursing on the subject of married women's economic servitude throws the narrator into "a state of profound depression" as he reflects on "how unconscious of their servitude most of these women are," yet his crowning of Sophronisba as a symbol of triumphant spinsterhood seems a crown with a thorn in it. Mon Amie, his most idealized portrait, the most loving, is the least shaded in irony, yet she too reduces the narrator not quite to a state of depression but to that wistful state Bourne was fond of attributing to youth with its vague, unfulfilled longings and desires. Mon Amie too looked upon marriage with disfavor, and thought most men usually *malhonnête;* she had concluded that friendship between a girl and a young man was almost impossible: "It was that they usually wished to love her." What made the narrator seem wistful, perhaps, was that she at least conceded "she might find some day a man of complete sympathy and complete loyalty."

Fearing that none of the free spirits he so ardently pursued would ever find him to be that man, even as he almost desperately assured them of sympathy with their cause, Bourne saw his own cruel dilemma made more so by that very cause itself.

In a largely unnoticed review of his, one of his rare contributions to *The Masses,* Bourne defined the protagonist in the triangular lesbian relationship of the novel under review, *Regiment of Women,* as a type of extreme feminist whose "philosophy of inverted sex-antagonism" was, he said, too much like that among some of the impressionable younger generation. He warned the Karens among his friends, as it were, that such a type harmed their cause and would inevitably become dominant "in the kind of man-less world which women are trying to create for themselves."[10]

Obviously the narrator of the sketches is speaking from Bourne's own felt dilemma. In actuality he was probably subjected more than most men to mere "ceremonial" treatment at the hands of his women friends, viewed as he was, as he knew he was, and as, ironically, in his pursuit of ideal friendship he invited women to view him, as above the battle of the sexes, safely perched on some Platonic plateau, out of the contest. But the tone of the narrative voice in the sketches is nonetheless remarkably different from that of the male lecturer in the review cited above, or that of the sometimes whimpering or outraged male ego of the letters. Whether the narrator wistfully yearns after Mon Amie, confesses his predatory urges in the presence of Karen, his impatience with her, the "violence" of his interest in her, or professes puzzlement at how Sophronisba has rid herself of "the virus of her New England conscience" and expelled "the perils of thwarted sex," or finds to his surprise that he envies her writing skill, especially the neatness with which she "piles her facts"—not supposed to be a feminine skill—the narrator is part of the comedy of personal relations which Bourne's generation experienced, suffered—and enjoyed. If each of his subjects is a representative feminist, so too the narrator is a representative youth confronting them, baffled, annoyed, amused, but finally an admirer, a supporter, and one with them, despite apparent contradictions.

This is more evident in those portraits where the subjects are also representative young men. In the sketch called "Making One's Contribution"[11] we have in effect four representative youths, each reacting in slightly different ways to their feminist friends. There is first of all the narrator again, "Max Coe," who signed the piece; "my friend Thomas," the chief subject; a "critic-friend" of Thomas; and a fourth youth whom the critic has suggested Thomas should emulate.

Thomas is introduced by the narrator as one who needs the comfort and warmth of companionship and good conversation, and who frequently escapes his lonely room for one of those half-public, half-private restaurants "where the women challenged one with their economic independence and the men with their air of being about some business that was for the amelioration of society"—a typical Greenwich Village setting. But a friendly critic, Thomas tells the narrator, has pointed out that he offends others—too often he monopolizes some one person, he ignores the amenities of group talk, and violates social etiquette by "not making his contribution." Thomas confesses bewilderment, all the more so because of his critic's contrasting him unfavorably with another youth who also had once lacked "a sense of social obligation." This youth had once thought all women foolish chatterers, had sought company instead in books, learned to cook in order to become a self-reliant Thoreau in the woods, and read Nietzsche and Whitman, thrilled by their "brave self-sufficingness." But then this youth had been redeemed: he married a woman who had been on the front line of masculine tyranny. "She had formed an alliance with other aggressive feminists, and it was into their dinner talk that this Nietzschean youth was introduced," often the only man present. Acquiescing, the youth had accepted the social code. "He knew his place, he smoked with them, he agreed with them, he made his contribution."

Thomas refuses to play the same "childish" game, feigning responses, becoming a mere social unit, "shedding satisfaction around." He would remain instead always personal, "and he would keep on disconcerting his friends by demanding personality of them." He could not understand how supposed radicals who had emancipated themselves from so much could still insist on the social code.

The narrator admonishes Thomas, reminding him that women who had had to struggle to free themselves from sex status had little energy left for "the flexible and time-consuming art of personal relations." But Thomas is unmoved. Henceforth he would always feel, with a group of feminists, "as if there was something ceremonial in the atmosphere. There were ways that one was expected to act. . . ." Their radicalism lay "in insisting that others please you where by the old code you had to please them." Thomas, the narrator says in concluding, "longed for the true freedom when nobody had to please anybody anymore"—when it was acceptable to do your own thing.

We have here four aspects of Randolph Bourne, surely, but also four representative responses of the youths of the day to their feminist counterparts. Thomas comes closest to the portrait of himself that Bourne most preferred to advance, the truly radical spirit, dodging all pressures. The Nietzschean youth who acquiesced, however, was one he sometimes wistfully longed to be, a longing regularly checked by the self-critic who knew all too well how abrasive he sometimes was to others. But finally there was the ironist in him who could see something of the contradictions among all these aspects of himself, and who sought resolution of them in art if not in life.

We have Bourne's word for it that "Fergus"[12] is a portrait of his college friend Edward Murray, a skilled violinist with whom he shared his love of music. It was with Murray, too, that he shared a cabin in Dublin, New Hampshire, that summer of 1915 (after the sketch was written and published) with Murray a very essential companion, since he, like that Nietzschean youth in the sketch above, had learned to cook whereas Bourne never did. But "Fergus" shares even more the personality of Bourne. Though clothed in the external details borrowed from Murray's life, Fergus has interior dimensions that resemble Bourne himself.

Bourne endowed Fergus with representative features of youth, and from the first sentence—"My friend Fergus has all the characteristics of genius except the divine fire"—to the last—"as his candor and his appreciations refresh me, I wonder if the next best thing to producing works of art is not to be, like Fergus, a work of art one's self"—we are in the presence of Bourne's characteristic self-judgments and those that speak his idealization of youth. The first echoes his frequent lament at his own inability "to start flowing the creative current" (said of Fergus in the next breath) and the last voices his creed and youth's creed about cultivating the art of personality. There are similar familiar touches in between. Of a mixed ethnic background, Irish and French-Canadian, Fergus is something of a transnational, described by the narrator as "the type that would be taken for a Spaniard in France and an Italian in Spain." He is plebeian in origin, but has the manners of an aristocrat. As others among Bourne's youths have rid themselves of a puritanic background or rebelled against family, Fergus, too, has shed "the influences of that close little Catholic society in which he was brought up," repelled by priests "whose 'will-to-power' background" he has analyzed for the narrator "with Nietzschean fidelity." He disdains his parents' anxiety that he "make something of himself," yet their restiveness with him "over a certain economic waste" is a trial for him—as Bourne often said of his Bloomfield relatives. Fergus, too, has suffered loneliness; for a while "the erotic world gnawed persistently at him," and he has been in love, though reticent about it. "A girl in his words"—though we know they are also the narrator's words, for he has used them about the women he has sketched—"is somewhat dark and inscrutable."

Fergus supports himself at odd jobs, playing organ for a small Catholic church, bearable only because he sees the irony of his doing so, trying out as an accompanist at a Bronx moving picture vaudeville theater, trying to teach, wanting to compose—a pattern like that of Bourne's pre-Columbian days. The sour-sweetness of unfulfilled ambition is nicely modulated: "But destiny has just clipped his wings so that he must live a life of noble leisure instead of artistic creation. His unconscious interest is the art of life." He is youth, "probably . . . not happy," but no matter, for he meets the world with candor, with the "calm speculation and artistic appreciation that Nietzsche glorifies."

Bourne's youth is unhappy because he is an ironist, and the life of irony, we remember, "cannot be peaceful . . . cannot even be happy," but it can perhaps be wise. One of Bourne's best attempts at offering wisdom was in the portrait of the saddened, unhappy young man of "Below the Battle." Destined to be born at a moment in history propitious for youth, as Bourne had announced in *Youth and Life*, Bourne's younger generation had its wings clipped by the same destiny. The advent of war into the life of youth dramatically uncovered youth's ironic fate. The sweet-sad tones prophesying that fate in all Bourne's earlier portraits, tinting them each with wistfulness, are made poignantly acute in "Below the Battle." The lines are etched precisely, carefully, ironically. They sting.

"Below the Battle" first appeared in the July 1917 issue of the *Seven Arts*,[13] following the American declaration of war on Germany in April and only weeks after the first registration for the military draft of over nine million young men between the ages of twenty-one and thirty-one, accomplished with little or no commotion, no organized resistance. General Pershing was already in Paris with the first small contingent of American troops. The reality of Americans committed to battle, however, still lay in the months and year ahead, with the full horror coming in the summer offensive of 1918. The mood of the country that first summer of the war was decidedly martial. Mobilization of its war resources was in full tilt, including organized efforts to sell the war to Americans, led by President Wilson's attempt, as one historian has put it, "to give a moral and altruistic meaning to American participation, to depict intervention in terms of the strong and pure democracy putting on the breast plate to do battle for the Lord."[14]

That's one context in which "Below the Battle" may be read, as one untimely essay among the several antiwar essays Bourne wrote during the early months of America's war involvement. But it is also one of his several nearly timeless portraits of youth. Set in that gallery, read as a kind of culminating portrait, almost elegiac, we get I think a better measure of Bourne's enduring and recurring appeal beyond the historical moment of his own time. It sets throbbing the chords of memory of the several generations since Bourne's time whose fate it was to be young when war coincided with their youth.

War confronts youth with its supreme crisis. The central conscious issue during youth, the tension between self and society, suddenly comes into sharp, painful focus. The major dilemma of youth, how to preserve the autonomous self and also perform an effective role in society, involving much ambivalence toward both desires, demands resolution, and the choices often seem reduced to simple, stark either/or terms. Youth being a time, phenomenologically, as Kenneth Kenniston noted, of alternating estrangement and omnipotentiality, the issue of war may precipitate one or the other, or just as likely result in a baffling mixture of both states of feeling at once. Bourne had observed with dismay crowds of German youths endorsing their country's war with songs and cheers of power. He would accuse his young colleagues on the *New Republic* and others of yielding, in effect, to a similar illusory will to power, and in doing so he became a leading spokesman of that "opposite but secretly related pole" in youth's world—estrangement.[15]

These opposite poles were related and joined in Bourne himself. *Youth and Life*, with one small undermining hint of doubt, had expressed youth's sense of omnipotence, of an almost "absolute freedom, of living in a world of pure possibilities, of being able to change or achieve anything."[16] It was, as I have suggested, a kind of manual of power for youth, defiant of society and the old order, speaking the language therefore of opposition and estrangement but buoyant with faith in youth's eventual triumph over the handicaps set in its way—if youth lived the life of adventure, the experimental life, viewed the world ironically, and remained thoroughly radical. Bourne's war essays, however, contain the opposite pole. They are icy expressions of furious dismay with a world become absurd. They express alienation, an angered sense of betrayal, but they come from the same youth, still using the language of power, arguing that the irreconcilable radical need not be reduced to irrelevancy or impotency.

"Below the Battle" is a dispassionate, coolly analytical portrait of that youth.[17] Alongside the war essays with which it is generally placed it is calm, without fury, but also with no hint of resignation or pathos. Using the fictional frame of his other portraits, a first-person narration about a "friend of mine," Bourne stepped aside from his polemical assault on a coercive war technique to achieve a candid, distanced perspective on himself and others of his friends suffering the same dilemma.

The narrator's friend is offered as representative, another emblem, "rather typical of a scattered race of young Americans of today." He shares the essential features of Bourne's other youths, including the usual detail about his national and cultural background, a necessary addition to the total irony of the portrait in this instance since this war objector has nought but English blood in his veins. As with Bourne's other young men and women, his desires are chiefly aesthetic—he works as an architect's assistant—and the dilemma posed by the war is most acute respecting those desires, "how he can best be true to his creative self?" But he is besieged by a host of other desires, always labeled "vague"; he has tried to write of the thoughts that have stirred him, but he could only express "of course, the usual large vague feeling of a new time that all of us feel." However vague his longings, the war program's failure to touch "remotely his aspirations, his impulses, or even his desires" paradoxically makes them all the more intensely felt. "He is always expecting he doesn't quite know what, and always being frustrated of he doesn't quite know what would have pleased him."

He is full of the anomalies and contradictions of youth, in short, but the narrator's ironic lens neatly redirects the confusion toward the war's advocates. His friend, he says, found that most of "the big men—intellectuals—whom he thought he respected had had so much of their idealism hacked away and got their nerves so frayed that they became at last, in their panic, willing and even eager to adopt the war-technique in aid of their government's notions of the way to impose democracy on the world." His friend, he adds with leveled tones, is "too naive and too young to effect this metamorphosis." With similar straight-faced irony the narrator confesses sharing his friend's awe for "the superb intellectual structure" erected by the likes of the *New Republic*, providing a "feast of eloquent idealism, with its appealing harbingers of a cosmically efficacious and well-bred war." The argument for American participation was convincing, but the youth was not convinced—"my friend is one of those unfortunate youths whose heart has to apprehend as well as his intellect, and it was his heart that inexorably balked." As with all Bourne's youths, feeling had to harmonize with thought.

True to youth's commitment to a life of irony, the narrator's friend feels alienated from the war strategy of the government and its intellectualist backers. He is "somehow in the nation but not of the nation." He is intelligent, idealistic; he wants democracy. "He still feels himself inextricably a part of this blundering, wistful, crass civilization we call America." But he refuses to be identified with it for warlike ends; he does not believe that the kind of democracy that may be achieved is worth the cost of world suicide.

He feels estranged, disconnected from a world gone mad. With the outbreak of the Great War "the world [had] turned out to be an entirely different place from what he had thought it." All progress and uplift seemed indefinitely suspended, all that he valued was "frozen until the horrible mess came to a close." Yet he struggled against any "pose of complete aliency." Weighing his alternatives—refusal to register for the draft, refusal to serve if drafted, conscientious objection status and alternative "service," or simply stoic submission—he lapses into a kind of paralysis, passive, apathetic, "waiting for the knife to fall." He may not, finally, rebel at all. "He may go in the mood of so many young men in other countries"—Bourne's international league of youth—"without enthusiasm, without idealism, without hope and without belief, victims of a tragically blind force behind them."

This was the near elegiac note which crept into Bourne's portrait, not so much a lament for what his youth himself has lost but for what America and the world loses in war—"the only genuinely precious thing in a nation, the hope and ardent idealism of its youth." The importance of this representative youth and his complicated attitudes toward war, the narrator concludes, lies in the suggestion that a "personal and social idealism" existed still in America, neither hurt by popular taunts of cowardice and slacking, nor kindled by patriotic slogans. It was there, but "out of reach of the most skillful and ardent appeals of the older order." His estrangement was not from America but from the older generation, from that lingering handicap of the past, from a fate that paradoxically destined youth, with its sense of power to leap beyond history, to be confronted by history.

"Below the Battle" contains one of Bourne's most compelling portraits of youth, catching him, as it were, at his most perilous moment, poised between two states of his being, when he may cease being a youth at all or, on the other hand, may yet endure, but more than ever, an outcast. He is still an anomaly. It is still a wistful portrait.

"Wistful," however, is not the word for any of Bourne's portraits of the older generation, those members of the older order who bar the way to youth's fulfillment. The mockery is all too evident. No sympathetic first-person narrator makes the direction of the ironies ambivalent. When he does fleetingly betray his presence it is still an omniscient voice that places his ironic words unmistakably on target.

We have at least three individualized portraits: "The Professor" and "One of Our Conquerors," both first in the *New Republic* and both reprinted by Brooks; and "The Architect," a slight *New Republic* piece only recently reprinted.

The model for the first of these was one of Bourne's former Columbia teachers, John Erskine, professor of English. Though their early relationship at Columbia may have been cordially proper as between teacher and student, at least on Erskine's side, Bourne had developed a profound dislike for the man. The hated Bligh had reminded him of Erskine along with his Uncle Halsey among the dominant personages who had put it over on him in the past. Subsequent to the appearance of "The Professor" the relationship understandably cooled further on both sides. During the following year they engaged in a chilling correspondence, feuding over their respective interpretations of the new education. Erskine had taken his own satiric stab at any educational theory resting on the assumption "that only the student's needs of the moment can be satisfied."[18] Bourne accused Erskine of misrepresentation; Erskine took Bourne to task for his bad manners in making the charge, and Bourne icily acknowledged that Erskine served his need "for a personal symbol for my intellectual bêtes noires."[19] Their intellectual differences were real enough. But all this being said about Bourne's source, "The Professor" remains a piece of fiction, the portrait of a recognizable type that still roams American college campuses, if only as a favorite caricature in the minds of undergraduates.

In fact, the animus in this portrait[20] is aimed less at the person of the professor than at the attitudes he embodies and at the culture and society which reward him with high status and esteem. Straighten the ironic twists in the diction, overlook some of its calculated inflation, uncritically accept the common meanings of its language—easily done in this subtly shaded portrait—and we might well read it as a tribute to the professor. He is first of all and surprisingly, a young man (Erskine was only six or seven years Bourne's senior). He had achieved distinction as a scholar at the age of twenty-three with a "masterly doctoral dissertation." And he is also a creative artist, a poet, having won fame while still an undergraduate, victor in a national poetry contest. He is popular with his students, he delivers model lectures, he has impeccable critical taste, he is an inspiration both in and outside the classroom with his "open-mindedness to radical thought," even encouraging his students to be radical. A rare, a genial sort. He should command admiration, envy at least.

Where is the irony, the malice in the apparent tribute? Well, first of all in the first line laid down. The professor is young, but he is clearly not a youth and has perhaps never experienced youth. His misfortune was in growing up too early, too fast, so that "he seems already like a mournful relic of irrevocable days." He is one of a type of Americans that Van Wyck Brooks shortly attacked, also prompted by a memory of his professors and of the "young instructors" he had met between Boston and San Francisco, preternaturally old, old-boys as he called them.[21] Growing up at a time, as Bourne put it, "when all was innocence in the heart of young America," his professor and other young men of that time are "still a race apart." The professor's doctoral dissertation was on "The Anonymous Lyrics of the Fourteenth Century"—as remote and irrelevant to the present, is the ironic implication, as was "Ganymede," the professor's prize poem whose "golden couplets" had won out over "the talent of all the best poets in America" (at a time when, Bourne's generation commonly agreed, America's poetic talent was mediocre, derivative, imitative, devoted to a hazy romantic past). The professor's popularity with his students gives him a strategic position, "incomparable opportunities for influencing the ideals of the young men under him"—an ominous note if read ironically, as intended. His impeccable critical taste is reserved for the classics only. Though a specialist in pre-Elizabethan literature he is "at home in all the ages," but he will venture no opinions that might guide his students "through the current literary maze." He will discuss Robert Louis Stevenson, recently "canonized," but G. B. S. and Galsworthy must await the judgment of time. If he is apparently responsive to the best radicalisms of the day, "he does not let their shock break the sacred chalice of the past." The narrator concludes on a note of feigned nostalgia:

> I think I like the Professor best in his study at home, when he talks on art and life with one or two respectful students. On the wall is a framed autograph of Wordsworth, picked up in some London bookshop; and a framed letter of appreciation from Richard Watson Gilder. On the table stands a richly-bound volume of "Ganymede" with some of the very manuscripts, as he has shown us, bound in among the leaves. His deep and measured voice flows pleasantly on in anecdotes of the Authors' Club, or reminiscences of the golden past. As one listens, the glamor steals upon one. This is the literary life, grave, respected, serene. All else is hectic rush, modern ideas a futile babel. It is men like the Professor

who keep the luster of scholarship bright, who hold true the life of the scholar and gentleman as it was lived of old. In a world of change he keeps the faith pure.

Scholarship, the literary life, the institutions that enshrine them, the students and public who are beguiled by them, all unduly reverential of the past and disdaining to confront and be involved in the present, averse to growth and change—these are the targets of Bourne's satirical portrait, not the professor himself but the genteel tradition contained in him.

The satiric scorn for "One of Our Conquerors" is aimed at the same genteel values, but it is much more decidedly placed upon the personage himself, "Dr. Alexander Mackintosh Butcher," president of "Pluribus University," the heavy-handed portrait of Nicholas Murray Butler, Columbia's long-time president (1902–1945) and almost permanent fixture on the national scene. Bourne despised the man and vented his scorn on the powerful multiversity he had made of Columbia, with its schools "numbered by the dozens, its buildings by the scores, its instructors by the hundreds, its students by the thousands, its income by the millions, and its possessions by the tens of millions." As a young philosophy instructor Butcher had preached an absolute idealism. He was also, therefore, an "immutabilist in politics"—see his famous treatise, "Why We Should Never Change Any Form of Government." But the "flexibility of his mind" is shown in his being a staunch Darwinian, never wearying of "expressing his robust contempt for the unfit who encumber the earth." His commencement addresses are always emphatic warnings to the thousands of graduates before him "against everything new, everything untried, everything untested." Hitting at several institutions where the power of the old mentality prevailed—Columbia, the Republican party, the American Academy of "All the Arts, Sciences, and Philosophies," the financial and corporate world, the various "peace" foundations on which the likes of Butcher/Butler served, beating "the swords of industrial exploitation into the ploughshares of universal peace" so as to prevent war's recurring "in *future* centuries"—Bourne compressed much of his wrath at the older generation into this one portrait.[22]

"The Architect,"[23] though slight, is an interesting addition to the same family gallery. Like the professor he too is a young man, but grown old too soon, without experiencing youth; and he is a type, representative of "a still complacent and cultivated American class which loves the old because it is right and because it is spiritual, which is still interested in the antithesis of spirit and matter. . . . Art he says...is the symbolical expression of otherwise inexpressible ideas. In a sense therefore the Architect himself is a work of art. . . the symbolical expression of this torpid old vague culture of ours. He is a symbol of our rootlessness, of that cultural colonialism which has so little left but smug comfort and polite aspiration." He is one with the older generation, of the genteel tradition, a puritan.

Bourne professed to see puritans everywhere. They were the real enemy of youth and progress. His generation made them so. Bourne, along with Brooks, Mencken, Lippmann, and some others, was among the leaders in creating the most notorious rhetorical dispute between the generations, dividing them into opposing camps of pagans and puritans. In less than a decade these young critics refashioned a former American hero and saint into the villain and chief sinner in the thwarting of the promise of America and youth. The puritan which they excoriated, peeling off his saintly visage, was something of a straw man, as Bourne knew, but he was a useful invention for the warfare between the generations, a perfect target for the ironist and satirist as he had been in other times and other places. Bourne gave full reign to his fictional impulse in his most devastating and devastatingly ironic portrait of the older generation, "The Puritan's Will To Power," his first contribution to the *Seven Arts*.[24] It appeared in April 1917, the month America declared war on Germany.

It does not pose as fiction, of course, but it belongs nevertheless in Bourne's gallery of portraits. Generalized, the puritan is presented as a type, the most pervasive and harassing presence for youth, for "the modern young person who tries to live well." He is everywhere, he cannot be got rid of. It is not a question of a puritanical age or a pagan age, "only a question of more puritans or less puritans." The Voltairean echo sets the tone: "If there were no puritans we should have to invent them."

So Bourne did just that. The piece defies succinct paraphrase or compressed summary without loss to its essential tones. Every line set down has several cutting edges. They slice even into young people, the new generations that find new ways of being puritanical, a new way of sacrifice, like the lusty young generation of Europe (and now America) going to "its million-headed slaughter," like the young intelligentsia who have finally achieved sexual freedom (or the "pious belief" in it) only to become terrorized by "a superstition like eugenics" and who must now face "idealistic girls [*sic*] and men coming out of the colleges to tell us of our social responsibility to the race."

It was important to understand the youth in "Below the Battle" so as to expose the fund of untapped personal and social idealism still available in America's youth. The ironic burden in that portrait rests upon an older generation that ironically ignored that idealism even as it demanded sacrifice in the name of its own absolute brand. It was the older generation that did not understand youth and thus threatened to snuff out its value to America. It was similarly important to explain and expose the puritan. "We must keep him before our eyes, recognize him as the real enemy, no matter in what ideal disguise he lurks." The burden of irony here, however, is upon youth, for whom the analyst speaks, because one must not be beguiled—or co-opted as a later youth might say—by the superstitious belief in his moral superiority. The will to power dogma would shatter that belief and reveal him, Bourne says, as "natural" a man as the most carnal sinner.

The puritan's instincts are neither canceled nor blocked, Bourne says, twisting the conventional explanation of the parlor Freudians. On the contrary, he gives his instincts full play, directing them into powerful channels, especially in the "cunningly organized satisfaction of two of his strongest impulses,—the self-conscious personal impulses of being regarded and being neglected." The powerful amalgam of these two apparently contradictory sentiments, the self-abasing and the self-regarding, constitute the essence of the puritan.

Indulging the first, the puritan renounces, "he puts on meekness, he sternly regiments himself, he makes himself unhappy in ways that are just not quite severe enough to excite pity and yet run no risk of arousing any envy." To do this he must, of course, exercise great self-control, but that in itself, however much puritan moralists might preach it as a virtue, is neither virtuous nor satisfying until it is idealized and until he becomes *proud* of his self-control. Then, having fully abased himself, the puritan brings into play his self-regard, becomes proud of his humility, enjoins it upon others, and thus gets his satisfaction out of his control over them.

The puritan gets his satisfaction exactly where the most carnal of natural men gets his, out of the stimulation of his pride. And in a world where renunciation has to happen to us whether we want it or not, the puritan is in the most impressive strategic position. In economy of energy he has it all over the head that is bloody but unbowed. For the puritan is so efficient morally that he can bow his head and yet exact control both out of the bowing and out of the prestige which his bowing gives him, as well as out of the bowing which he can enforce on others. . . . In the compelling of others to abstain, you have the final glut of puritanical power. For in getting other people to renounce a thing you thereby get renewed justification for your own renouncing. And so the puritan may go on inexhaustibly rolling up his satisfactions, one impulse reinforcing the other. The simultaneous play of these two apparently inconsistent personal impulses makes the puritan type one of the stablest in society. While the rest of us are longing for power the puritan is enjoying his.[25]

If we have not guessed it from some of his other portraits, Bourne tells us here: "The puritan is a case of arrested development." He has not the capacity to grow. Youth, on the other hand, is capable of growing beyond the puritan to find subtler ways of satisfying the desire for power—for Bourne's youth, a very strong desire. "We never can quite become proud of our humility." Renunciation for youth is a genuine going without, sacrifice is real, and like the youth of "Below the Battle," and again ironically phrased, "we are too naive to pretend that there are compensations. There *is* a loss. We are left with a vacuum. There is only depression and loss of control."

To this analyst of the puritan, renouncing leaves him only with the sense of degradation. "I had rather beat my head rhythmically and endlessly against an unyielding wall. For the pagan often breaks miraculously through the wall. But the puritan at his best can only strut outside." Bourne concluded: "Most of us, therefore, after we have had our puritan fling, sown our puritan wild oats as it were, grow up into devout and progressing pagans, cultivating the warmth of the sun, the deliciousness of love-experience, the high moods of art. The puritans remain around us, a danger and a threat. But they have value to us in keeping us acutely self-conscious of our faith. They whet our ardor. Perhaps no one can be really a good appreciating pagan who has not once been a bad puritan."[26]

CHAPTER 5

Mythographer of Youth

BEGIN with an individual, and before you know it you have created a type, F. Scott Fitzgerald said in one of his own tales. Invariably that was the route Bourne's fictional impulse followed. For the puritan he had any number of individuals to start with, any one and all of those dominating people who had thwarted his desires in one way or another—the pillars of his hometown society, Bloomfield, his Uncle Halsey, Bligh, Erskine, Butler, many others. After them there were those he sparred with in the intellectual arena, the humanist critics like Paul Shorey, Paul Elmer More, Stuart Sherman, W. C. Brownell, and then some of his own contemporaries, those who had yielded to the puritan's will to power, the "liberals" who not only supported the war but boasted of having willed American intervention. But he had also, as always, started with himself—and created a type, in this instance, the bad puritan devoutly desiring the sun's warmth, the deliciousness of love, the high moods of art—the typical, ideal youth.

These experiments in fiction remain, however, just that and only that. They are sketches, portraits of types, meant to be emblematic. The figures in their frames are not yet characters. They hang in a gallery. They do not move in any world outside their frames, though they may resemble personalities who do. It will not do to extend Van Wyck Brooks's suggestion. Bourne was no novelist.

His desire to write a novel should not be confused with his achievement. He did a little better than his Karen who had nothing to show that "her novels unfolded anywhere but in her mind as they interpreted the richly exciting detail of her personal contacts"—which may have been his wryly oblique way of confessing his sensitivity to the distance between his own ambitions and achievement. But the autobiographical novel he was indeed working on remained unfinished at his death. Stories of a lost manuscript contribute to legend but not to a reputation as a novelist. The fragmentary evidence that survives adds to his claim upon us as a fictioneer, but of another kind than he aspired to.

"An Autobiographic Chapter," the surviving fragment of Bourne's novel, and "History of a Literary Radical," both included in Brooks's posthumous collection, are the significant additions to his other fictional experiments on which, taken all together, I think that claim rests and rests securely. They each display a skillful advance in control over the materials of his own experience. The portrait of Miro, the literary radical, might well have become a later chapter in the novel, for Miro is only Gilbert, the boy, become a youth. One can well imagine, in fact, that other figures who sat for his portraits would have appeared in the novel as it progressed, removed from their frames and given a habitude, a world to move in and become characters. Several of their representative types are already present or foreshadowed. A brief outline of the novel's theme left among his papers indicates intentions to make it a story of the dramatic conflict between the generations, the issue that emerges from the ironic tones in all his portraits.

The proposed cast of characters matches those in Bourne's own family (minus one sister), plus two young women, the protagonist's "sweetheart" and "another girl whom he partly loves," setting up the familiar triangular relationship Bourne so often got mixed up in and mixed up about. His summary outline of his novel's theme is as follows, in its entirety, as put down in his own hand:

Theme: The father has been false to the mother, & left her to bring up the children which she has done, through the aid of her brother & sister. The father wishes to return but faces the hostility of the latter. The son hates his father and feels the shame of his mother. He is in love with a girl who has given herself to him and who distrusts him. He is uncertain whether he can marry her, though he wishes it. She fears his desertion. He is inconstant. But his horror at his father's hypocrisy combined with the girl's brave self-sufficiency create a situation which contrasts dramatically with the sterile situation of the mother. The new candor of the young man of to-day and the economic independence of the young woman make a relation possible which may be poignant and unhappy but which will not be complicated by all the fears and scruples and righteous hypocrisies of the older generation.[1]

It is not fair, of course, to pass judgment on a mere outline's promise, but one would guess from this that Bourne was following his usual route, from individual to type, even toward stereotypical relationships among his characters. The proof of anything more must lie in the performance, and we have only a fragment. There is enough there, however, to suggest that he could have turned the trick. He might have achieved a memorable novel. He might have created a memorable character in the full story of Gilbert/Miro's coming of age, a story at once distinctive and representative.[2]

The point of view in the fragment is strictly limited to the third-person sensibility of the boy, Gilbert (as "History of a Literary Radical" is limited to that of "my friend Miro"). The narrator is not overtly commenting, surmising, intruding his own personality, but presenting a world as seen from the perspective of innocence, that of youth and of childhood, youth's prologue and preparatory experience. Place and setting loom importantly as determinants of personality: for Gilbert, the physical setting of his small world, limited to house and rooms, a dark musty-smelling basement dining room, a blacker kitchen, the more comforting upstairs bedrooms, a fearsome outhouse, a marvelous yard and barn, or the outer world's restricted extension from house to church and the church itself, its pews, distant ceiling, and enormous chandeliers; for Miro, the intellectual and cultural setting of the world he inherits, before college, during, and after, a world marked by the clash between the old orthodoxies and the new, the dead classics and the new prophets, the older critics and the new critics, conservatives and radicals. The contradictions, the ironies are contained in the settings. We see them or their symbolic foreshadowing as Gilbert does not, as Miro, recognizing them, tries to reconcile them with his own desires and grow beyond them toward a new cultural attitude, possibly "a new classicism."

The advance is not only in the handling of point of view, but also in style: crisp, succinct, more dense with detail and that more concrete and particular. The subject is still youth and life, the chief originating source still Bourne himself. But he has moved beyond abstraction and released from himself a figure of some solidity, and set him in a world his comprehending audience could identify as their own.

We know Gilbert—"Gilbert Shotwell Harden" as stamped in golden letters in the Bible given him—only as a boy of six and seven, the same age of Ernest in Bourne's earlier sketch, "Ernest: or Parent for a Day." The interest in that sketch is evenly divided, however, between the narrator, amusingly recording the experiment which shatters his theories of parenthood (not, of course, Bourne's own theories), and Ernest, the self-reliant institutional orphan who spends the day and night with him. "Ernest," it may be inferred, was a preparatory sketch for the novel, but it is a contrast rather than any identity between Ernest and Gilbert which throws some suggestive light on Bourne's intentions in the novel. Ernest's robust self-reliance, his intelligence, and his capacity to enjoy himself make the narrator envious, and he concludes that Ernest's having had no home or parents has been an advantage: he has escaped so much "bringing up . . . there was nothing repressed about him, nothing institutionalized, and certainly nothing artificial." He envies Ernest's peaceful slumber and recalls how in his own childhood such a sense of security had come only after nightly assurances from his mother that she would be home for the night. So too, "Gilbert got in the habit of asking his mother every night whether she was going out," needing her comforting presence, unlike Ernest.

Expectedly, Ernest and Gilbert share some of the natural attributes of childhood, both delighting in the pleasures of the eye and of the senses generally, both displaying an instinctive intelligence, each betraying a rebellious streak. Interested in exploring Ernest's "intellectual background," his parent for the day records the delight Ernest took in naming everything he sees around him. He is already living the life of adventure and experiment, "living in life's essential,—excitement," and learning through his keen senses from the world immediately before him. He has had some religion in his career, the narrator infers, but he seems unbothered by any of the "easy mythologies"; he chortles incredulously at the narrator's recital of the biblical tale of David and he is not awed by an account of the majesty of Moses. The narrator refrains from trifling with Ernest's intellectual honesty and decides not to tell him about Adam and Eve or to correct Ernest's insistence on seeing pictures of the Greeks as men and women, not as gods.

Gilbert, on the other hand, is clearly in for all sorts of repressions and artificialities likely to inhibit his natural intelligence and instincts. His senses teach him one thing, his elders and the books he reads, another. Despite the ominous absence of a father and the foreboding hints of a shamed, distressed, and unloving mother—it is only Garna, the grandmother with whom they live, that Gilbert is sure he loves—his is to be the now conventional story of being brought up absurd. Along with his terrors of the dark (associated with nighttime walks down the long path to the outhouse) and nighttime fears that mother would be gone, there are all sorts of prohibitions he must abide by, and guilt clutches fiercely at him whenever he dares a clandestine violation. He will have a lot of bringing up to escape, but at a later time than the more fortunate Ernest, and chiefly from the church, Sunday school, and the Bible ("a magical book that you must not drop on the floor" as the older Miro recalled it).

The stories from the Old Testament Gilbert finds plausible enough for teaching little boys and girls to be good, to honor and obey their parents, and go regularly to church and Sunday school, but they did not succeed in persuading him to love God, even though he knew it was "the most important thing in life that he could do." Sin, constantly expounded upon, remained a vague idea on the whole, except for the horrifying pictures derived from Miss Figg's Sunday school temperance lectures. He had never seen any spirituous liquors, but he imagined "a dark, evil-smelling brew, a sort of religious urine, which foul and wicked men put into their stomachs, so that at once houses were wrecked, and mothers and children brought to abject want."

The repressive notes are countered somewhat by Gilbert's sensual pleasures in the Eden-like garden and surrounding yard, recalling the idyllic summertimes of Tom Sawyer. But the "tedium vitae" of some summer days made him feel "as if alive in a tomb," and got translated "into the colossal ennui of heaven," an "appalling sense of eternity" where time ticked on but nothing ever happened. Heaven became as fearful a prospect as hell. School brings none of the promised relief. Having already learned to read, he finds his reading lessons absurd, school as a whole "an enormous joke" and a bore. He retaliates by teasing the teacher and amusing his classmates at her expense. The last glimpse we have is of a Gibert " drunk with power, " refusing all inducements to be good, and, like D. H. Lawrence's rocking horse winner, riding "his high horse until the mill whistles blew twelve o'clock and they all went home for the day."

Miro's rebellion and bid for power begin in boredom, too. Bright, but docile in accepting all the pronouncements of his teachers about the greatness of literature, he had been initiated into culture as into a kind of religious mystery. He never doubted the wisdom of the "serious, puckered women who had the precious manipulation of his cultural upbringing in their charge," and learned to grieve with them, not quite knowing why, that "the millions pursued cheap and vulgar fiction instead of the best that had been thought and said in the world." The early years of college did nothing to deprive him of his cultural loyalty, but although he remained "almost inconceivably docile, he found himself being bored." The literary life he had aspired to proves less exciting than he had expected. College permitted no escape from "the closed dichotomy of culture," a culture split between the "classic" and the "popular," or "highbrow" and "lowbrow" (echoing Van Wyck Brooks's mournful denunciation of that same split).

No less a "literary radical" than Professor William Lyon Phelps began Miro's emancipation—with an audacious lecture, at the Lyceum Club of Miro's village, on "the modern novel," Hardy, Tolstoy, Turgenev, Meredith, "even Trollope"! Phelps so charmed his audience that "the virgin shelves of the village library were ravished for days to come by the eager minds upon whom these great names dawned for the first time." So at college Miro explores these "forbidden realms."

> It was as if some devout and restless saint had suddenly been introduced to the Apocrypha. A new world was opened to Miro that was neither "classic" nor "popular," and yet which came to one under the most unimpeachable auspices. There was, at first, it is true, an air of illicit adventure about the enterprise. The lecturer who made himself the missionary of such vigorous and piquant doctrine had the air of being a heretic, or at least a boy playing out of school. But Miro himself returned to college a cultural revolutionist. His orthodoxies crumbled. He did not try to reconcile the new with the old. He applied pick and dynamite to the whole structure of the canon. Irony, humor, tragedy, sensuality, suddenly appeared to him as literary qualities in forms that he could understand. They were like oxygen to his soul.[3]

He reads *Resurrection* while his literature class is making an "intensive" study of Tennyson. He rises in revolt, foreswears literary courses forever as "dead rituals in which anaemic priests mumbled their trite critical commentary," and becomes "as violent as a heretic as he had been docile as a believer." Nothing that was "mere literature" would do, "social purpose" had to shine in any writing that would rouse his enthusiasm.

The story of his continuing radicalism charts an ironic curve, however. Starting in rejection, Miro seeks a new affirmation, not merely an extension of the cultural dichotomy in new guise, no mere continuation of the old battles between the ancients and the moderns. One result of his rebellious awakening has been the discovery that he really had no standards of critical taste—a confession few of Miro's contemporaries would have made since that is precisely what their older opponents charged against them. Mere reverence for the classics had left Miro with no capacity for making preferences, yet "dealing with the raw materials of letters, he had to become a critic and make selection." Impeccable revolutionary thought in a book could not redeem it if it was badly written. The new fashion among some of the promising young instructors to study literature as the record of ideas ("and not merely as a canon of sacred books") was welcome, but the accompanying attempt to treat literary studies as a science, not an art, left Miro cold. His own apprehension of literature's significance "only as the expression of personality or as an interpretation of some social movement" had no counterpart in the scholastic mind.

After college Miro finds that the old battles continue, now between the "older critics" and the new young critics, and though he is clearly on the side of the young, neither camp satisfies him. He is amused at the last ditch defense of the "classics" still enduring in the attacks on the "new education." Other conservatives—the new humanists, to whose leading spokesman, Irving Babbitt, Bourne had once given fleeting allegiance—although they shared with the cultural revolutionists a hatred of some of the "arrogant and mechanical psychologies and sociologies that reduced life to figures or organisms," were too defensive, too unwilling to discriminate among current writers (lumped all together as "anarchic" and "naturalistic," the latter an evil word in their lexicon) and altogether too obstructive of the creative spirit. Moreover, their own polemics showed none of the urbanity and command of thought and ideas that was supposed to result from preparation in the classics.

But if the older critics seemed inhospitable, tired, even "a little spitefully disconsolate," the newer ones were so intent on "their crusades against puritanism and philistinism" as to have little time for constructive assistance. The likes of Mencken and Dreiser, in their raging battle with the Philistines, were creating a new orthodoxy with as much moralism, bigotry, and tastelessness as that of their enemies. Miro believed he needed at least an inoculation of the virus of each orthodoxy, but he sought to transcend both:

> He would have to look for the critics among the young men who had an abounding sense of life, as well as a feeling for literary form. They would be men who had not been content to live on their cultural inheritance, but had gone out into the modern world and amassed a fresh fortune of their own. They would be men who were not squeamish, who did not feel the delicate differences between "animal" and "human" conduct, who were enthusiastic about Mark Twain and Gorki as well as Romain Rolland, and at the same time were thrilled by Copeau's theater.[4]

Rather than follow Mencken and fight the Philistine in the name of freedom, or the young but misguided apologist for humanism, Stuart P. Sherman, and fight "the vulgar iconoclast in the name of wholesome human notions," Miro resolved in the spirit of Voltaire "to write for one's own brand of comprehenders."

The rest was prophesy. Looking ahead to postwar America, Bourne has Miro anticipate a new internationalism and a new classicism for his new man of culture. The American writer must still be a nationalist, drawing upon the materials of the life in which he is saturated, but he must be international "in the sense that he works with a certain hopeful vision of a 'young world,' and with certain ideal values upon which the younger men, stained and revolted by war, in all countries are agreeing."

Youth thus remained an important part of Miro's cultural vision, a youth still a little more "certain" about what he rejected than about the still vague "certain values" he hoped for. Some virtues of youth would also make for a classicism for Miro far different than what had been "so unintelligently" handed down to him. It would be a classicism "worked out and lived into," doing "what Van Wyck Brooks calls 'inventing a usable past,'" and it would rescue Thoreau and Whitman and Mark Twain. In an ironic marriage of some of the favorite words of his youth with those favored by humanists, Miro concluded: "If the classic means power with restraint, vitality with harmony, a fusion of intellect and feeling, and a keen sense of the artistic conscience, then the revolutionary world is coming out into the classic." To the end, Bourne's youth, Miro, remained a lover of paradox and the life of irony.

His fictional efforts make Bourne something else, neither more nor less, than a novelist, but perhaps something as valuable to culture. He provided images that Americans have had to contend with in trying to understand themselves. He was the mythographer of an American radical youth, a type and emblem he created out of the materials of his own personality.

That personality would not have become known in the mythical dimensions it assumed, nor been revived again and again by successive younger generations as someone who had shaped some feature of their own experience as youth, had he not created the image in the first place.

CHAPTER 6

The Young Radical and War

IN the early months of 1916 the European war still seemed distant to most Americans, particularly the prospect of their own involvement. President Wilson appeared determinedly resolved to maintain America's neutrality and, as the national election in November would demonstrate, a majority of American voters endorsed that resolve. Still, as international events alternately heightened tensions first in German-American relations, then those with Great Britain and her allies, and as hopes for an American mediating role rose and collapsed, the divisions among Americans had become sharper and also more complicated and confusing. The relatively simple act of voting aye or nay for a president whose final campaign weeks stressed his having "kept us out of war" concealed a complex of responses to the dreary, deadly continuation of a war that was not supposed to have been possible in the first place. When they thought about the war most Americans were still trying to make up their minds, still sorting out their conflicting emotions amid variant claims upon their allegiances.

The first allegiance of all good young Progressives was, of course, to the power of reason. Reacting to the first shock of the war's initial explosion, the *New Republic*'s editors had stoutly declared: "We cannot abandon the labor of thought."[1] A year and a half later, in the still uncertain spring of 1916, Randolph Bourne concluded that they had done just that. In their own pages he obliquely reminded his colleagues of their first allegiance. He tucked his warning within the folds of another issue, but the application to the increasingly interventionist stance of Croly and Lippmann is unmistakable. "Middle-Class radicalism," he said, had become "too easy"—not exercising the labor of thought—and was tending "to drift." "The young radical today is not asked to be a martyr," he said, "but he is asked to be a thinker, an intellectual leader."[2]

Ironies in Bourne's story abound, but none seem more tragic than the consequences of his being bestowed with the mantle of martyrdom to the war, which he would have scorned, in ironic payment for the intellectual clarity he provided on issues that included the war but also went beyond that of war. The unhappy coincidence of his death within weeks of the war's end immediately cast him into the role of a war casualty. The first posthumous publication in 1919 of *Untimely Papers*, collecting his *Seven Arts* war essays and two of his most pessimistic writings, the fragments "Old Tyrannies" and "The State," reenforced that role. Amid the postwar disillusionment which set in so quickly after the initial euphoria with victory, James Oppenheim's introductory offering of the book as "the only living record of the suppressed minority...the prophecy of that minority's final triumph," set the pitch for a chorus of reviewers and eulogists who added to the country's mounting second thoughts on the war just ended. The war had checked and tripped Bourne, these coincidences suggested, and then had "shot the spirit on" in the singular direction of a prophet of the postwar awakening to the truth about war.[3]

The misty veils of legend settled around his memory: that for his dissident opinions he had been hounded by federal agents; that he had been denied a forum for his views; that he was the chief cause of the ending of the *Seven Arts;* that he was cut off from a livelihood and died nearly destitute; that he was, in short, a martyr. The sum of such half-truths is legend, the legend of his martyrdom. John Dos Passos painted them all into his portrait of Bourne in *1919* (and added some legendary colors of his own). His oft-quoted lines about the ghost of Bourne

> Hopping along the grimy old brick and brownstone streets left in
> downtown New York,
> crying out in a shrill soundless giggle:
> *War is the health of the state*

made for an indelible outline of the spirit.

If some of the legends have since been corrected with other portions of the truth,[4] dying hard, they still tint the myth with martyrdom to war. A member of a later wartime younger generation, finding much else in Bourne difficult for his generation to understand—especially the alleged boundless optimism of his college years—found only in Bourne's response to the war crisis "a familiar chord."[5] Insofar as the crisis of war is the crucial one for youth, one can understand why other generations have similarly responded to Bourne in their wartimes. But estimates of Bourne have continued to emphasize his wartime role as victim, the war as his maturing experience, and the war essays as his most mature expression. The historian Henry May could confidently speak of "the famous case" of Randolph Bourne's "wartime metamorphosis"—from a "somewhat naive insurgent" to a "profound inquirer, a defender of freedom in what he had learned was a hostile world"—and then May placed a weighty assessment upon that metamorphosis as "the precise moment" when the innocence of a whole American era had come to an end.[6] If that is too much historical responsibility to assign any one person and too much precision for such a moment in history, it is fitting to assign a symbolic moment, as Professor May finally makes it, to a figure already endowed with mythical purport. Such uses of Bourne testify to his persisting availability as a myth; but they also reveal how the still echoing legends of the war's tripping and checking him, provoking precipitous change, sudden maturity, and martyrdom to war, have been mixed and stirred with the motives of later critics and students of Bourne, often skewing and limiting understanding of that myth's power to endure.

He was no martyr to the war.

Martyrdom is a complex state of being, more easily pronounced after the fact than discernible before, more often bestowed, rarely invited. There is little evidence to suggest that Bourne underwent any anguish resembling, say, that of T. S. Eliot's Becket; nor can he be called an unwitting martyr, innocent of the probability of suffering for persevering in his convictions. He had his moments of despair, often profoundly agonizing ones—for friends facing the impossible choices war demanded of them, for friendships that cooled or collapsed over differences on the war, friendships he had so desired and courted. But he already had more reason than most men to know how hostile the world could be; he needed no war, however startlingly depressing when it came, to discover that. The protective doublet of irony he had learned to wear had him better prepared than most young men of his generation to face the world's hostility. Suffering and despair he felt, and all the more acutely no doubt, because of the ironic protective immunity of his handicap. But he translated that suffering into personal triumph, not defeat. The war neither checked nor tripped him; it spurred him on. 1917 and 1918, his last two years, were his most productive, his most brilliant—and with all due respect for the irony provided by the context of those war years—his most joyous, satisfying his most ardent desires, both intellectually and emotionally.

These were the years following the arrival of Van Wyck Brooks's stirring manifesto, *America's Coming-of-Age*, a call to the younger generation to keep the fiddles tuning, to remember that humanity was older than puritanism. That book had been, Waldo Frank said, the prolegomenon to the *Seven Arts*, which sent out its notice of arrival during the summer of 1916: a magazine, its editors James Oppenheim and Frank said, that was to be a channel for the flow of "new tendencies: an expression of American life . . . not a magazine for artists but an expression of artists for the community." In November 1916 its first number appeared. The year before, about the time the book was published, Bourne and Brooks had finally met, following correspondence between them and Brooks's earlier solicitation for an article from Bourne for the *Century* magazine. The friendship ripened quickly. The resonating similarities of their aims and ambitions proved mutually stimulating, with Bourne's visionary glance toward the future provoked by Brooks and rising beyond Brooks's in some respects. During the last two summers of his life Bourne lived some parts of the time with the Brookses, exulting in the nonstop conversations on the highest of planes. Bourne reported on his "delightful days" with Brooks in Provincetown, "where Greenwich Villagers are as thick as the mosquitoes," a "rarified two weeks" in all, with much enthusiastic planning for a communal living group that would include the Brookses, some other compatible friends, and Bourne and "E"—Esther Cornell. The summer before, 1916, he had moved in with Esther and Agnes de Lima, sharing living quarters with them in Caldwell, New Jersey, within easy reach of New York City. Recovering at the time from another rebuff at love, he had promptly fallen in love again; this time there was promise of its being returned. By August of the following year he confidently counted Esther into those plans with the Brookses. "I already have E" he told Agnes de Lima. He was riding high.[7]

Yet this was the same summer he was writing and publishing his furious assaults on his fellow intellectuals, possibly the summer he wrote "Old Tyrannies," probably the summer he commenced "The State." The public Bourne may have appeared then, and in immediate retrospect more so, to be bidding for martyrdom. Crying "betrayal" in the *Seven Arts*, he was subsequently revealed to have yielded to a bleak determinism, resigned to the "inexorable" march of events. So it appeared, and so in part this desperate side of Bourne's response to the war is true. But only in part.

The private Bourne was riding high, soaring even, on a confident realization and exercise of his powers. He was counting for something, at least with the comprehending audience he spoke to.

The real months of despair and depression were behind him, during the winter of 1915-1916: a lovelorn affair, a ruptured friendship with Carl Zigrosser and other old friends, the growing certainty of divergent views on the war with his *New Republic* colleagues and others, deepening doubts about his ability to write, to write honestly, fully, clearly about all his conflicting passions. These had provided cause for pessimism. By contrast, the ensuing and final months left to him contained mounting assertions of his will to power and his enjoyment of it. He found a new love. He moved into a new circle of friends, fellow intellectuals who shared his vision of an America fulfilling its promise, coming of age: Brooks, others of the *Seven Arts* set, Oppenheim, Frank, and Paul Rosenfeld. He finally met Max Eastman, liked him, discovered in him "the firm bond of a common enemy." On the same occasion he met Horace Kallen whose assault on the "melting-pot" metaphor for America matched Bourne's—another firm bond. He had been to Chicago, talking at a young women's college, hosted by a Unitarian minister, "one of the most industrious propagandists of 'Youth and Life.'" He had a constituency. He enjoyed the sense of his importance to others. The midwest—where the war was least popular—was "one of the few American scenes where I am appreciated," he wrote. But he was in demand elsewhere and appreciated elsewhere. Earlier, the reverberations from his *Atlantic Monthly* article, "Trans-National America," had brought him an invitation to speak in Cambridge before the Harvard Menorah Society. He was introduced there, he reported to Alyse Gregory, "in the most cosmic terms," and with the "reverential awe" usually reserved for an international figure. He enjoyed it all thoroughly. If the world was darkening around him and others, he felt he could nevertheless be "a little fountain of light." He counted for something.[8]

Of course he continued to have his ups and downs, his characteristic lapses into depression. But such alternations of moods *had been* characteristic, so much so as to invite his self-conscious probing of the anomaly, converting it into a virtue of youth. To point out an apparent contrast in the larger pattern of alternating tones between the public Bourne and the private Bourne is not simply to adjust legend, or to suggest the paradoxical figure of a happy pessimist, but to remark the emergence of a Bourne in nearly full command of the role he had created for himself: the ideal youth whose antipodes of being, his sense of power, his sense of estrangement, joined in mutual reenforcement to promote desire for a beloved community beyond war.

Bourne underwent no sudden metamorphosis, certainly not regarding his position toward the war. True, when it came, he was as shocked at his innocent obliviousness to its coming as was nearly everybody else. Besides his own confession of the obtuseness of his vision while he was in Europe, we have hindsight's judgment of the naive optimism of some of his earliest pronouncements on war, made while it was still an abstraction, but on the very eve of its coming. The reversal in mood from early optimism to later pessimism is readily apparent in a simple comparison between them and his wartime essays. But we should look more closely.

In "The Tradition of War," one of two pamphlets Bourne wrote for the American Association for International Conciliation (which included on its council distinguished names in the prestigious peace movements of the day, like Lyman Abbott, Charles Francis Adams, Andrew Carnegie, Charles W. Eliot, David Starr Jordan, and, yes, Nicholas Murray Butler), this one published in June 1914 while he was still in Europe, Bourne could flatly assert that war had become almost unimaginable, so far had civilization progressed. The historic change in the modern world from "a feudal society based on isolation and force to an industrial creative society based on co-operation and exchange has definitely and for all time relegated war to the dusty limbo of the past," he wrote. It was a fact, he said; "the military game is up."[9] Naive, of course. He was wrong. So was nearly everybody else. But if history had rudely and, within another brief month's time, embarrassingly canceled this "fact" of his, it did not cause him to reverse other features in his reasoning about war and about the hostile world around him, a world whose special hostility seemed reserved for thought itself.

"The Tradition of War" rests solidly upon the Progressive era's faith that progress, at every level, international and national, public and private, could be achieved, as Bourne put it, by "the substitution of conscious rational control of environment for the unconscious yielding to the traditional forces of inertia and habit."[10] Along with many others he overestimated the fact of that substitution, but unlike many others he did not abandon his insistence in the increased necessity for it.

Bourne was guilty in the pamphlet of the rhetorical gambit, common to propaganda, of declaring that to be true which he was really trying to argue *should be* true. The event of war exposed the fallacy, but also confirmed his opening point: "One of the most important things that we can learn in regard to this world about us is that ideals and institutions are far less rational than they generally purport to be"—especially those having to do with war and the preparation for war. When he subsequently turned his wrath upon his fellow intellectuals it was precisely aimed at the *purported* rationalism they claimed in their advocacy of the war. No change there. Similarly, if his assertion that the fanatical irrationalism of militarism was simply incompatible with a rational modern world proved to be a vain expression of hope, his lengthy analysis of the continuing strength of militarism's appeal seemed only confirmed by the event of war. The pamphlet had warned that the tradition of war could be overcome only through "a resolute insistence upon seeing things as they are, unblinded by sentiment or class-prejudice."[11] When the war came, it followed that Bourne indeed saw it as a consequence of the failure to see things as they are, as a yielding to sentiment and prejudice. Moreover, that early pamphlet's analysis of the sources of militarism's strength amounts to a forecast, in outline, of his later castigation of the "war-technique."

When Bourne later accused his fellow intellectuals of lapsing into the primitive ways of thought of militarists, he was simply repeating the warning of his pamphlet about militarists who "befuddle the wits of masses of people with shibboleths of 'patriotism,' identifying the war ideals with love of country, and representing hatred of militarism as in a way synonymous with disloyalty to country." The refrain notoriously threaded through "The State"—"War is the health of the state"—is obversely and ironically adumbrated in the pamphlet's cocky declaration that "any intelligent person will recognize in an instant that the power for war is one of the least of the glories of the state." Similarly, the attempt in the later fragment to distinguish between the state, which provides support to militarism and a nation's political life, and country and national character, which alone can enlist "true patriotism," had already been advanced in the earlier pamphlet.[12]

His ironic observation in 1917 that "the pacifist is roundly scolded for refusing to face the facts, and for retiring into his own world of sentimental desire"[13] is almost an exact echo of his 1914 pamphlet's opening causticism that "the workers for peace are jeered at as sentimentalists who will not see things as they are"—in both instances used as points of departure for reversing the charge that it is the so-called and self-proclaimed "realists" who prove to be least capable of controlling the forces of war. Even his alleged sudden resignation to the inexorable deterministic force of the war's coming was anticipated in the pamphlet's recommendation that enthusiasts "for war as a science or game," something they could therefore control, should read Tolstoy's *War and Peace* to understand "the helplessness of even the greatest generals in the grip of elemental forces and uncontrollable masses of men, and the pure fortuitousness of battle."[14]

The war, in short, when it came, confirmed his worst fears and admonitions as much as it dashed his hopeful optimism about rationalism's power to prevail. Always perilously poised between hope and despair, Bourne could give simultaneous expression to both, and frequently did. Paradoxical as it may appear, that capacity made for remarkable consistency in the nature of his criticism, whether addressed to the issues of youth, of education, of feminism, of militarism and war, or to the ultimate concern of nearly all his writing, that of the self-conscious realization of a national culture. Hope and despair, optimism and pessimism, were the two sides of his steady insistence on seeing things as they are. When what he saw was the persisting ascendency of the irrational, he despaired; when he pointed to what might be, he grew eloquent in affirmation. When he brought both visions together, as was more often his way, irony emanated from his effort to smart the eyes of his readers into sharing his hopeful vision by scoring their presumed "practical" realism or "hard-headed" rationalism.

What steadily matured, while the basic outline of his thinking and feeling about war's irrational nature remained intact, was his rhetorical skill at exposing the contradictions between the proposed aims and the methods of the strategists for war. "The State," too often overrated as an essay at political theory, is essentially an expansion upon "The Tradition of War." It refines and carries further the distinctions he had made among state, nation, and government; it develops in more detail the argument that the tradition of war is entrenched in social caste and class interests; it supports the whole argument with an excursion into American history as well as with the broad sweeps into the European past he had made in the earlier tract. It is a better piece of writing, but as a piece of analysis just as naive in its pessimism as the former was for its incongruous optimism. It is a better piece of writing because it is more concrete, its words invoking and pointing to recent realities rather than to remote probabilities (though still on the abstract side, with reliance upon the contemporary currency of intellectual jargon like "the herd" and a general air of psychologizing about social forces). But it is questionable whether it is any more profound an inquiry into the irrational persistence of war as an instrument of the state than was his earlier foray into the same grounds, the one buoyed on the hope that it was no more, the other anchored to the despairing acknowledgment that it was.

The real profundity of his resounding attack on the war technique grew from his imaginative grasp and rhetorical command of the contending forces of the old and the young, of tradition and youth, and from his steady insistence on the exercise of clear thought in the service of honest emotions. Though denied a role in the policy-making decisions on the *New Republic,* he got his licks in when he could. Very early in his tenure on the *New Republic* he deplored the "distressingly moral plane" on which discussion of the war was being conducted. It was all too much in terms of justification and responsibility, he said, "as if this were a world where things are justified."[15] He had been misled and misleading in that early pamphlet of his, so he now called for an analysis of the role that intellect and passion played, in both the warring countries and those that were still neutral—at home, in America. A few months later, in early January 1915, he warned that American assessments of the war had failed to recognize that the war had been fueled by the differences of national cultures; the American assessments deferred instead to the language of morality with which the English articulated their side, a language Americans understood, as they did not the "language of culture" (not, of course, as used by the Matthew Arnold cult). Anticipating his theme of transnationalism he counseled looking beneath the uniform features of European life—those in business and technology—to the stubbornly persisting distinctions in art, literature, and thought. Such differences should be welcomed, he said, since no one would want a slow washing out of diverse values into a "colorless European mass." At that point, with American involvement still remote, he could voice a shared *New Republic* hope that the war might prove to be "a vast liberating movement, clearing the way for this more conscious intenser world," though he would stop short of using that hope as justification for America's entry into the war (this not being a world where things are justified).[16]

That last note became characteristic of the way, increasingly, he looked beyond the war, using the war as a field for analysis of larger concerns. By throwing into stark relief the contrasting cultures, the war might provide opportunity to sift and sort out the creative contributions from diverse national cultures that a modern world could use. In September 1915, as anti-German sentiment began to build, Bourne had the courage—and the freedom still—to argue that America might profitably use some German ideals, that the intense feelings about the war should not lead to total refusal of everything German. German organization, German collectivism, German social art (with its styles speaking the ideal of form through function)—these ideals, in contrast to those of nations still "living on their funded nineteenth-century spiritual capital," England and France, for instance, were destined to become part of the modern world, whatever the war's outcome. It behooved America not to repudiate them lest it isolate itself from the modern world, or, rejecting them, then it must assume the responsibility of setting up even worthier ideals, ideals carved from our own "still pioneer, still struggling American spirit," and "in terms of values which secure all the vital fruits of the German ideals, [but] without the tragic costs." For the German will, fatally shattering the world's sympathies, Americans must substitute "a great desire" for ideals that would attract from ahead rather than push from behind. And of course—in the inevitable accompaniment to Bourne's appeal to "desire"—the spirit for such an enterprise was already available "in the thought of a younger generation."[17]

The younger intelligentsia, he argued, repeatedly and consistently, must heed the pragmatic imperative provoked by the spectacle of the European war to chart a course for a more creative America. Consistently and repeatedly he sought to "use," in faithful pragmatic fashion, the issues raised by the war to direct the sights of his fellow intellectuals beyond the war, to address the question "What shall we do with our America?" Had the war's reverberations revealed, to the consternation of America's dominant Anglo-Saxon class, the apparent failure of the "melting pot"? Then the younger intelligentsia must perceive in this reality the incalculable potentialities for a new cosmopolitan ideal, one that would not simply mimic "the weary old nationalism" of Europe, "belligerent, exclusive, inbreeding," whose poison made for war, but would be "a trans-nationality, a weaving back and forth" of the "threads of living and potent cultures." The war had revealed this process already going on, a blind striving of diverse cultures trying to weave themselves into a novel international nation. "It is for the American of the younger generation," Bourne urged, "to accept this cosmopolitanism and carry it along with self-conscious and fruitful purpose."[18]

The great danger the war posed to America, Bourne warned, was "not so much that we become militarists" as that we might yield to a delusive unity and to an expression of "Americanism" in noncreative activities. But if the war had indeed provoked a desire to serve America, why then not direct that desire into life-enhancing ways? So, to such ends he proposed "A Moral Equivalent for Universal Military Service," a pragmatic application of William James's "moral equivalent for war." The instrumentality for making James's one-time utopian-sounding proposal practically possible was already available in the systems of public education, he pointed out. He would have all children remain in school till the age of sixteen, then spend two years in national service before they reached twenty-one, a service whose aim would be constructive and communal, for "the improvement of the quality of our living." He envisioned, he said, "an army of youth" providing services "of neatness and mercy and intelligence," teaching us "how to live rather than die," becoming creators, "not engines of destruction"—the whole vision an embryonic prophecy of a later realized Civilian Conservation Corps and still later VISTA.[19]

While America was still officially uncommitted, and whenever and wherever he could, in short—and more frequently than has sometimes been recognized or acknowledged—Bourne applied his rhetorical and analytical powers against the war not simply in shrill cries against militarism, moralism, and sentimentalism, but also in behalf of positive alternatives which, he stressed time and again, the war had ironically made visible and available. He remained the practical idealist, the pragmatic intellectual, the young radical dodging pressures, proposing radical ideas, demonstrating for other young radicals the proper stance toward the war in Europe and what it meant for America's promise. And he still rested his faith on youth as the best guarantee of fulfilling that promise.

When America finally did declare war he was neither driven into isolation nor into silence. If he saw less of many of his earlier friends that was as much because he chose to see more of a few new ones—like Esther Cornell—as because he was shunned or ignored. Had there been no war the strategies of courtship would have called for a narrowing of his circle. April 1917, the month of American entry into the war, may well have been something of a high point for Bourne's appearances in print: his book, *Education and Living,* three pieces in the *New Republic,* one in the *Dial,* and his first essay in the *Seven Arts.* After that anything less might be counted a falling off, but not into silence. In fact, better than one fourth, nearly a third, of all the pieces published in his lifetime appeared in the twenty months between April 1917 and his death in December 1918, and something from his pen appeared in print in distinguished quarters in every one of those months but one (August 1918).

True, the frequency and regularity of his contributions to the *New Republic* fell off distinctly, and understandably, but its columns remained open to him, and I count his presence in them at least eighteen times from April 1917 on. These were nearly all in the form of book reviews, but a review by Bourne was always a chiseled essay advancing his own radical appreciations, never simply journeyman's work. Moreover, his absences from the *New Republic* were more than matched by the longer reach permitted him in his several essays for the *Seven Arts,* and by the increasing frequency of his appearance in the rejuvenated *Dial,* whose young financial backer, Scofield Thayer, wanted Bourne very much as an associate editor,[20] along with an occasional piece for his old patron, the *Atlantic Monthly,* and the still radical but chastened and renamed *Masses,* now the *Liberator.* If most of this output consisted also of reviews—the *Seven Arts* essays, *Atlantic Monthly*

("Ernest") and *Liberator* ("The Cult of Convention") contributions aside—they nevertheless permitted him to comment, in his fashion, upon the whole range of issues (including the war) and interests (increasingly literary) that had always been his.

One story of one article rejected because, allegedly, of his radical views on the war, no matter how often repeated or alluded to, is insufficient evidence to add up to enforced isolation and silence.[21] That Bourne perceived himself as a loner, an outcast, the embattled spokesman for a minority viewpoint is not, after all, surprising. Stigmatized by his handicap, he had very early accepted that role as one assigned him; he had carefully, even proudly, cultivated it. Not so much opposed to war as he was for directing "America's promise," America's official entry into the war nevertheless indubitably cast him, officially as it were, into the role of dissenter. It could not have been otherwise. But none of this disturbs the fact that he did have his say, and he said it brilliantly, courageously, in perhaps the best sustained series of attacks on the apologists for war that anyone issued during the war years themselves.

The argument of those essays is dense, not readily summarized, nor its peculiar acerbic wistfulness conveyed without extensive quotation. Biting as his words were in castigation of the war apologists' use of rationalism in defense of the irrational, they were accompanied by a mounting cry of anguish at lost opportunities, yet still defiant, with no trace of sentimental resignation. Insofar as the argument can be reduced to the simplest of terms, it was an Orwellian exposure of the contradictions, ironies, and hypocrisies in the defense of the indefensible.

But the full force of his dissent reverberates from the style and tone that conveyed it, and especially from the way it is stretched between the two antipodes of his rhetorical imagination—youth, and the older generation; the young pagan intelligence and sensibility, and the old puritan mentality and sentiment. Protagonist and antagonist are the same ones he had created and confronted in their abstract regalia in *Youth and Life*, the issue of war now throwing them into sharper outline, more stark opposition to each other, and in starker relief against a still vague background of hope for "America's promise."

Nearly all that he had to say against the apologists and strategists of the war, for instance, is contained within and between the two fictive attempts, "The Puritan's Will to Power" and "Below the Battle." The first written and submitted at least two months before American entry into the war,[22] fittingly appeared that very month of the illusory triumph of those who would boast that it was their power that had willed American intervention; the second appeared as the reality of conscription compelled the Bournian youth to confront his supreme crisis. Many of the same rhetorical tropes that govern in both essays appear again and again in the more direct assaults of the argumentative essays that define his case against the war proponents and for the young "irreconcilables" and "malcontents."

As he had warned that the puritan must be recognized as "the real enemy, no matter in what ideal disguise he lurks," so he charged that intellectuals who had thrown their support to the war technique had forgotten that "the real enemy is War," however they might try to drape over it a mantle of idealism. "Idealism should be kept for what is ideal." Moreover, those intellectuals were not content with simply confirming American belligerency: "They are now complacently asserting that it was they who effectively willed it . . . ," and they were slowly impressing upon the American people a picture of themselves as "gently guiding a nation through sheer force of ideas into what other nations entered only through predatory craft or popular hysteria or militant madness!" (The puritan "puts on meekness," is "proud of his self-control . . . becomes proud of his humility, enjoins it upon others. . . .") "Not only is every one forced into line" by tactics of the intellectuals, "but the new certitude becomes idealized." To what they allege are the "futile obstruction and the cowardly refusal to face facts" of the pacifist, the intellectuals opposed "a noble realism." "The realist" Bourne wrote in "The War and the Intellectuals" (from which all these phrases are taken)[23] "thinks he at least can control events by linking himself to the forces that are moving." ("It is control over others that yields [the puritan] his satisfaction of power.")

"The puritan then gets the satisfaction of his will to power through the turning of his self-abasement into purposes of self-regard," Bourne had written. Five months into the war he looked back in "A War Diary" to remark "something incredibly mean and plebeian about the abasement into which the war partisans tried to throw us all."[24] That dependence upon renunciation for his sense of power, Bourne had earlier noted, placed the puritan "in a world where renunciation has to happen whether we want it or not . . . in the most impressive strategic position." In "The War and the Intellectuals" he wrote:

> But the intellectuals whom the crisis has crystallized into an acceptance of war have put themselves into a terrifyingly strategic positon. It is only on the craft in the stream, they say, that one has any chance of controlling the current forces for liberal purposes. If we obstruct, we surrender all power for influence. If we responsibly approve, we then retain our power for guiding. We will be listened to as responsible thinkers, while those who obstructed the coming of war have committed intellectual suicide and shall be cast into outer darkness. Criticism by the ruling powers will only be accepted from those intellectuals who are in sympathy with the general tendency of the war. Well, it is true that they may guide, but if their stream leads to disaster and the frustration of national life, is their guiding any more than a preference whether they shall go over the right-hand or the left-hand side of the precipice? Meanwhile, however, there is comfort on board. Be with us, they call, or be negligible, irrelevant. Dissenters are already excommunicated. Irreconcilable radicals, wringing their hands among the debris, become the most despicable and impotent of men. There seems no choice for the intellectual but to join the mass of acceptance. But again the terrible dilemma arises,—either support what is going on, in which case you count for nothing because you are swallowed in the mass and great incalculable forces bear you on; or remain aloof, passively resistant, in which case you count for nothing because you are outside the machinery of reality.[25]

How to counter this "strategic position" of the puritan/intellectual? What way out of the dilemma of the "irreconcilable" against the war who, like Bourne, still wanted to count for something, still wanted to assert his own power? Like the pagan youth who, rather than indulge a puritanic renunciation, preferred to beat his head "rhythmically and endlessly against an unyielding wall," Bourne replied in rhythmically pounding parallelism:

> There is work to be done to prevent this war of ours from passing into popular mythology as a holy crusade. . . . There is work to be done in still shouting that all the revolutionary by-products will not justify the war, or make war anything else than the most noxious complex of all the evils that afflict men. There must be some to find no consolation whatever, and some to sneer at those who buy the cheap emotion of sacrifice. There must be some irreconcilables left who will not even accept the war with walrus tears. There must be some to call unceasingly for peace, and some

to insist that the terms of settlement shall not only be liberal but democratic. There must be some intellectuals who are not willing to use the old discredited counters again and to support a peace which would leave all the old inflammable material of armament lying about the world. There must still be opposition to any contemplated "liberal" world order founded on military coalitions. The "irreconcilable" need not be disloyal. He need not even be "impossibilist.". . . The old ideals crumble; new ideals must be forged. . . . If the American intellectual class rivets itself to a "liberal" philosophy that perpetuates the old errors, there will then be need for "democrats" whose task will be to divide, confuse, disturb, keep the intellectual waters constantly in motion to prevent any such ice from ever forming.[26]

That was Bourne's formula for dissent, as it had been for the pagan, who "often breaks miraculously through the wall" while the puritan could only strut outside.

The one ironic compensatory value in being surrounded by puritans, Bourne had said, lay in their "keeping us acutely self-conscious of our faith. They whet our ardor." Similarly his formula for dissent included the argument that the irreconcilables' apathy toward the war "should take the form of a heightened energy and enthusiasm for the education, the art, the interpretation that makes for life in the midst of a world of death," and in "A War Diary" he conceded that "for many of us resentment against the war has meant a vivider consciousness of what we are seeking in American life."

It was his ideal youth he spoke for here, the pagan youth capable of responding to "the allure of fresh and true ideas, of free speculation, of artistic vigor, of cultural styles, of intelligence suffused by feeling, and feeling given fiber and outline by intelligence."

Whence can come this allure? Only from those who are thorough malcontents. Irritation at things as they are, disgust at the continual frustrations and aridities of American life, deep dissatisfaction with self and with the groups that give themselves forth as hopeful, out of such moods there might be hammered new values. The malcontents would be men and women who could not stomach the war, or the reactionary idealism that has followed in its train. They are quite through with the professional critics and classicists who have let cultural values die through their own personal ineptitude. Yet these malcontents have no intention of being cultural vandals, only to slay. They are not barbarians, but seek the vital and sincere everywhere. . . . They will be harsh and bad-tempered, and they will feel that the break-up of things is no time for mellowness.

They will have a taste for spiritual adventure, and for sinister imaginative excursions. It will not be Puritansism so much as complacency that they will fight. A tang, a bitterness, an intellectual fiber, a verve, they will look for in literature, and their most virulent enemies will be those unaccountable radicals who are still morally servile, and are now trying to suppress all free speculation in the interests of nationalism. Something more mocking, more irreverent, they will constantly want. They will take institutions very lightly, indeed will never fail to be surprised at the seriousness with which good radicals take the stated offices and systems. Their own contempt will be scarcely veiled, and they will be glad if they can tease, provoke, irritate thought on any subject. These malcontents will be more or less of the American tribe of talent who used either to go immediately to Europe, or starved submissively at home. But these people will neither go to Europe, nor starve submissively. They are too entangled emotionally in the possibilities of American life to leave it, and they have no desire whatever to starve. So they are likely to go ahead beating their heads at the wall until they are either bloody or light appears.[27]

With that final sentence in this, one of his last published papers on the war, we have come full circle back to "The Puritan's Will to Power." The basic outline and terms of that essay had lent themselves as premise for his analysis of the otherwise "unanalyzable feeling," as he put it, of liberal intellectuals, "that this was a war in which we had to be. . . ."[28]

Rather fond of that wall metaphor, even as used above without any clear definite reference—is it the wall of complacency rather than of puritanism? (but Van Wyck Brooks had called Americans' self-complacency "Puritanism's obverse and twin brother")[29] — Bourne recurred to it at least once again, shifting its position, when he concluded "A War Diary" with an exhortatory call to his fellow malcontents: "Let us compel the war to break in on us, if it must, not go hospitably to meet it. Let us force it perceptibly to batter in our spiritual walls." But there is no mistaking the ring of defiant embattlement and resistance which sounds off those "walls," definite or indefinite.

Nor is there any mistaking the targets of his scorn in his ironic variations upon Walter Lippmann's theme in *Drift and Mastery*—the book Bourne wished he had written—as in the caustic allusion in a passage quoted above to the "comfort on board" the intellectuals' ship that floats on a stream which may lead to "disaster and the frustration of national life." The liberal strategy for peace had become subverted by "the war-technique" into a strategy for prolonged war, and "in the war, we are a rudderless nation. . . ."[30] Or again, in this sustained extension of the metaphor of drift:

If after all the idealism and creative intelligence that were shed upon America's taking up of arms, our State Department has no policy, we are like brave passengers who have set out for the Isles of the Blest only to find that the first mate has gone insane and jumped overboard, the rudder has come loose and dropped to the bottom of the sea, and the captain and pilot are lying dead drunk under the wheel. The stokers and engineers, however, are still merrily forcing the speed up to twenty knots an hour and the passengers are presumably getting the pleasure of the ride.[31]

Other rhetorical tricks skillfully powered his indictment of the war proponents and the emerging war strategy, or rather, as he saw it, that strategy's collapse. The strokes of his pen slanted the once proudly worn labels of "intellectual," "liberal," "pragmatist," and "realist," even "radical" (labor leaders and socialists) into derisory fools' caps placed on the heads of those who had used them in justification of the war, and then he reset them, erect once more, on the younger generation of irreconcilables, the malcontents and the pacifists. He had tried in his earlier pamphlet, "The Tradition of War," to proclaim pacifists as the only true "realists," but now he had events on his side. As the country confusedly and hastily organized for war through the summer of 1917, introducing conscription, censorship, and other coercive measures of "the war-technique," Bourne could readily underscore the paradox of a "democratic war" and point up the way American intervention had "practically" thwarted its alleged purposes. Thus, in "The Collapse of American Strategy," in the August *Seven Arts*, with a series of short, punching lines he pointed out how the event of war had betrayed those liberal intellectuals who had thrown their support to the president in the belief that American intervention assured them active participation on an independent basis:

We have not ended the submarine menace. We have lost all power for mediation. We have not even retained the democratic leadership among the Allied nations. We have surrendered the initiative for peace. We have involved ourselves in a moral obligation to send large armies to Europe to secure a military decision for the Allies. We have prolonged the war. We have encouraged the reactionary elements in every Allied country to hold out for extreme demands. We have discouraged the German democratic forces. . . . All this the realistic pacifists foresaw when they held out so bitterly and unaccountably against our entering the war. The liberals felt a naïve faith in the sagacity of the President to make their strategy prevail. They looked to him singlehandedly to liberalize the liberal nations. They trusted him to use a war-technique which should consist of an olive-branch in one hand and a sword in the other. They have had to see their strategy collapse under the very weight of that war-technique. Guarding neutrality, we might have counted toward a speedy and democratic peace. In the war, we are a rudderless nation, to be exploited as the Allies wish, politically and materially, and towed, to their aggrandizement, in any direction which they may desire.[32]

"For once," he said a month later, returning to his theme of the "inexorable" nature of war, "for once the babes and sucklings seem to have been wiser than the children of light."[33]

"Creative intelligence" also became almost a sneering phrase in Bourne's use of it as he attacked John Dewey and his followers for betrayal of their own pragmatic principles, for using them in the service of the war technique. In its place, as with his replacement of other labels, Bourne argued the greater need for "creative skepticism" and for "creative desire," both long since claimed by him as the special possessions of youth.

Bourne's assault on the war proponents was not, of course, simply a matter of skillful rhetoric. That is what made it sting, what was calculated to make his opponents' consciences gag on the memory of their own words that had appealed to reason and intelligence, to mastery and control, and what has made it memorable in the long years that have followed the event of the Great War. He saw American intervention as a tragic consequence of the failure of the liberal intelligence to use reason to prevent it; he saw and spelled out with a controlled, cold fury, the ironic contradiction in the arguments of those, like John Dewey, that America's entering the war was a historical necessity, yet thought they could manipulate and control it to assure a benign outcome, a spreading of democratic forces and the betterment of social control the world over. "If the war is too strong for you to prevent, how is it going to be weak enough for you to control and mold to your liberal purposes?"[34] Once entered into, war *then* became "inexorable"—the word he repeatedly intoned in his bitter-sad dismissal of John Dewey's philosophy, exposed as inadequate before the crisis of war.

It is a mistake to conclude that the war drove Bourne into resigned acceptance of pessimistic determinism. The burden of his argument against the war and its proponents was that it could have been prevented—through the exercise of intelligence supported by a passionate desire for the true, the good, and the beautiful, through thought fused with emotion. It was the commitment to war which made for the inexorable and the deterministic, and which meant, therefore, an abandonment of any philosophy of pragmatism, a philosophy which simply had no place for the inexorable. "I find the contrast between the idea that creative intelligence has free functioning in wartime, and the facts of the inexorable situation, too glaring," he said. The pragmatism of William James, "with its gay passion for ideas, and its freedom of speculation," had allowed for a moral equivalent of war, for a constant searching for democratic values; the instrumentalism of Dewey and his followers, in adjusting so easily to the inexorable nature of war, revealed its effective abandonment of values in deference to the application of techniques. The "pragmatic" supporters of war were the slaves of the inexorable, of determinism. Bourne chose otherwise for himself: to remain "aloof."[35]

From his ironic vantage point "below the battle," Bourne saw the paradox of a "democratic war" with greater clarity than most of his contemporaries. His consummate mastery of the ironist's style enabled him to turn back upon the war's apologists their own rhetorical and logical defenses, shattering them, showing them to be empty or full of contradictions. He had his eye sharply on events, but he attacked chiefly the manner in which his opponents perceived and translated those events. He phrased the democratic dilemma succinctly: war, or America's promise. One must choose, he said. "One cannot be interested in both." That remains the democratic dilemma whenever America goes to war. Bourne's "war essays" remain available and usable whenever that dilemma rises again.

CHAPTER 7

The Young Radical and a National Culture

ONE had to choose—the war, or American promise. Bourne chose the latter. "One keeps healthy in wartime not by a series of religious and political consolations that something good is coming out of it all, but by a vigorous assertion of values in which war has no part," he had written.[1] The other side of his attack on the war mentality had consisted of his own vigorous assertions of what young intellectuals could have been doing that might have prevented war, and then when the event and its inexorable nature had effectively canceled any pragmatic use of it, what the younger generation of malcontents *should* be doing—pursuing America's promise. For Bourne this meant the self-conscious creation and development of an American national culture, one as distinctive and expressive of America as were the various "homogeneous" national cultures he had admired in Europe.

America's going to war had not newly directed that choice of his, but it had made, as he said, for "a vivider consciousness" of what he was seeking in American life. He had made his commitment to that search early, on his return from Europe. In those first gloomy months of the European war he had resolved to brace himself against the war, not waste his energy in despair or recrimination, and try instead to "slowly sting people into new ideals and tastes," the only thing one could do, he had said to Alyse Gregory. Almost four years later, deep into the first year of American active involvement in the war, having indulged his bout of recrimination but still neither acquiescing to the war nor lapsing into despair, he reiterated his commitment to the only pragmatic cause he could give his allegiance. "I imagine," he wrote to Van Wyck Brooks, that "people must be appealed to to desire certain things mightily."[2]

He wrote to Brooks on the eve of the latter's publishing his *Letters and Leadership*, a collection of *Seven Arts* articles and one or two others arranged into another manifesto directed at the younger generation, calling for "an organized higher life" to be created by young poets, novelists and critics, acting in concert as a class—much as Whitman had called for. Bourne exulted in the "superb youthful arrogance" of Brooks's implication "that it is we and our friends who are to be the masters." Mastery was still an ambition of this one-time bad puritan, mastery over and leadership of his fellow malcontents. He was confident that there were members of the younger generation who were ready to respond to Brooks and himself, those irreconcilables who had been driven from the liberal camp, who, like himself, wanted "an idealism which is not full of compromises, which is more concerned with American civilization than with American politics, which is more desirous for American life, liberty, and the pursuit of happiness than for a model constitution and a watertight political-democratic system." This "malcontented class" needed "a new gospel," and would understand, he said to Brooks, "what you are driving at."[3]

What *was* Brooks driving at, and Bourne with him? What new ideals and tastes, what new gospel and what new things did they mightily desire for American civilization?

It is easier in answering these questions to say what they rejected first, as it was also easier for them. The route of rebellion proceeded for them, as perhaps it does for all rebels, toward affirmation from rejection. When they looked ahead they spoke as prophets of possibilities, but the achievement of what they foresaw was premised on the shattering of the obstacles in the way.

Much of what Bourne rejected is contained in all that he had to say against the older generation and puritans, against America's colonial mentality and cultural humility, against the dominant role in cultural matters of the Arnold cult of the best and of Anglo-Saxon values generally. He spent his critical energy over a wide range of iconoclastic enterprises in an endeavor to unseat "the ruling classes" in American education in school and university; in American art and letters; to a much lesser extent in American politics, and only as the war became the all-encompassing political issue of his generation. He was an antagonist and critic of the exploitative nature of American capitalism, cast his sympathies with the lot of the working class and his ire and disdain at American millionaires and industrialists, but while he was acutely aware of the social consequences and resulting class divisions in American society, he rarely leveled his sights on economic power as such. He called himself a radical and socialist, but he was no advocate of revolution except in the realm of personality and culture. At bottom he rejected whatever manifested itself as a lingering, uncritical acceptance of some value from the past that operated in the present to restrain and limit critical thought and the expansive growth of the personality.

Independently Van Wyck Brooks had already articulated the same rejections, often in remarkably similar language, and from the same commitment to the importance of cultivating the whole personality. By the time Brooks and Bourne had joined forces on the *Seven Arts* they had between them pretty nearly completed the catalog of values rejected by their generation. In essay, story, and poem, other contributors to the *Seven Arts* offered what read like extended footnotes to *Youth and Life* and *America's Coming-of-Age*. And by the time the *Seven Arts* ceased publication, Brooks and Bourne between them had added two more rejections to their catalog: the philosophy of pragmatism, rejected for its lack of "a poetic vision," and that of humanism as articulated by Irving Babbitt, Paul Elmer More, Stuart P. Sherman, and others, rejected for fostering a "culture of the intellect" that was not borne out by a corresponding "culture of the feelings" (Brooks's terms).

Rejections, of course, imply affirmations in their opposites. If pragmatism was rejected for lacking poetic vision, it follows that a pragmatism with such vision was desired; if an arid intellectualism devoid of feeling was deplored, it follows that, Bourne so often said, thought must be "fused" with feeling, just as every other deplorable dichotomy in American life implied the need for resolution into some organic whole.

But two positive words that recur with great frequency in the writing of both critics suggest better than these contrary implications what they were each seeking in a national culture: "desire" and "creative."

The first of these, as we have seen, had long been a favored value for Bourne. To say he desired for Americans the capacity to desire itself may seem tautological, yet it is an accurate description, I think, of what he hoped to arouse in Americans. They must be appealed to "to desire certain things mightily," he had said to Brooks. They must want to be proud, for instance, to be proud of what American artists had achieved, even "against the obstacles of our cultural humility. . . . For only pride is creative." From desire came creativity. The "attainment of culture" for Americans could come only from cultivation of "an intense self-consciousness" of, and a desire to perpetuate, "the American ideals and qualities, our pulsating democracy, the vigor and daring of our pioneer spirit, our sense of *camaraderie*, our dynamism, the bigheartedness of our scenery, our hospitality to all the world," as expressed by the genius of such writers as Whitman, William James, Emerson and Thoreau, the composer MacDowell, and the sculptor Saint-Gaudens. "We shall never be able to perpetuate our ideals except in the form of art and literature; the world will never understand our spirit except in terms of art."[4]

Similarly Brooks argued that thought alone could not bring about a radically more beautiful civilization for Americans. "Only desire can do this," he said, and that was what the younger generation of Americans had come to feel. "They feel this, I say," he added, "they feel it very deeply. How deeply they desire another America, not like the America of today, *grande et riche, mais désordonnée*, as Turgenev said of Russia, but harmonious and beneficent, a great America that knows how to use the finest of its gifts!" But no genuine change would occur in America until a race of artists appeared to bring Americans face to face with their own experience, "and set working in that experience the leaven of the highest culture. For it is exalted desires that give their validity to revolutions, and exalted desires take form only in exalted souls." Leaders would have to appear to conceive these desires, formulate them, and "press them home."[5] Getting down to cases, Bourne singled out Theodore Dreiser as deserving of admiration because in his novels he caught hold "of the thread of human desire," made "desire," in fact, the "hero." "Desire" for Bourne often carried a sexual connotation, appropriate enough in his use of it in discussing Dreiser, but appropriately consonant also with Brooks's call for a race of artists who would bring Americans face to face with their experience. He located Dreiser's service to the American imagination in his "going gravely to the business of picturing sex as it is lived in the personal relations of bungling, wistful, or masterful men and women."[6]

For both writers the notions of "desire" and the "creative" readily merged, with Bourne perceiving and providing the sexual nexus between them. It was "creative desire" that was needed, Bourne had said, countering Dewey's call for the exercise of "creative intelligence"; and for Brooks, "Young America," if still deficient in "creative power," already had "more creative desire than it knows what to do with."[7]

From that joining of those two notions a definition of the culture each was seeking emerges, and may be put somewhat as follows: Taking off on the wings of desire, art, the creative act, the expression of thought fused with feeling, would itself lead the way toward the creation of an American culture. Engaged with and confronting the actualities of American experience rather than aloof from and stranded high and dry above it, art, the poetic vision, would point beyond politics to a democratic culture. Culture, put more succinctly, was life organized by art in the service of a democratic community for the realization and satisfaction of personal, hence social, ends.

This culture would be, as Brooks declared it, "the highest culture," for it would be the high culture of Matthew Arnold but "leavened" by the personal encounter with actuality. In the ideal school of Bourne's Miro, for instance, "One's acquaintance with the best that had been said and thought should be encouraged . . . to follow the lines of one's temperament." For Miro, therefore, Bourne said, "The new culture would be more personal, but it would not be held as personal property. It would be democratic in the sense that it would represent each person's honest spontaneous taste."[8] Personal, yet democratic and social, in short, and leading to the discovery of community.

"Where was a better program for culture, for any kind of literary art?" Bourne's Miro asked. "Culture as a living effort, a driving attempt both at sincere expression and at the comprehension of sincere expression wherever it was found! Appreciation to be as far removed from the 'I know what I like' as from the textbook impeccability of taste! If each mind sought its own along these lines, would not many find themselves agreed?"[9] Yes, they would, Brooks said; in fact, young Americans needed only to be reminded of the "Young Italy" of Mazzini's day and to look at the "Young Ireland" of the present to realize that the world had witnessed "again and again that sudden fusion of great natural aggregations of men by which all their elements have been set beating together at the highest pitch. . . ." What had happened elsewhere could happen in America. The *Seven Arts* gave further witness to the emergence of self-conscious national cultural communities elsewhere by featuring a series of articles that pointed to the signs, not only in "Young America," by Brooks, but also in "Young Japan," "Young Spain" (by young John R. Dos Passos), "Youngest Ireland," and "Young India"—all notably led by the "young," the notorious possessors of "creative desire." "Civilization ought to be a symphony," Brooks contended, saying that all these signs of creative desire in the younger generations of the world betrayed "in mankind an orchestral instinct . . . clamoring at the gates of consciousness."[10]

In all these assertions we have what might be called a vision of culture, and a "poetic vision" insofar as culture and civilization (interchangeable terms as used by both writers) were viewed as susceptible to being shaped like works of art, but hardly yet a "program of culture," though each writer repeatedly announced that conditions were ripe for one. He was prepared to join with Brooks in the orchestration of Young America's creative desire, but Bourne himself posed a puzzled query to his friend as to "the technique you have in mind." He had some notions of his own, he said.

What Brooks had in mind is somewhat easier to answer now than it was then. We have an answer contained in all its density in the volume of writing Brooks turned out in the long career after Bourne's death until his own in 1963—contained in the ways he responded to his own call for the creation of a usable past for American writers, in the ways his example provoked others into revaluation of America's literary heritage, and especially in his culminating work, his imaginative creation of a community of American writers and artists intricately connected to one another through their lives and work over space and time as he presented it in his monumental five-volume study, *Makers and Finders* (1936–1952). For Bourne, however, we must decipher his search for culture from its initial probings only, and in these as they lie scattered in short articles and reviews, and in the fragments he left behind.

Brooks and Bourne complemented each other in their early work. Their respective contributions to the *Seven Arts*, with Brooks's essays dominating the first half of the magazine's life and

Bourne's the last half, amount to a collaborative counterpointing enterprise in a scorching of the American scene to rid it of noxious weeds so that desire might grow in its own soil (a commonly used metaphor). They agreed in their diagnosis of what inhibited or warped the emergence of an American culture. They seem to have shared a common vision of culture. Their names inevitably were linked, especially in the twenties and thirties, with frequent references to the Brooks-Bourne "school" of critics or to the Brooks-Bourne "thesis," and nearly always still are linked in any historical glance at the 1910s. All this has made plausible the speculative assumption that Bourne, had he lived, would have carried out a program in pursuit of a national culture similar to Brooks's. There are, however, some essential distinctions, if not clear-cut differences, between their respective visions of American culture.

Two of these distinctions are matters of emphasis, perhaps, not altogether absent from Brooks's vision, at least in its early articulation, but so emphatic in Bourne's as to be nearly controlling concepts without which, indeed, we might find their visions identical. The first of these in priority and importance is the controlling concept in all his work—that of youth; the second, one of the important by-products of his European experience and his dissent with the war, in his argument for a transnational America.

Both of these concepts, left in a state of suspended abstraction by Bourne's early death, and therefore still ballooning with possibilities, may account for the difference in the succeeding reputations of the two writers. Brooks's long career endured through a series of critical debates amid changing literary, social, and political climates that altered estimates of his role from that of literary radical to that of genteel apologist for a too narrowly conceived national culture, an estimate from which he has yet to be fully rescued. Bourne, on the other hand, still appears the literary radical, with a radical vision of culture for America.

The route that Brooks traveled took him on a long and painstaking search through the American past, there to discover and create from the materials of his discovery an American culture composed of the lives and imaginative expressions of America's artists. Those two pervasive concepts in Bourne's search led him, however, as he himself put it, "to perpetrate the paradox that our American cultural tradition lies in the future."[11] Although a revolutionary change in a judgment of the past such as Brooks's work effected may also change "our vision of the future," as Malcolm Cowley suggested,[12] Bourne's perpetration of his paradox offers the more open-ended vision, with room for more radical possibilities, especially to youth grown restive or discontented with a past that seems to have been thrust upon it.

Like Brooks, Bourne had returned from Europe impressed by and envious of the homogeneity of national life and culture on the Continent, and mightily desiring something comparable for America. The "squalor and vulgarity" of the American scene he found on his return only sharpened the memory of "superior" civilizations in Europe. He found himself "constantly rejecting" American things, looking for something to affirm.[13] Sorting through his impressions, he had to contend with the paradox that lay between his envy and his desire: the very kind of envy he had of those "superior" European civilizations was responsible for America's "cultural humility" and posed the chief barrier to producing any "true indigenous culture." The only remedy, he had concluded, was a conscious cultivation of "a new American nationalism," shaped and perpetuated in the only way ideals could be, "in the form of art and literature."[14]

But Bourne had also witnessed, and been shocked and dismayed by, the spectacle of nationalism transformed by war overnight into uncritical chauvinism. As signs increased of a similar coercive transformation in America, he was compelled to have second thoughts about the "most harmless of patriotisms" in the "cultural chauvinism" he had so brashly proposed.[15] In a near turnabout from his original call for a new American nationalism he flatly suggested that perhaps "we shall have to give up the search for our native 'American' culture."[16]

The European war provoked and intensified renewed concern among nativist elements—Bourne's Anglo-Saxon "ruling class"—for the unassimilated multitudes of new immigrants that had poured in from Europe in ever-increasing numbers over the previous three or more decades. The popular success of Israel Zangwill's play *The Melting Pot* (produced on Broadway in 1909) had released upon the public consciousness a metaphor whose implications of an American ideal, or of the somewhat mystical process by which an American ideal achieved realization, had been latent in American thought since at least the time of de Crèvecoeur.[17] The dramatic denouement of the play implied that the melting pot worked. The passions and conflicting emotions released by the war suggested otherwise, and led to growing demands not only for restrictive controls over immigration but also for more conscious efforts to achieve "Americanization." Predictably Bourne was bound to resist those pressures, coupled as they came to be with the war technique. The metaphor itself, suggesting as he put it, a resulting "tasteless, colorless fluid of uniformity," was also anathema to him.

What is of interest here is the way Bourne pulled back from his call for a purely "national" culture and proposed a quest for "a new and more adventurous ideal," and thus modified his vision of an American culture. To the extent that he did, his search differs from that of Van Wyck Brooks. He never entirely abandoned his conviction that artistic expression gave shape and direction to culture, but his probings provided a sociological dimension to his vision of culture that was largely missing from Brooks's. The "trans-national America" he proposed, expressed in his own preferred metaphor of a woven fabric, approaches an anthropological concept of culture, insisting as it does on recognition of "an actual situation." He put it this way:

> With the exception of the South and that New England which, like the Red Indian, seems to be passing into solemn oblivion, there is no distinctively American culture. It is apparently our lot rather to be a federation of cultures. This we have been for half a century, and the war has made it ever more evident that this is what we are destined to remain.[18]. . . America is coming to be, not a nationality but a trans-nationality, a weaving back and forth, with other lands, of many threads of all sizes and colors. Any movement which attempts to thwart this weaving, or to dye the fabric any one color, or disentangle the threads of the strands, is false to this cosmopolitan vision. . . . What concerns us is the fact that the strands are here. We must have a policy and an ideal for an actual situation. Our question is, What shall we do with our America? How are we likely to get the more creative America—by confining our imaginations to the ideal of that melting-pot, or broadening them to some such cosmopolitan conception as I have been vaguely sketching?[19]

Vague in some respects this essay is, more a contention of metaphors than one resting on documented fact. It is also not without its contradictions and some strange prejudices. While asserting that there was no distinctively American culture, he could still insist that there had been, nevertheless, "expressions of indigenous genius that could not have sprung from any other soil," and that when such expressions were of "the pioneer spirit" then one *could* speak of "the American culture"[20] (another modulated difference with Brooks, for whom "the pioneer mentality" was a pejorative equated with "the Puritan mentality"). And in an otherwise commendable expression of liberal sentiment he could say, "Let us speak, not of inferior races," and then add, "but of inferior civilizations,"[21] and go on to suggest that those critics of the foreign-born who were angered at "the alien who works in America for a few years and returns to his own land, only perhaps to seek American fortune again" thought in narrow nationalistic terms, did not see the "cosmopolitan significance" of that migration, and ignored "the fact that the returning immigrant is often a missionary to an inferior civilization," with America "thus educating these laggard peoples from the very bottom of society up, awakening vast masses to a new-born hope for the future."[22] Such echoes sounding off the old nineteenth-century backboard of manifest destiny and the snobbery of American superiority seem oddly inconsistent with the critical scorn Bourne had for others who expressed these attitudes.

One always has the uneasy suspicion with Bourne that he may intend irony, as he may have intended here in the allusion to "laggard" peoples and in all his talk of "superior" and "inferior" civilizations. He liked to play upon the counterwords of his opposition. In an essay so deadly serious in its tone as is this one, however, the irony does not work; the prejudices sound like his own and not like satirical allusions to persons sitting in darkness. Moreover, the contradictions, and perhaps the prejudices, are inherent in the aim of his argument which tried to resolve, as he finally recognized it, "a crucial dilemma" for American idealism.

He voiced this in a companion piece to the first essay, one originally delivered as an address to the Harvard Menorah Society sometime in early November 1916, an invitation that had followed from the appearance of the first article in the *Atlantic Monthly* the summer before. It is the better of the two attempts to define his vision, since the illustration of Zionism "as a pattern for American trans-nationalism" fills in some of the vagueness of the first.[23]

"Cultural self-consciousness," he reiterated to his Harvard audience, "such as the French possess . . . is the most precious heritage a nation can have." Then he posed the dilemma: "Yet apparently this intense national feeling leads straight into chauvinistic self-assertion, into conflict with other nationalisms, into a belligerency which drags the world down in mutual ruin." The solution, the very salvation of America, in fact, he said, might be found in the current Jewish ideal of Zionism. Transnationalism was a Jewish idea, he said, the very term stolen by him from a Jewish college mate of his, his own thinking set to work by Horace Kallen's articles in the *Nation*, "Democracy versus the Melting-Pot" (1915). To his Jewish audience he singled out for praiseworthy mention and as the final "proof of the practicability of the co-operative American ideal" of transnationalism, members of "the younger generation of Jewish intelligents [*sic*]" like Felix Frankfurter, Horace M. Kallen, Morris R. Cohen, and (perhaps as an oblique provocation to the conscience of his friend and *New Republic* associate) Walter Lippmann, men whose "Jewish idealism [their sympathy, as Bourne surmised it, with Zionism] has not in the least vitiated their peculiarly intimate insight into American problems. . . ." Their example suggested that transnationalism held out the possibility of keeping one's "cultural allegiance" intact and distinct from one's "political allegiance." This in turn was possible because of the "very modern conception" of the distinction between state and nation—that conception Bourne had first approached in his pamphlet, "The Tradition of War," and which he would elaborate upon in "The State." It made possible and desirable a kind of dual citizenship—one could preserve his cultural heritage, yet still cooperate loyally "with all other nationals in the building-up of America. . . ."[24]

This refined and extended attempt to define a vision of a transnational American culture is wholly that, a vision of a desirable yet still future possibility. Nowhere is there reference to an American past in this second essay, no allusion to expressions of indigenous genius that might provide a thread of an American culture, nowhere, in fact, any resort to the metaphor of weaving, of a national cultural fabric in which some such thread might be central. This second essay shows some signs of Bourne trying to reply to some of the criticism of the first. Perhaps he had become aware that the metaphor implied a weaver, potentially as coercive as the melting-pot programs he despised. In any event, he here disclaimed any intention to promote "an artificial stimulation of trans-national feeling,"[25] asking only that it be free to operate—making it no less mystical a process than that of the melting-pot. He conceded risks in those transnational groups who might color their cultural allegiance too strongly with political loyalties, or who continued to cultivate the culture left behind them after it had become "superseded at home." These pitfalls could be avoided, however, if transnationalism remained resolutely modern and if it emulated the Jewish ideal; if, in short, it heeded present actualities and kept its eyes on the future.

The future came swiftly. War suspended the vision for its duration. But the vision is still available. Bourne's expression of it in these two essays is dated in some respects, still echoing the quarrels of earlier times. The contradictions are still there, unresolved. History has rendered some of it ironic, in ways, for once, he did not intend. But none of this cancels the idealism, none of the hope. The "crucial dilemma" of an American idealism still exists, political and cultural allegiances still coincide. But whenever a new generation of American idealists confronts the dilemma, those idealists may find that Bourne has anticipated their own desires.

Bourne's desires for American culture are, finally, all subsumed under the desires of youth, of youth as he conceived it. After all is said that can be said about the centrality of his allegiance to the romantic tradition in Emerson, Thoreau, and Whitman, in William and Henry James and Mark Twain—to name only the most frequently mentioned of his indigenous geniuses; and to the importance he gave to art and literature as the formulator of ideals; about his transnational ideal; about the culture of personality and that of community; about the culture of intellect and the culture of emotion—we come back to his culture of youth. We come back to it because Bourne always came back to it, linking all his expressions of cultural desire to those of youth, of the younger generation, the young intelligentsia. Culture stretched out ahead, into the future, a constant sloughing off of the old in favor of the new, the modern—adventurous, experimental, spontaneous and daring, perpetually young, full of promise. Genuine culture expressed and contained the secret of perpetual youth and was in some sense identical with "a young world."

The linkages he made between culture and youth are constant, consistent, and pervasive in his writing. Each of his ideal youths in his several portraits is an artist, or aspires to be one, or possesses an artistic conscience, or is an artist of life itself; each is blessed with a touch of the transnational, or sounds the "cosmopolitan note" of the future international culture. They are living examples of transnational America, the new Americanism coming into being.

Bourne appreciates Dreiser, excuses his clumsy style, because he has "the artist's vision," because he is "a true hyphenate" whose talent is therefore "thoroughly American," evidenced all the more as "specifically American" when Dreiser "writes more about his youth."[26] (To Dreiser himself Bourne wrote in enthusiastic admiration of the autobiographical *A Hoosier Holiday,* finding it, he said, "incredibly American" and wishing "Young America" would "soak itself in a book like this, [for] then I think we might really get some real fiction with some of the warmth of the soil and the beauty and sting of youth. . . .")[27] Dreiser's clumsiness of style was like the clumsiness of youth, "groping" for beauty, but it was therefore also a sign, almost an analogue of American culture itself, of American culture taking shape. "He [Dreiser] expresses an America that is in the process of forming."[28]

As with Dreiser's "happy and unlabored" *A Hoosier Holiday,* so too with Hamlin Garland's autobiographical *A Son of the Middle Border,* which Bourne called a "revealing drama . . . of brave and sensitive youth," a story "the rawest young malcontent [would] read with enthusiasm and delight."[29] The personal accounts of both writers contained the social drama of youth in America, of "wistful" youth trying to find its bearings.

Of Dreiser's boyhood he wrote: ". . . [it] is so typical of the uncritical and careless society in which wistful American talent has had to grope. . . . Talent in America outside the ruling class flowers very late, because it takes so long to find its bearings. It has had almost to create its own soil. . . . It is born shivering into an inhospitable and irrelevant group."[30] Read "youth" for "talent," and "culture" for "soil" and we have a linkage that comes not only from a conjunction of rhetorical echoes but from a mind that interprets the universe as alive and all things in it as organically connected.

The groping progress of youth is like the groping progress of the new American culture. If we recall all that went into Bourne's conception of youth, we can see that concept merging with his conception of culture—in the Garland review, for instance.

Writers like Garland and Dreiser, Bourne wrote in that review, writers who had been unlucky enough to be born in a country without a strong literary tradition, and who had been hampered in their education, would, expectedly, he said, have difficulty with literary construction. They would "suffer a long handicap from not starting with the cultural capital with which a mind in a more intensive civilization is endowed. . . . They would have almost to create for themselves the standards, preferences, techniques of expression." They would struggle with conventional forms at first, "fight to get their bearings and make a living" (like the handicapped youth), but eventually, gradually, they would attain "the true sincerity of their talent, and feel themselves as significant," as men who counted; "so that their story," the story of themselves, "when it came, would be much more than a mere personal record, it would be a drama of a social movement or a struggling class." [31]

"When it came"—in the future. Like the promise of youth, the promise of culture always loomed just ahead, beyond the horizon. Dreiser and Garland were signs of its coming. Vachel Lindsay, also a late blooming talent, was another. They were winning the struggle with the old orthodoxies and conventions, winning it in the very act of recording the struggle. Bourne's Miro appreciated Amy Lowell because she made clear (in her book, *Tendencies in American Poetry* [1917]) "the struggles of contemporary men and women with the tradition and against 'every affectation of the mind'" (and because, as Bourne had written earlier, she made of Carl Sandburg a powerful figure "with his brave novelty of the America that is in the making"; because, too, her book demonstrated the younger generation's determination not to permit the war to penetrate the domain of literary art. A "young world," he said, had "its treasures for other heavens!"). Bourne applauded the appearance of Willa Cather's *My Antonia* (1918) for its "indestructible fragrance of youth," as a "masterpiece of wistful youth," one that took her out of the rank of "provincial writers" and classed her "with the modern literary art the world over that is earnestly and richly interpreting the spirit of youth" (it was also, of course, a story of transnational America).[32]

The "true autobiographies," told by the best autobiographers, the masters of fiction, those he had said in *Youth and Life* that the world needed, were being written—interpretations of the spiritual shocks and changes, of that "tense shrinking from life and yet the ardor for life" which characterized youth. Though he felt no one had yet achieved Dreiser's "largeness of utterance," Bourne announced that young writers everywhere were shaking loose from the older generation and exercising "thoroughly American and wholly un-English" talents. The vers-librists "teem" with the hitherto suppressed hyphenate, he said. The gifted young poets among the imagists, with their "naive, cool vision of beauty, and in their sense of flowing life," were providing "new vistas." The spiritual biographies of youth were being written, creating a personal culture, or a culture of personalities, but revealing a community too, for everywhere Bourne saw the personality of youth. Dorothy Richardson's novel, *Honeycomb* (1918), an "imagist novel," his review called it,[33] captured "the very fibre of sensitive youth," not only "the very essence of quivering youth, but of youthful femininity." The books were being written. Youth was telling its story, creating an American culture. And of course, Randolph Bourne, a late flowering talent, was at work on an autobiographical novel.

"The mind that aspired towards 'culture,'" Bourne's Miro had concluded, needed to be instructed "not to conform or worship," to dodge pressures; it needed to be told to "search out its group, its own temperamental community of sentiment, and there deepen appreciation through sympathetic contact." Bourne devoted himself to that task, to bring about a new cosmopolitanism, a transnational, and beyond that, an international culture. Miro looked ahead:

> The American has to work to interpret and portray the life he knows. He cannot be international in the sense that anything but the life in which he is saturated, with its questions and colors, can be the material for his art. But he can be international—and must be—in the sense that he works with a certain hopeful vision of a "young world," and with certain ideal values upon which the younger men, stained and revolted by war, in all countries are agreeing.[34]

The vision of culture is the vision of youth, a "young world." But that vision contains little that can be called "certain." Bourne's youth, as he said of one ideal candidate, "is always expecting he doesn't know quite what, and always being frustrated of he doesn't quite know what would have pleased him." Youth has about it, as he characterized youth in his review of that imagist novel, "the air of standing, half-contemptuously but stirred before a closed door, on the other side of which is an obscure, not even imagined happiness."[35]

So too the young radical's wistful desire for culture.

When the war ended Bourne rejoiced along with everyone else. He witnessed the celebrations in the streets of New York, amused by the antics of the crowds, the drunken sailors and soldiers. As a pacifist, he said, he rejoiced especially "at the innocent uprising of the unconscious desire on the part of the populace for peace. . . ." With the war over he felt people might speak freely again and one could dare to think. "It's like coming out of a nightmare."[36]

In the next month or so he was busy at his writer's trade, translating a French book, *Les Vagabonds de la Glorie* by René Milan, an irksome task, but it paid a little and provided "excellent practice in stretching one's own style." There was his own writing too; he had agreed to write two articles a month for the *Dial*. His friend Brooks had gone west to Carmel, California, to write a book on Mark Twain, but other friends, like Paul Rosenfeld, were returning to the city, and with the draft calls ended and the prospect of no more friends being sent overseas, Bourne found the air altogether "blither and freer. . . .!"[37]

Besides, a door had recently opened for him. Esther Cornell and he had agreed to marry, and marry soon. When he fell ill, late in December, just before Christmas, it seemed natural that he move from his own cold flat on Charles Street and into the apartment on West 8th Street which Esther shared with Agnes de Lima. It was there, despite the ministrations of his friends, that he died of the flu a few days later, on December 23, 1918. It was a sad ending; there had been so many possibilities, so much imagined happiness.

Notes and References

Preface

1. Kenniston, *Youth and Dissent: The Rise of a New Opposition* (New York: Harcourt Brace Jovanovich, 1971), pp. 4–5. Bourne had read Hall. See his reference in *Education and Living* (New York: Century, 1917), p. 162.

2. Kenniston, p. 7.

Chapter One

1. John Adam Moreau, *Randolph Bourne: Legend and Reality* (Washington, D.C.: Public Affairs Press, 1966), p. 105. See also Sedgwick's *The Happy Profession* (Boston: Little Brown and Co., 1947), p. 223; and Moreau, p. 36. Letter, Beulah Amidon to Alyse Gregory, October 4, 1948, Bourne Papers, Columbia, quoted with permission. See also Van Wyck Brooks, "Randolph Bourne," in *Fenollosa and His Circle* (New York: Dutton, 1962), p. 291.

2. Amidon to Gregory, letter cited above. Christopher Lasch quotes Amidon, from this letter, on Bourne's appearance, but ignores her qualifying follow-up: Lasch, "Randolph Bourne and the Experimental Life," in *The New Radicalism in America, 1899–1963: The Intellectual As a Social Type* (New York: Vintage, 1967), p. 75. See also Waldo Frank, *In The American Jungle, 1925–1936* (New York: Farrar & Rinehart, 1937), p. 60; Moreau, pp. 24–25; Brooks, "Introduction," in *History of a Literary Radical* (New York: B.W. Huebsch, 1920), pp. xii, xiv.

3. Rosenfeld, "Randolph Bourne," in *Port of New York: Essays on Fourteen American Moderns* (New York: Harcourt, Brace, 1924), p. 217; and Dreiser, "Appearance and Reality," in *The American Spectator Yearbook* (New York: Frederick A. Stokes, 1934), pp. 204–9. Dreiser's poem echoes a line from Bourne's essay review, "Theodore Dreiser," *New Republic*, 2 (April 17, 1915), pt. 2, p. 7. Asserting a penchant among other American novelists for the theme of redemption, and their irresistible itch to effect a moral transformation of their characters "before our astonished eyes," Bourne wrote: "The eyes of the blind are opened, the crooked are made straight." Dreiser, of course, changes the direction of

the irony. See Oppenheim, "R. B.," in *History of a Literary Radical*, p. vii.

4. Mumford, "The Image of Randolph Bourne," *New Republic*, 64 (September 24, 1930), 151–52; Schlissel, "On Creating a Usable Randolph Bourne," in *The World of Randolph Bourne* (New York: Dutton, 1965), p. xv.

5. For these and other biographical details about his family background, I have drawn upon Moreau.

6. Moreau, p. 6.

7. See my *Van Wyck Brooks* (New York: Twayne, 1969), pp. 24–25. For at least one reference to himself as prophet, see Bourne's letter to Prudence Winterrowd, March 2, 1913, #17 in Eric Sandeen's *The Letters of Randolph Bourne: A Comprehensive Edition* (Troy, N.Y.: Whitston Publishing Co., 1981); transcript in Bourne Papers, Columbia University.

8. First published as "An Autobiographic Chapter," *Dial*, 68 (January 1920), 1–21; here cited from "Fragment of a Novel," its title in *History of a Literary Radical*, pp. 300–343. Some other autobiographic "chapters" often drawn upon are "The History of a Literary Radical," "A Philosophy of Handicap," "What Is Exploitation?" But see Chapter 4.

9. To Prudence Winterrowd, March 2, 1913, #17, in Sandeen, *Letters*, p. 75; to Dorothy Teall, June 14, [1915], #122, Sandeen, *Letters*, p. 303; transcripts at Columbia.

10. The phrase is from Van Wyck Brooks, seconding Voltaire, in his *Scenes and Portraits: Memories of Childhood and Youth* (New York: Dutton, 1954), p. 9.

11. Kenniston, *Youth and Dissent*, p. 8.

12. Bourne, "A Philosophy of Handicap," *Youth and Life* (Boston: Houghton Mifflin, 1913), p. 343.

13. "The Dodging of Pressures," in *Youth and Life*, p. 254.

14. "Diary for 1901," *Twice-a-Year*, nos. 5–6 (Fall–Winter, 1940; Spring-Summer, 1941), 89–98.

15. Moreau, pp. 10–13.

16. "A Philosophy of Handicap," in *Youth and Life*, p. 341; italics mine. I quote the words as they appear in the first, anonymously published form of the essay entitled "The Handicapped—By One of Them," *Atlantic Monthly*, 108 (September 1911), 320–29. In the revised essay for the book Bourne dropped the word "deformed" in favor of the euphemistic "handicapped." One effect is to make the later version available to a wider response. Any young reader with the least sense of alienation can fit himself into Bourne's account.

17. "A Philosophy of Handicap," in *Youth and Life*, pp. 344–45.

18. Ibid., p. 348.

19. "History of a Literary Radical," in *History of a Literary Radical and Other Essays*, pp. 7–8, 16.

20. Quoted with permission from the manuscript in the Bourne Papers, Columbia.

21. See Louis Filler, *Randolph Bourne* (Washington, D.C.: American Council on Public Affairs, 1943), p. 31. See also Moreau, p. 26.

22. Filler, p. 32.

23. To Winterrowd, November 3, 1913, #56, Sandeen, *Letters*, p. 170; transcript at Columbia.

24. Comer, *Atlantic Monthly*, 107 (February 1911), 145–54.

25. Hard, *Atlantic Monthly*, 107 (April 1911), 545–46. I have cited from Bourne's article as it appears in *Youth and Life*, pp. 29–52.

26. Moreau, p. 59.

27. Bourne to Carl Zigrosser, July 25, [1913], #33, Sandeen, *Letters*, p. 119; MS. at University of Pennsylvania. "Impressions of Europe, 1913–14," his report to Columbia Trustees, in *History of a Literary Radical*, pp. 230–65.

28. Bourne to Arthur Macmahon, January 30, 1914 #71, Sandeen, *Letters*, p. 218; transcript Columbia.

29. *Columbia Journal*, 9 (September 12, 1912), 530–31.

30. The letters of Bourne to Bligh have yet to surface. I cite, with permission, from Bligh's letters among the Bourne Papers, Columbia. Bligh's first letter, August 14, 1912, granted permission for Bourne to use his phrase "the dodging of pressures" as a title. The "mental affinity" note was struck several times, but as expressed here is in a letter of December 5, 1912, along with the allusion to Montaigne.

31. Bligh to Bourne, October 2, 1912, and December 7, 1912, p. 3 of letter.

32. Bligh to Bourne, November 11, 1912, p. 3. Bligh appears to be quoting from a letter of Bourne's.

33. Bligh to Bourne, the same letter as the one dated December 7, 1912, but apparently resumed and dated December 9, 1912; p. 6.

34. Bligh to Bourne, April 5, 1913, p. 3.

35. Bligh to Bourne, February 20, 1913, p. 2.

36. Bligh to Bourne, November 11, 1912.

37. Bligh to Bourne, April 5, 1913; December 5, 1912.

38. Bligh to Bourne, October 2, 1912, p. 4; November 11, 1912, p. 2.

39. Bligh to Bourne, December 5, 1912.

40. To Alyse Gregory Bourne wrote, much later: "My life is beset by women in pairs" (August 2, 1918, #210, Sandeen, *Letters*, p. 420).

41. Bligh to Bourne, December 7, December 9, 1912. 7 pages, typed.

42. In "Randolph Bourne," *Port of New York*, p. 226.

43. *Youth and Life*, pp. 81–84.

44. Bligh to Bourne, December 9, 1912, p. 7.

45. Bligh to Bourne, April 5, 1913, p. 2.

46. Moreau, p. 60.

47. Bourne to Alyse Gregory, September 8, 1913, #39, Sandeen, *Letters*, pp. 131–33, passim.

48. Bourne to Henry W. Elsasser, September 17, 1913, #43, Sandeen, *Letters*, p. 142; MS. Columbia.

49. Bourne to Elsasser, October 10, 1913, #48, Sandeen, *Letters*, pp. 153–54; MS. Columbia. Bourne was, on the surface at least, actually attacking the psychological theories of Hugo Muensterberg.

50. Bourne to Sarah Bourne, September 12, 1913, #41, Sandeen, *Letters*, p. 136; MS. Columbia.

51. Bourne to Arthur Macmahon, January 30, 1914, #71, Sandeen, *Letters*, p. 218; transcript Columbia.

52. Bourne to Alyse Gregory, November 1, 1913, #54, Sandeen, *Letters*, pp. 165–66.

53. Bourne to Carl Zigrosser, November 16, 1913, #57, Sandeen, *Letters*, p. 175. See also #58, to Zigrosser, November 21, [1913], for the account of the meeting with Wells; transcript Columbia.

54. Bourne to Dorothy Teall, June 14, [1915], #122, Sandeen, *Letters*, p. 303; transcript Columbia.

55. Brooks, *Scenes and Portraits*, pp. 211–12; for the meeting with Lippmann, Wells, Chesterton, see p. 217.

56. Brooks, *The World of H. G. Wells* (New York: Mitchell Kennerley, 1915), pp. 166-69.

57. Bourne to Mary Messer, February 7, 1914; as published in *Twice-a-Year*, 2 (Spring–Summer 1939), 80–81 (omitted from Sandeen, *Letters*, in the absence of positive verification).

58. Bourne to Alyse Gregory, September 8, 1913, #39, Sandeen, *Letters*, p. 132.

59. Brooks, *The Malady of the Ideal* (Philadelphia: University of Pennsylvania Press, 1947), p. 21.

60. Stanley Edgar Hyman, *The Armed Vision* (New York: Alfred A. Knopf, 1948), p. 122, is one who credited the inspiration for *America's Coming-of-Age* to "Bourne's crusading fury." For Brooks's attack on Lee, see his chapter, "Apotheosis of the 'Lowbrow,'"in *America's Coming-of-Age* (New York: B.W. Huebsch, 1915). See also Bourne to Carl Zigrosser, February 18, 1914, #73, Sandeen, *Letters*, p. 222; MS. Pennsylvania. See the repetition from this letter in Bourne's "Our Cultural Humility," *History of a Literary Radical*, p. 42 (first published in *Atlantic Monthly*, 114 [October 1914]). Bligh to Bourne, Dec. 9, 1912, p. 7, referring to Bourne's suggestion.

61. The "slip" along with his praise of James occurs in Bourne to Alyse Gregory, January 5, 1914, #66, Sandeen, *Letters*, p. 199 (italics mine); The reference to James's *Princess Casamassima* in Bourne to Carl Zigrosser, November 3, 1913, #55, Sandeen, *Letters*, p. 168.

62. Bourne to Alyse Gregory, June 14, 1913, #23, Sandeen, *Letters*, p. 89; to Carl Zigrosser, November 16, 1913, #57, Sandeen, *Letters*, p. 175.

63. Bourne to Carl Zigrosser, February 18, 1914, #73, Sandeen, *Letters*, p. 222; to Zigrosser, March 6, [1914], #76, Sandeen, *Letters*, p. 225; Brooks, *Fenollosa*, p. 277.
64. Brooks, *America's Coming-of-Age*, pp. 118–19.
65. Bourne to Alyse Gregory, January 5, 1914, #66, Sandeen, *Letters*, p. 199.
66. Brooks's introduction to *History of a Literary Radical* mistakenly reported their first meeting in November 1914; his essay on Bourne in *Fenollosa* corrected the year to 1915 (p. 308). See Moreau, p. 218, n. 40, who notes the error; and James Hoopes, *Van Wyck Brooks: In Search of American Culture* (Amherst, Mass.: University of Massachusetts Press, 1977), p. 120, who repeats it. See also Bourne's "Our Cultural Humility," in *History of a Literary Radical*, pp. 40–41.
67. "Impressions of Europe 1913–14," in *History of a Literary Radical*, p. 235, 239–41.
68. "Impressions," p. 245.
69. Bourne to Alyse Gregory, November 19, 1916, #181, Sandeen, *Letters*, p. 385.
70. Bourne to Mary Messer, December 28, 1913, in *Twice-a-Year*, 5–6, (Fall–Winter 1940, Spring–Summer 1941), pp. 86-87; omitted from Sandeen, *Letters*, in the absence of verification of the original. With this precautionary note in mind, I nevertheless judge it consistent with Bourne's utterances elsewhere and to other correspondents.
71. Kenniston, *Youth and Dissent*, p. 16; Brooks, "Introduction," *History of a Literary Radical*, pp. xxv–xxvi.
72. "Mon Amie," as published in *History of a Literary Radical*, pp. 66–81.
73. *The Great War and Modern Memory* (New York: Oxford University Press, 1975), pp. 7-8.
74. "Impressions," p. 231.
75. Ibid., p. 232.
76. Fussell, p. 8, quoting from *The Letters of Henry James*, ed. Percy Lubbock, 2 vols (New York: Scribner's, 1920), II, 384.
77. August 25, 1914, #96, Sandeen, *Letters*, p. 266.
78. Bourne to Alyse Gregory, September 28, 1914, #97, Sandeen, *Letters*, p. 276.

Chapter Two

1. *Youth and Life*, p. 166.
2. "Youth," pp. 15–16.
3. Ibid., pp. 7–8.
4. "The Adventure of Life," p. 169.
5. Ibid., p. 171.
6. "Youth," p. 23.

7. "The Life of Irony," pp. 129–30.
8. All from "Youth."
9. "For Radicals," p. 291; "Youth," p. 19.
10. Henry F. May, *The End of American Innocence: A Study of the First Years of Our Own Time 1912–1917* (New York: A.A. Knopf, 1959), p. 14.
11. Francis Greenwood Peabody, "This Younger Generation," *Atlantic Monthly,* 116 (December 1915), 105; *Dial,* 54 (May 16, 1913), 420.
12. Filler, p. 41.
13. May, *End of American Innocence,* p. 28.
14. Bourne, "The Suicide of Criticism," *Columbia Monthly,* 8 (March 1911), 189; Babbitt to Bourne, April 2, 1911, in Bourne Papers, Columbia.
15. "The Experimental Life," p. 227, 243–44.
16. "Virtues and Seasons of Life," pp. 71–73.
17. Ibid., p. 74.
18. May, *End of American Innocence,* p. 29.
19. "Seeing, We See Not," pp. 218–19, 223.
20. "The Adventure of Life," p. 182.
21. *Youth and Life,* p. 356.
22. Kenniston, *Youth and Dissent,* pp. 8–11, 12ff; italics in original.

Chapter Three

1. See his essay, "Emily Dickinson," in *On the Limits of Poetry, Selected Essays: 1928–1948* (New York: Swallow Press & William Morrow & Co., 1948), p. 208 and passim.
2. *America's Coming-of-Age,* p. 161; italics mine.
3. "Reality in America," in *The Liberal Imagination* (New York: Doubleday, 1953), p. 22.
4. "The Life of Irony," in *Youth and Life,* p. 129.
5. Ellen Williams, *Harriet Monroe and the Poetry Renaissance: The First Ten Years of Poetry, 1912–22* (Urbana: University of Illinois Press, 1977), p. 18.
6. In "Life, Art and America," *Seven Arts,* 1 (February 1917), 373.
7. Bourne to Mary Messer, December 28, 1913, in *Twice-a-Year,* 5–6 (Fall–Winter 1940; Spring-Summer 1941), 84; not included in Sandeen, *Letters.*
8. In his review of Mencken's *A Book of Prefaces* (New York: A.A. Knopf, 1917), in *New Republic,* XIII (November 24, 1917), 102-103.
9. Eastman, *Love and Revolution: My Journey Through an Epoch* (New York: Random House, 1964), pp. 12–21.
10. Dell, *Intellectual Vagabondage: An Apology for the Intelligentsia* (New York: George H. Doran, 1926), pp. 113–14; Eastman, *Love and Revolution,* p. 15.

11. Eastman, *Love and Revolution*, p. 22.

12. Years later Beulah Amidon wrote that *she* "never was in love with Randolph," thinking, naively, that his deformity had insulated him from sex (Amidon to Alyse Gregory, October 4, 1948, Bourne Papers, Columbia). Since, as she confessed to Gregory, she destroyed Bourne's letters to her, we have only Bourne's remarks about Amidon to others, notably to Dorothy Teall whose unpublished manuscript on Bourne Amidon called, in 1948, "a very distorted picture," written, she said, with "bitterness"—all of which compounds the usual difficulty of disentangling Bourne's actual state of feeling from his ironies and self-deprecating mockeries and his often ingenuous outbursts of delight or pique with some one of his woman friends. Then too there was Bourne's propensity for idealizing the women he admired, seeing them as symbolic of youth, as when he wrote to Teall of how Amidon "dramatized her whole generation . . . so passionate and yet so intellectual" (Bourne to Teall, [April 29, 1915], #116, Sandeen, *Letters*, (pp. 297–98). For his proposal of marriage to Amidon, see Bourne to Teall, [May 2, 1915], #117, Sandeen, *Letters*, p. 298. See the several letters to Cornell, especially those of December 1916, #185, #186, Sandeen, *Letters*, pp. 388–91. For the Amidon relationship, see Moreau's account, pp. 101–2; on the "free spirit" (probably Lucille Deming) see Carl Zigrosser to Moreau, April 12, 1964 (Bourne Papers, Columbia), ibid., p. 106; on the Cornell courtship, ibid., pp. 195–97.

13. "Youth," in *Youth and Life*, p. 3.

14. Croly to Bourne, June 3, 1914; September 15, 1914; Bourne Papers, Columbia.

15. *Education and Living*, pp. v–vi.

16. Originally anonymous, "The Reply," *New Republic*, 10 (February 10,1917), 46–47; Hamilton, "Interesting Schools," side by side, pp. 45–46.

17. Some professors already had organized. Bourne's essay first appeared in the *New Republic*, 3 (July 17, 1915), 269–70. On January 1–2, 1915, some 650 professors, responding to a call issued in the spring of 1913 by eighteen professors at Johns Hopkins University, Arthur O. Lovejoy a leading figure among them, met and organized the American Association of University Professors and elected John Dewey as its first president.

Chapter Four

1. See Bourne to Elizabeth Shepley Sergeant, June 25, 1915, #124, Sandeen, *Letters*, p. 306; to Alyse Gregory, January 21, 1916, #162, Sandeen, *Letters*, p. 362. For the *New Republic*'s developing "new kind of war" policy, see Charles Forcey, *The Crossroads of Liberalism: Croly, Weyl, Lippmann and the Progressive Era, 1900–1925* (New York: Oxford University Press, 1961), pp. 234–72. ("By the end of 1915, in fact, the *New Republic* men wanted war," p. 242.) See also Bourne to Alyse

Gregory, July 24, 1915, #129, Sandeen, *Letters*, pp. 311–12.

2. Bourne to Alyse Gregory, January 5, 1914, #66, Sandeen, *Letters*, p. 201.

3. See Bourne to John Erskine, April 29, 1916, #166, Sandeen, *Letters*, p. 369.

4. June 25, [1915], #124, Sandeen, *Letters*, p. 305.

5. See #124, to Sergeant; to Sergeant, December 6, 1916, #184, Sandeen, *Letters*, p. 388; to Alyse Gregory, [December 1914?], #102, Sandeen, *Letters*, p. 282; to Simon Pelham Barr, September 13, 1913, #42, Sandeen, *Letters*, p. 138 (about Bligh).

6. Since this was written, "The Architect" has been reprinted in *The Radical Will: Randolph Bourne, Selected Writings, 1911–1918*, ed. Olaf Hansen (New York: Urizen, 1977), pp. 279–81. Hansen has also published, for the first time, some additional "portraits" from among the manuscripts in the Bourne Papers, Columbia, swelling the record further. These should be included, therefore, among Bourne's fictional efforts: "The 'Scientific' Manager," pp. 290–93; "The Artist in Wartime," pp. 408–13; "Suffrage and Josella," pp. 453–56; "'A Little Thing of Brunelleschi's ,'" pp. 528–31 (about another architect friend).

7. To Alyse Gregory, [January 1915?], #103, Sandeen, *Letters*, pp. 283–84. Quotations from the portraits are from those in *History of a Literary Radical*, except where otherwise noted.

8. In a letter among the Bourne Papers, Columbia, one Frances Lundquist acknowledges that "Karen" may have been partly drawn from her, but "I was not the feminist." See Sandeen's note, 4, to #153, *Letters*, p. 340, identifying Lundquist as the source for "Karen." I am indebted to Mr. Sandeen for identifying the woman in the letter to Gregory as "probably Lillian Soskin Rogers" (letter to me, January 11, 1979).

9. Bourne to Gregory, January 13, 1915, #105, Sandeen, *Letters*, pp. 285–86.

10. "The Vampire," *Masses*, 9 (June 1917), 35–36. Bourne does not speak of the relationship as "lesbian," however.

11. *New Republic*, 8 (August 26,1916), 91–92.

12. First published in *New Republic*, 3 (May 22, 1915), 62–64; cited here from *History of a Literary Radical*, pp. 82–90. See Bourne to Dorothy Teall, August 13, 1915, #136, Sandeen, *Letters*, p. 318; and to Carl Zigrosser, September 12, 1915, #144, Sandeen, *Letters*, p. 328.

13. Cited here from *Untimely Papers*, ed. James Oppenheim (New York: Huebsch, 1919), pp. 47-60.

14. Arthur S. Link, *American Epoch: A History of the United States Since the 1890's*, 3 vols. (New York: A.A. Knopf, 1963), I, 192.

15. Kenniston, *Youth and Dissent*, p. 9.

16. Ibid., p. 9. Bourne in "Youth": "It is the glory of the present age that in it one can be young. Our times give no check to the radical tendencies of youth" (*Youth and Life*, p. 25).

17. Essentially he resembles Bourne himself, but Bourne may have drawn upon others of his friends, like Paul Rosenfeld and possibly Roderick Seidenberg, a conscientious objector (see Bourne to Seidenberg, July 12, 1918, #209, Sandeen, *Letters*, p. 418).

18. John Erskine to Bourne, April 28, 1916 (Bourne Papers, Columbia), replying to Bourne's letter of April 25, 1916, #165, Sandeen, *Letters*.

19. Bourne to Erskine, April 29, 1916, #166, Sandeen, *Letters*, pp. 368–69.

20. First published in the *New Republic*, 3 (July 10, 1915), 257–58; here quoted from *History of a Literary Radical*, pp. 96–97.

21. Brooks, "Old America," in *Letters and Leadership* (New York: B.W. Huebsch, 1918), pp. 7–10. ("As a class they seem never to have been young. . . .") See George Santayana's "The Genteel Tradition in American Philosophy," in *Winds of Doctrine* (New York: Scribner's, 1913), pp. 185–215: "America is a young country with an old mentality: . . . it has been a wise child. But a wise child, an old head on young shoulders, always has a comic and an unpromising side." Bourne's sketch tried for the comic side.

22. First published in *New Republic*, 4 (September 4, 1915), 121–23; here quoted from *History of a Literary Radical*, pp. 98–106.

23. By "Juvenis" in *New Republic*, 5 (January 1, 1916), 238–39.

24. I cite from *History of a Literary Radical*, pp. 176– 87.

25. Ibid., pp. 183–84.

26. Ibid., pp. 186–87.

Chapter Five

1. "Outline . . ." in Bourne Papers, Columbia; quoted with permission.

2. From *History of a Literary Radical:* "History of a Literary Radical," pp. 1–30; "Ernest: or Parent for a Day," pp. 140–68 (first published in *Atlantic Monthly,* 116 [September 1915], 385–91); and "Fragment of a Novel," 300–343 (first published in the *Dial*, 68 [January 1920], 1–21).

3. *History of a Literary Radical*, pp. 11–12.

4. Ibid., pp. 25–26.

Chapter Six

1. [Walter Lippmann], editorial, 1 (November 7, 1914), 7; reprinted as "Force and Ideas," in *Walter Lippmann: Early Writings*, ed. Arthur Schlesinger, Jr. (New York: Liveright, 1970), pp. 3–6.

2. "The Price of Radicalism," *New Republic*, 6 (March 11, 1916), 146.

3. Oppenheim, editor's foreward, *Untimely Papers*, p. 7; Phrase and paraphrase from Robert Frost's "A Soldier."

4. Notably by Moreau. Daniel Aaron, reviewing Olaf Hansen's collection, *The Radical Will,* steers by some of the legends but still asserts that "when the United States entered the war, Bourne went into seclusion"— which seems to me an unwarranted inference—and starts his essay review with allusion to Dos Passos' biography of Bourne and Dos Passos' "penchant for martyrs" ("American Prophet," *New York Review of Books,* 25 [November 23, 1978], 36–40).

5. Vincent L. Broderick, "Randolph Bourne" (History Department undergraduate thesis, Princeton University, 1941), p. 2. Broderick's thesis marked the beginning of scholarly inquiry into Bourne's significance.

6. *The End of American Innocence* (New York: A.A. Knopf, 1959), p. 395.

7. Bourne to Alyse Gregory, July 27, [1917], #193, Sandeen, *Letters,* p. 398; and to Agnes de Lima, August 6 [1917], #194, Sandeen, *Letters,* p. 399.

8. Bourne to Alyse Gregory [January 1917], #188, Sandeen, *Letters,* on meeting Eastman and Kallen and the Unitarian minister; to Alyse Gregory, November 10, [1916], #179, Sandeen, *Letters,* on his Harvard visit.

9. "The Tradition of War" (New York, June 1914), pp. 12, 13.

10. Ibid., p. 7.

11. Ibid., p. 14.

12. Ibid., p. 9.

13. "The War and the Intellectuals," in *Untimely Papers,* p. 42.

14. "Tradition of War," p. 11.

15. "Bumptious Psychology," *New Republic,* 1 (November 28, 1914), 26; [a review of Hugo Muensterberg's *The War and America*].

16. "Continental Cultures," *New Republic,* 1 (January 16, 1915), 14–16.

17. "American Use for German Ideals," *New Republic,* 4 (September 4, 1915), 117–19.

18. "Trans-National America," *Atlantic Monthly,* 118 (July 1916), 86–97; here quoted from *History of a Literary Radical,* pp. 266–99.

19. *New Republic,* 7 (July 1, 1916), 217–19.

20. According to Bourne. See his letters to his mother, Sarah Bourne, October 12, 1918, and November 4, 1918, #214, #215, Sandeen, *Letters,* pp. 423–24.

21. See Moreau, p. 198, who betrays some skepticism about the story.

22. See Bourne to Van Wyck Brooks, February 16, 1917, #189, Sandeen, *Letters,* p. 395.

23. As published in *Untimely Papers,* pp. 44, 33, 23, 42.

24. Ibid., p. 108.

25. Ibid., pp. 43–44.

26. Ibid., pp. 45–46.

27. "Twilight of Idols," in ibid., pp. 136–38.
28. "A War Diary," in ibid., p. 96.
29. "Our Awakeners," in *Letters and Leadership*, p. 107.
30. "The Collapse of American Strategy," in *Untimely Papers*, p. 89.
31. "A War Diary," in ibid., p. 99.
32. *Untimely Papers*, pp. 88–89.
33. "A War Diary," in ibid., p. 101.
34. "Twilight of Idols," in ibid., p. 122.
35. Ibid., pp. 118,139.

Chapter Seven

1. "A War Diary," in *Untimely Papers*, p. 106.
2. To Alyse Gregory, September 28, 1914, #97, Sandeen, *Letters*, p. 276; to Brooks, March 27, 1918, #205, Sandeen, *Letters*, p. 414.
3. To Brooks, March 27, 1918, #205, Sandeen, *Letters*, pp. 410–14.
4. "Our Cultural Humility," in *History of a Literary Radical*, pp. 40–43.
5. Brooks, "Toward the Future," in *Letters and Leadership*, pp. 125–28.
6. "The Art of Theodore Dreiser," in *History of a Literary Radical*, p.199; first published in the *Dial*, 62 (June 14, 1917), 507–9. Bourne wrote two other pieces on Dreiser: "Theodore Dreiser," *New Republic*, 2 (April 17, 1915), pt. 2, pp.7–8; and his review of Dreiser's *The "Genius,"* "Desire as Hero," *New Republic*, 5, (November 20, 1915), pt. 2, pp.5–6.
7. Brooks, "Our Critics," in *Letters and Leadership*, p. 63.
8. "History of a Literary Radical," p. 24; p. 22.
9. Ibid., p. 26.
10. Brooks, "Toward the Future," in *Letters and Leadership*, pp. 126–27.
11. "Trans-National America," in *History of a Literary Radical*, p. 284.
12. Cowley, "Van Wyck Brooks: A Career in Retrospect," *Saturday Review of Literature*, May 25, 1963, p. 18; reprinted as the introduction to Brooks, *An Autobiography* (New York: Dutton, 1965), p. xxxiii.
13. To Alyse Gregory, September 28, 1914, #97, Sandeen, *Letters*, p. 276.
14. "Our Cultural Humility," *History of a Literary Radical*, pp. 40, 43.
15. Ibid., p. 40.
16. "Trans-National America," in *History of a Literary Radical*, p. 282.
17. See Philip Gleason, "The Melting-Pot: Symbol of Fusion or Confusion?" *American Quarterly*, 16 (Spring 1964), 20–46.

18. "Trans-National America," pp. 282–83.
19. Ibid., p. 297.
20. Ibid., pp. 283–84.
21. Ibid., p. 271.
22. Ibid., p. 295.
23. "The Jew and Trans-National America," *Menorah Journal*, 2 (December 1916), 277–84; here quoted from its reprinting in *War and the Intellectuals: Essays by Randolph S. Bourne, 1915–1919*, ed. Carl Resek (New York: Harper and Row, 1964), pp. 124–33.
24. Ibid., pp. 125, 128, 132, 129.
25. Ibid., p. 131.
26. "The Art of Theodore Dreiser," in *History of a Literary Radical*, pp. 201–3.
27. To Dreiser, April 19, 1917, #190, Sandeen, *Letters*, pp. 395–96.
28. "The Art of Theodore Dreiser," p. 204.
29. "The American Adventure," *New Republic*, 12 (October 20, 1917), 333–34.
30. "The Art of Theodore Dreiser," p. 201.
31. "The American Adventure," p. 333.
32. "History of a Literary Radical," p. 26 on Amy Lowell; the earlier remark on Lowell in "Traps for the Unwary," *Dial*, 64 (March 28, 1918), 278; on Cather, in "Morals and Art from the West," *Dial*, 65 (December 14, 1918), 557.
33. All quotations in this paragraph, except the allusion to Dreiser and hyphenates among the vers-librists (from "The Art of . . . Dreiser") from Bourne's "An Imagist Novel," *Dial*, 64 (May 9, 1918), 452 (a review of *Honeycomb* by Dorothy M. Richardson).
34. "History of a Literary Radical," pp. 28–29.
35. "An Imagist Novel," p.452.
36. To Van Wyck Brooks, November 12, 1918, #216, Sandeen, *Letters*, pp.424–25; to Sarah Bourne, November 21, 1918, #217, Sandeen, *Letters*, p. 425.
37. To Brooks, November 12, 1918, #216, Sandeen, *Letters*, p.425; "Milan" was a pseudonym of Maurice Larrouy. Bourne's translation was published in 1919 as *Vagabonds of the Sea*.

Selected Bibliography

PRIMARY SOURCES

Since all the books by Bourne are collections of articles and reviews that, for the most part, first appeared in periodicals, I have indicated in parentheses at the end of each item that was subsequently republished an abbreviated title of the collection in which it later appeared. I have listed under a book publication those essays that first appeared therein. The abbreviated titles are as follows:

EL	*Education and Living* (1917)
HLR	*History of a Literary Radical* (1920)
THLR	*The History of a Literary Radical and Other Papers* (1956)
TRW	*The Radical Will: Selected Writings, 1911-1918* (1977)
UP	*Untimely Papers* (1919)
WI	*War and the Intellectuals: Essays, 1915–1919* (1964)
WRB	*The World of Randolph Bourne: An Anthology of Essays and Letters* (1965)
YL	*Youth and Life* (1913)

1. Publications during lifetime

1910

"Some Aspects of Good Talk." *Columbia Monthly,* 7 (January 1910), 92–97.

"Chesterton's "Orthodoxy," *Columbia Monthly,* 7 (March 1910), 170–72.

["Aurelius."] "Prof. Peck's 'Studies." *Columbia Monthly,* 7 (March 1910), 176. Review of *Studies in Several Literatures* by Harry Thurston Peck.

"On Hero-Making." *Columbia Monthly,* 7 (April 1910), 178–81.

"The Function of a College Literary Magazine." *Columbia Monthly,* 8 (November 1910), 3–7.

"The Blue Bird for Happiness," *Columbia Monthly,* 8 (December 1910), 61–64.

1911

"On Playing at Five Hundred." *Columbia Monthly,* 8 (January 1911), 105–10.

["Aurelius Bloomfield."] "The Prayer of a Materialist." *Columbia Monthly,* 8 (February 1911), 165–67.

Review of *Socialism and Christianity* by Percy S. Grant. *Columbia Monthly,* 8 (February 1911), 183–85.

"The Suicide of Criticism." *Columbia Monthly,* 8 (March 1911), 188–92.

Review of *The Social Basis of Religion* by Simon N. Patton. *Columbia Monthly,* 8 (April 1911), 269–70.

Review of *A Defense of Prejudice and Other Essays* by John Grier Hibben. *Columbia Monthly,* 8 (May 1911), 313–15.

"The Two Generations." *Atlantic Monthly,* 108 (May 1911), 591–98 (*YL,* 31–52).

"The Editor on Examinations—with Apologies to F. Bacon." *Columbia Monthly,* 8 (June 1911), 344–46.

"Over the Quadrangle." *Columbia Monthly,* 8 (August 1911), 401–3.

"The Handicapped." *Atlantic Monthly,* 108 (September 1911), 320–29 (*YL,* 339–65; *WRB,* 15–30; *TRW,* 73–87).

"The College: An Undergraduate View." *Atlantic Monthly,* 108 (November 1911), 667–74 (*YL,* 313–36).

Review of *The Mind of Primitive Man* by Franz Boas. *Columbia Monthly,* 9 (November 1911), 31–32.

1912

"A Letter to Mr. John Galsworthy." *Columbia Monthly,* 9 (January 1912), 88–90.

"Individuality and Education." *Columbia Monthly,* 9 (January 1912) 88–90.

"The Mystic Turned Radical." *Atlantic Monthly,* 109 (February 1912), 236–38 (*YL,* 207–13; *TRW,* 174–77).

"Seeing, We See Not." *Columbia Monthly,* 9 (February 1912), 133–36 (*YL,* 217–24).

"Law and Order." *Masses,* 3 (March 1912), 12 (*TRW,* 352–54).

"Youth." *Atlantic Monthly,* 109 (April 1912), 433–41 (*YL,* 3–27; *WRB,* 3–15; *TRW,* 93–105).

"Poker and Veronica." *Columbia Monthly,* 9 (April 1912), 175–79.

"Some Thoughts on Religion." *Columbia Monthly,* 9 (May 1912), 229–32 (*YL,* 191–201).

Review of *The Moral Life* by W. R. Sorley. *Journal of Philosophy, Psychology and Scientific Methods,* 9 (May 9, 1912), 277.

"Student Life." *Columbia University Quarterly,* 14 (June 1912), 341–42.

Review of *Nietzsche* by Paul Elmer More. *Journal of Philosophy, Psychology, and Scientific Methods*, 9 (August 15, 1912), 471–73.
"College Life Today." *North American Review*, 196 (September 12, 1912), 365–72.
Review of *The Desire for Qualities* by Stanley M. Bligh. *Journal of Philosophy, Psychology and Scientific Methods*, 9 (September 12, 1912), 530–31.
"Socialism and the Catholic Ideal," *Columbia Monthly*, 10 (November 1912), 11–19.
"The Excitement of Friendship." *Atlantic Monthly*, 90 (December 1912), 795–800 (*YL*, 135–51; *WRB*, 30–38; *TRW*, 106–14).

1913

"The Social Order in an American Town." *Atlantic Monthly*, 111 (February 1913), 227–36.
"The Life of Irony." *Atlantic Monthly*, 111 (March 1913), 357–67 (*YL*, 101–31; *TRW*, 134–48).
Youth and Life. Boston: Houghton Mifflin Co., [March] 1913; Edinburgh: Constable, [May] 1913. First publication of "The Virtues and the Seasons of Life," pp. 55–98; "The Adventure of Life," pp. 155–88; "The Experimental Life," pp. 227–46 (*TRW*, 149–58); "The Dodging of Pressures," pp. 249–87 (*WRB*, 39–58; *TRW*, 115–33); "For Radicals," pp. 291–310.
"The Next Revolution." *Columbia Monthly*, 10 (May 1913), 221–27.
"The College Lecture Course as the Student Sees It." *Educational Review*, 46 (June 1913), 66–70.
"Stoicism." *The Open Court: A Monthly Magazine*, 27 (June 1913), 364–71.
"Arbitration and International Politics." New York: American Association for International Conciliation, no. 70, September, 1913. A pamphlet.
"Sabotage." *Columbia Monthly*, 10 (November 1913), 1–2 (*TRW*, 90–92). Free-verse poem.
Review of *History as Past Ethics: An Introduction to the History of Morals* by Philip Van Ness Myers. *Journal of Philosophy, Psychology and Scientific Methods*, 10 (November 6, 1913), 641–42.

1914

"In the Mind of the Worker." *Atlantic Monthly*, 113 (March 1914), 375–82.
"An Experiment in Cooperative Living." *Atlantic Monthly*, 113 (June 1914), 813–31.

"The Tradition of War." New York: American Association for International Conciliation, no. 79, June 1914. A pamphlet.

Review of *The Making of Character: Some Educational Aspects of Ethics* by John MacCunn. *Journal of Philosophy, Psychology and Scientific Methods*, 11 (June 4, 1914), 332–33.

"An Hour in Chartres." *Atlantic Monthly*, 114 (August 1914), 214–17.

"Maurice Barres and the Youth of France." *Atlantic Monthly*, 114 (September 1914), 394–99.

"Our Cultural Humility." *Atlantic Monthly*, 114 (October 1914), 503–7 (*HLR*, 31–43).

"Berlin in War Time." *Travel*, 24 (November 1914), 9–12, 58–59.

"In a Schoolroom." *New Republic*, 1 (November 7, 1914), 23–24, (*EL*, 41–48; *WRB*, 61–64; *TRW*, 185–88).

"Holy Poverty." *New Republic*, 1 (November 14, 1914), 25. Review of *The Ragged-Trousered Philanthropists* by Robert Wessall ("The Ragged-Trousered Philanthropists" in *THLR*).

"Maeterlinck and the Unknown." *New Republic*, 1 (November 21, 1914), 26. Review of *The Unknown Guest* by Maurice Maeterlinck and *The New Philosophy of Henri Bergson* by Edouard Le Roy.

"Bumptious Psychology." *New Republic*, 1 (December 5, 1914), 26–27. Review of *The War and America* by Hugo Muensterberg.

"Sincerity in the Making." *New Republic*, 1 (December 5, 1914), 26–27. Review of *The Congo, General William Booth Enters into Heaven* and *Adventures While Preaching the Gospel of Beauty* by Vachel Lindsay.

"Paul Claudel's East." *New Republic*, 1 (December 19, 1914), 26. Review of *The East I Know* by Paul Claudel.

"Town Planning and the Law." *New Republic*, 1 (December 19, 1914), 27–28. Review of *Carrying Out the City Plan* by Flavel Shurtleff.

"A Danish Epic." *New Republic*, 1 (December 19, 1914), 28. Review of *Pelle The Conqueror* by Martin A. Nexö.

"Good People." *New Republic*, 1 (December 26, 1914), 18.

1915

"Puzzle Education." *New Republic*, 1 (January 2, 1915), 10–11 (*EL*, 26–31).

"What Might Be in Education." *New Republic*, 1 (January 2, 1915), 28. Review of *What Is and What Might Be* by Edmond Holmes.

"Continental Cultures." *New Republic*, 1 (January 16, 1915), 14–16.

"The Schools from the Outside." *New Republic*, 1 (January 30, 1915), 10–11 (*EL*, 77–83).

"A Glance at German Culture." *Lippincott's Monthly*, 95 (February 1915), 22–27.

"A Substitute for Schools." *New Republic*, 2 (February 6, 1915), 25–26.

"When We Went to School." *New Republic*, 2 (February 27, 1915), 101–3 (*EL*, "Learning Out of School," pp. 32–40).
"Mon Amie." *Atlantic Monthly*, 115 (March 1915), 354–59 (*HLR*, 66–81; *THLR*, 43–54; *TRW*, 435–42).
"Impressions of Europe, 1913–14." *Columbia University Quarterly*, 17 (March 1915), 109–26 (*HLR*, 230–65; *THLR*, 75–101).
"Class Struggle in Education." *New Republic*, 2 (March 6, 1915), 135. Review of *School Discipline* by William Chandler Bagby.
"John Dewey's Philosophy." *New Republic*, 2 (March 13, 1915), 154–56 (*TRW*, 331–35).
"Schools in Gary." *New Republic*, 2 (March 27, 1915), 198–99.
"Communities for Children." *New Republic*, 2 (April 3, 1915), 233–34 (*EL*, 104–15).
"Really Public Schools." *New Republic*, 2 (April 10, 1915), 259–61 (*EL*, 116–26).
"Theodore Dreiser." *New Republic*, 2 (April 17, 1915), supp. 7–8 (*TRW*, 457–61).
"A Map of the Public." *New Republic*, 2 (April 17, 1915), supp. 11–12. Review of *Problems of Community Life* by Seba Eldridge.
"Apprentices to the School." *New Republic*, 2 (April 24, 1915), 302–3 (*EL*, 136–45).
"The Natural School." *New Republic*, 2 (May 1, 1915), 326–28 (EL, 136–45).
"The School Room." *New Republic*, 2 (May 1, 1915), 333. Review of *School Hygiene* by Leo Burgerstein.
"The Failing Church." *New Republic*, 3 (May 15, 1915), 49. Review of *The Reconstruction of the Church* by Paul Moore Strayer.
"Fergus—A Portrait." *New Republic*, 3 (May 22, 1915), 62–64 (*HLR*, 82–90; *THLR*, 55–61; *TRW*, 448–52).
"The Inside of a Settlement." *New Republic*, 3 (May 29, 1915), 87–89.
"The Wasted Years." *New Republic*, 2 (June 5, 1915), 120–22 (*EL*, 18–25; *TRW*, 189–92).
"Platitude." *New Republic*, 3 (June 19, 1915), 183–84. Review of *Play in Education* by Joseph Lee; *Education Through Play* by Henry S. Curtis.
"The Issue in Vocational Education." *New Republic*, 3 (June 26, 1915), 191–92 (*EL*, "An Issue . . . ," pp. 182–88).
"Our Unplanned Cities." *New Republic*, 3 (June 26, 1915), 202–3. (*THLR* 140–46; *TWR*, 275–78).
"Our Educational Prospect." *New Republic*, 3 (June 26, 1915), 210–11. Review of *Schools of Tomorrow* by John Dewey and Evelyn Dewey.
"The Heart of the People." *New Republic*, 3 (July 3, 1915), 233. Review of movie, *The White Terror* (*WI*, 171–74).
"The Professor." *New Republic*, 3 (July 10, 1915), 257–58 (*HLR*, 91–97; *THLR*, 62–67).

"Educating the Educators." *New Republic*, 3 (July 10, 1915), 263–64. Review of *The Hygiene of the School Child* by Louis M. Terman.
"Who Owns the Universities?" *New Republic*, 3 (July 17, 1915), 269–70 (*EL*, 215–21; *WRB*, 72–75; *TRW*, 216–18).
"A French Glimpse at America." *New Republic*, 3 (July 24, 1915), 318. Review of *America and Her Problems* by Paul H. B. d'Estournelle.
"Studies in Tone Poetry." *New Republic*, 4 (August 7, 1915), 26–27. Review of *Nature in Music* by Lawrence Gilman.
"The Organic School." *New Republic*, 4 (August 21, 1915), 64 (*EL*, 100–103).
"Medievalism in the Colleges." *New Republic*, 4 (August 28, 1915), 87–88 (*EL*, 230–36; *THLR*, 153–58; *WRB*, 64–68).
"Social Workmanship." *New Republic*, 4 (August 28, 1915), 108. Review of *The Field of Social Service*, edited by Philip Davis.
"This Older Generation." *Atlantic Monthly*, 116 (September 1915), 385–91 (*HLR*, 107–27; *THLR*, 294–309, *TRW*, 159–68).
"American Use for German Ideals." *New Republic*, 4 (September 4, 1915), 117–19 (*WI*, 48–52).
["Juvenis."] "One of Our Conquerors." *New Republic*, 4 (September 4, 1915), 121–23 (*HLR*, 98–106; *THLR*, 68–74).
"To Make Undergraduates Think." *New Republic*, 4 (September 4, 1915), 134–35. Review of *College and the Future* by Richard Rice, Jr.
"Mental Unpreparedness." *New Republic*, 4 (September 11, 1915), 143–44.
"What Is Opinion?" *New Republic*, 4 (September 18, 1915), 171–72.
"The Undergraduate." *New Republic*, 4 (September 25, 1915), 197–98 (*EL*, 222–29; *THLR*, 147–52).
"The Fortress of Belief." *New Republic*, 4 (October 16, 1915), 283–84.
"The Democratic School." *New Republic*, 4 (October 23, 1915), 297–99 (*EL*, 146–53; *TRW*, 202–5).
"The Reality of Peace." *New Republic*, 4 (October 30, 1915), 322–23.
"Religion in Public Schools." *New Republic*, 5 (November 13, 1915), 33–34 (in *The Gary Schools*, pp. 160–63).
"Sophronisba." *New Republic*, 5 (November 13, 1915), 41–43 (*HLR*, 57–65).
"Desire as Hero." *New Republic*, 5 (November 20, 1915), supp. 5–6. Review of *The "Genius"* by Theodore Dreiser.
"Anna Howard Shaw." *New Republic*, 5 (November 20, 1915), supp., 22,24. Review of *The Story of a Pioneer* by Anna Howard Shaw.
"American Heights." *New Republic*, 5 (November 20, 1915), supp., 24. Review of *Letters to a Friend* by John Muir.
"What Is College For?" *New Republic*, 5 (December 4, 1915), 127–28. Review of *College Sons and College Fathers* by Henry Seidel Canby; and *Through College on Nothing a Year* by Christian Gauss.

"Diminuendo." *New Republic*, 5 (December 11, 1915), 153–55. Review of *The Song of the Lark* by Willa Cather.

1916

The Gary Schools. Introduction by William Wirt. Boston: Houghton Mifflin Co., 1916.

["Juvenis."] "The Architect." *New Republic*, 5 (January 1, 1916), 222–23 (*TRW*, 279–81).

"The Portland School Survey." *New Republic*, 5 (January 8, 1916), 238–39 (*EL*, 84–90).

"The Cult of the Best." *New Republic*, 5 (January 15, 1916), 275–77 (*EL*, 49–56).

"The School Situation in New York." *New Republic*, 6 (February 5, 1916), 6–8.

"Politics Against the School." *New Republic*, 6 (February 12, 1916), 32–33.

"Real Estate and the City Plan." *New Republic*, 6 (February 19, 1916), 60–61.

"Parents and Children." *New Republic*, 6 (February 19, 1916), 81–82. Review of *How to Know Your Child* by Miriam Finn Scott.

"House Keeping for Men." *Atlantic Monthly*, 117 (March 1916), 430–32.

"Education in Taste." *New Republic*, 6 (March 4, 1916), 122–24 (*EL*, 57–65).

"Education For Work." *New Republic*, 6 (March 11, 1916), 145–46 (*EL*, 197–205).

"The Price of Radicalism." *New Republic*, 6 (March 11, 1916), 161 (*WI*, 139–41). Review of *The Pillar of Fire* by Seymour Deming.

"Smoking." *Atlantic Monthly*, 117 (April 1916), 573–75.

"Paul Elmer More." *New Republic*, 6 (April 1, 1916), 245–47 (*WI*, 165-70; *TRW*, 467–71). Review of *Aristocracy and Justice.*

"The Self-Conscious School." *New Republic*, 6 (April 8, 1916), 260–61 (*EL*, 11–17).

"Learning to Write." *New Republic*, 6 (April 22, 1916), 326. Review of *How the French Boy Learns to Write* by Rollo Walter Brown.

"Organized Labor on Education." *New Republic*, 7 (May 6, 1916), 8–9 (*EL*, 189–196).

"Guiding the City." *New Republic*, 7 (May 13, 1916), 47–48. Review of *City Planning*, edited by John Nolen.

"On Discussion." *New Republic*, 7 (May 27, 1916), 87–89 (*HLR*, *168–75*).

"Continuation Schools." *New Republic*, 6 (June 10, 1916), 143–45 (EL, 206–14).

"The World's Second Worst Failure." *New Republic*, 7 (June 17, 1916), 177–78. Review of *The American College*, a collection of addresses with introduction by William H. Crawford, president of Allegheny College.

"Trans-National America." *Atlantic Monthly,* 118 (July 1916), 86–97 (*HLR,* 266–69; *THLR,* 260–84; *WI,* 107–23; *TRW,* 248–64).

"A Moral Equivalent for Universal Military Service." *New Republic,* 7 (July 1, 1916), 217–19 (*EL,* 66–76; *THLR,*188–96; *WI,* 142–47).

"Training for Public Service." *New Republic,* 7 (July 8, 1916), 140–41.

"The Business Man in Office." *New Republic,* 7 (July 15, 1916), 267–68.

"Very Long and Sunny." *New Republic,* 7 (July 15, 1916), 282–83. Review of *We* by Gerald Stanley Lee.

"Education as Living." *New Republic,* 8 (August 5, 1916), 10–12 (*EL,* 3–10; *WI,* 148–51).

["Max Coe."] "Making One's Contribution." *New Republic,* 8 (August 26, 1916), 91–92.

"The Gary Public Schools." *Scribner's Magazine,* 60 (September 1916), 371–80.

["Max Coe."] "Karen: A Portrait." *New Republic,* 8 (September 23, 1916), 187–88 (*HLR,* 47–56; *TRW,* 443–47).

"Americanism." *New Republic,* 8 (September 23, 1916), 197. Review of *Straight America* by Frances A. Kellor.

[Edited.] *Towards an Enduring Peace: A symposium of Peace Proposals and Programs, 1914-1916.* With an introduction by Franklin N. Giddings. New York: American Association for International Conciliation, [October] 1916.

"Heroics." *New Republic,* 8 (October 7, 1916), 249. Review of *Americanization* by Royal Dixon.

"Perishable Books." *New Republic,* 8 (October 14, 1916), 258–59.

"The Will to Lynch." *New Republic,* 8 (October 14, 1916), 261–62.

"What is Exploitation?" *New Republic,* 9 (November 4, 1916), 12–14 (*THLR,* 178–83; *WI,* 134–38; *TRW,* 285–89).

"The Jew and Trans-National America," *Menorah Journal,* 2 (December 1916), 277–84 (*WI,* 124–33).

"Magic and Scorn." *New Republic,* 9 (December 2, 1916), 130–31. Review of *Industrial Preparedness* by C. E. Knoeppel; and *Inviting War to America* by Allen R. Benson.

"France of Yesterday." *New Republic,* 9 (December 9, 1916), 156, 158. Review of *French Perspectives* by Elizabeth Shepley Sergeant.

"Seeing it Through." *Dial,* 61 (December 28, 1916), 563–65. Review of *Mr. Britling Sees it Through* by H. G. Wells.

1917

"Extending the University." *New Republic,* 9 (January 6, 1917), 259–60.

"Emerald Lake." *New Republic,* 9 (January 6, 1917), 267–68.

"Joseph Fels." *New Republic*, 10 (February 3, 1917), 28–29. Review of *Joseph Fels: His Life-Work* by Mary Fels.

"The Reply." *New Republic*, 10 (February 10, 1917), 46–47 (in part, *EL*, 161–72). Answer to Edith Hamilton, "Interesting Schools."

"A Policy in Vocational Education." *New Republic*, 10 (February 17, 1917), 63-65 (*EL*, 182–88).

"1917—American Rights—1798." *New Republic*, 10 (February 17, 1917), 82. Letter advertisement signed by Bourne, Max Eastman, Amos Pinchot, and others of the "Committee for Democratic Control," in reply to Agnes Repplier and Lyman Abbott, the "American Rights League."

"New Ideals in Business." *Dial*, 62 (February 22, 1917), 133–34. Review of *America and the New Epoch* by Charles P. Steinmetz; and *An Approach to Business Problems* by A. W. Shaw.

"Do the People Want War?" *New Republic*, 10 (March 3, 1917), 145. Advertisement, signed by Bourne and others of the "Committee for Democratic Control."

"The Charm of Distance." *New Republic*, 10 (March 10, 1917), 170–73. Review of *The Emperor of Portugallia* by Selma Lagerlöf.

"A Modern Mind." *Dial*, 62 (March 22, 1917), 239–40. Review of *Social Rule* by Elsie Clews Parsons.

"The Puritan's Will to Power." *Seven Arts*, 1 (April 1917), 631–38 (*HLR*, 176–87; *WI*, 156–61; *TRW*, 301–6).

"American Independence and the War." *Seven Arts*, 1 (April 1917), a nine-page supplement (unsigned).

"A Stronghold of Obscurantism." *Dial*, 62 (April 5, 1917), 303–5. Review of *Problems of Secondary Education* by David Snedden.

"Experimental Education." *New Republic*, 10 (April 21, 1917), 345–47 (*EL*, 91-99; *TRW*, 197–201).

Education and Living. New York: Century Co., 1917. With the addition of a preface, republishes articles from the *New Republic*.

"An Epic of Labor." *New Republic*, 10 (April 21, 1917), supp., 8–10. Review of *Pelle the Conqueror: Daybreak* by Martin Nexö.

"Two Amateur Philosophers." *New Republic*, 10 (April 28, 1917), 383–84. Review, *The Amateur Philosophers* by Carl H. Grabo; and *Philosophy: An Autobiographical Fragment* by Henrie Waste.

"International Dubieties." *Dial*, 62 (May 3, 1917), 387–88 (*WRB*, 207–11). Review of *A League to Enforce Peace* by Robert Goldsmith; and *American World Policies* by Walter E. Weyl.

"A Reverberation of War." *New Republic*, 11 (May 17, 1917), 86–87. Review of *A Soldier of Life* by Hugh de Selincourt.

"Ernest: or Parent for a Day." *Atlantic Monthly*, 119 (June 1917), 778–86 (*HLR*, 140–67; *THLR*, 102–23).

"The War and the Intellectuals." *Seven Arts*, 2 (June 1917), 133–46 (*UP*,

22–46; *THLR*, 205–22; *WI*, 3–14; *TRW*, 307–17).
"The Vampire," *Masses*, 9 (June 1917), 35–36. Review of *Regiment of Women* (a novel) by Clemence Dane.
"The Art of Theodore Dreiser." *Dial*, 62 (June 14, 1917), 507–9 (*HLR*, 195–204; *THLR*, 124–31; *TRW*, 462–66).
"The Immanence of Dostoevsky." *Dial*, 62 (June 28, 1917), 24–25 (*HLR*, 188–94).
"Below the Battle." *Seven Arts*, 2 (July 1917), 270–77 (*UP*, 47–60; *WI*, 15–21).
"The Collapse of American Strategy." *Seven Arts*, 2 (August 1917), 409–24 (*UP*, 61–89; *WI*, 22–35).
"Conspirators." *Seven Arts*, 2 (August 1917), 528–30.
"The Later Feminism." *Dial*, 63 (August 16, 1917), 103–4. Review of *Towards a New Feminism* by William Meikle; and *Motherhood* by C. Gascquoine Hartley.
"Thinking at Seventy-Six." *New Republic*, 12 (August 25, 1917), 111–13. Review of *The New Reservation of Time* by William Jewett Tucker.
"An American Humanist." *Dial*, 63 (August 30, 1917), 148–50. Review of *The Assault on Humanism* by Paul Shorey.
"A War Diary." *Seven Arts*, 2 (September 1917), 535–47 (*UP*, 90–113; *THLR*, 223–40; *WI*, 36–47; *TRW*, 319–30).
"Conscience and Intelligence in War." *Dial*, 63 (September 13, 1917), 193–95 (*THLR*, 197–204; *WRB*, 129–33).
"Twilight of Idols." *Seven Arts*, 2 (October 1917), 688–702 (*UP*, 114–39; *THLR*, 241–59; *WI*, 53–64. *WRB*, 191–203; *TRW*, 336–47).
"The Belgian Carthage." *Dial*, 63 (October 11, 1917), 353–54. Review of *The New Carthage* by Georges Eekhoud.
"Those Columbia Trustees." *New Republic*, 12 (October 20, 1917), 328–29 (*THLR*, 184–87; *WRB*, 76–78).
"The American Adventure." *New Republic*, 12 (October 20, 1917), 333–34 (*TRW*, 532–36). Review of *A Son of the Middle Border* by Hamlin Garland.
"Denatured Nietzsche." *Dial*, 63 (October 25, 1917), 389–91 (*WRB*, 211–14). Review of *The Will to Freedom* by John Neville Figgis.
"Mr. Hillquit for Mayor." *New Republic*, 12 (October 27, 1917), 356–57. Letter signed by Bourne and others.
"Sociologic Fiction." *New Republic*, 12 (October 27, 1917), 359–60 (*WI*, 175–78). Review of *King Coal* by Upton Sinclair.
"Gorky's Youth." *New Republic*, 13 (November 3, 1917), 26–27. (*THLR*, 135–39, "In the World of Maxim Gorky"). Review of *In the World* by Maxim Gorky.
"The Idea of a University." *Dial*, 63 (November 22, 1917), 509–10 (*WI*, 152–55).
"H. L. Mencken." *New Republic*, 13 (November 24, 1917), 102–3 (*WI*,

162–64; *TRW*, 472–74). Review of *A Book of Prefaces* by H. L. Mencken.
"Mr. Huneker's Zoo." *New Republic*, 13 (December 1, 1917), 130–31. Review of *Unicorns* by James Huneker.
"The Industrial Revolution." *Dial*, 63 (December 20, 1917), 642. Review of *The Town Laborer, 1760-1832* by J. L. and Barbara Hammond.

1918

Review of *Applied Psychology* by H. L. Hollingsworth and A. T. Poffenberger. *New Republic*, 13 (January 12, 1918), 323.
"A Primer of Revolutionary Idealism." *Dial*, 64 (January 17, 1918), 69 (*WRB*, 214–16). Review of *Political Ideas* by Bertrand Russell.
Review of *Suggestions of Modern Science Concerning Education*, by H. S. Jennings et al. *New Republic*, 13 (January 19, 1918), 355.
Review of *Housemates* by J. D. Beresford. *New Republic*, 13 (January 26, 1918), 387.
"Americans in the Making." *New Republic*, 14 (February 2, 1918), 30–32. Review of *An American in the Making* by M. E. Ravage; and *The Rise of David Levinsky* by Abraham Cahan.
"Quadrangles Paved With Good Intentions." *Dial*, 64 (February 14, 1918), 121–22. Review of *The Undergraduate and His College* by Frederick P. Keppel.
"The Guild Idyl." *New Republic*, 14 (March 2, 1918), 151–52. Review of *Old Worlds for New* by Arthur J. Penty.
"Adventures in Miniature." *New Republic*, 14 (March 9, 1918), 180–82. Review of *Persian Miniatures* by H. G. Dwight.
"A Vanishing World of Gentility." *Dial*, 64 (March 14, 1918), 234–35 (*TRW*, 537–39). Review of *These Many Years* by Brander Matthews.
"Traps for the Unwary." *Dial*, 64 (March 28, 1918), 277–79 (*WI*, 179–83; *TRW*, 480–84).
"Clipped Wings." *Dial*, 64 (April 11, 1918), 358–59. Review of *The House of Conrad* by Elias Tobenkin.
"The Brevity School in Fiction." *Dial*, 64 (April 25, 1918), 405–7. Review of *On the Stairs* by Henry B. Fuller.
"Making Over the Body." *New Republic*, 15 (May 4, 1918), 28–29. Review of *Man's Supreme Inheritance* by F. Matthias Alexander.
"An Imagist Novel." *Dial*, 64 (May 9, 1918), 451–52 (*WRB*, 216–19). Review of *Honeycomb* by Dorothy M. Richardson.
"Our Enemy Speaks." *Dial*, 64 (May 23, 1918), 486–87. Review of *Men in War* by Adele Seltzer.
"Other Messiahs." *New Republic*, 15 (May 25, 1918) 117. Letter.
"The Cult of Convention." *Liberator*, 1 (June 1918), 38–39. Review of *On Contemporary Literature* by Stuart P. Sherman.

"Purpose and Flippancy." *Dial*, 64 (June 6, 1918), 540–41. Review of *His Second Wife* by Ernest Poole; and *The Boardman Family* by Mary S. Watts.

"Oxford Ideas." *New Republic*, 15 (June 15, 1918), 214. Review of *The Oxford Stamp* by Frank Aydelotte.

"Mr. Bennett is Disturbed." *Dial*, 65 (July 18, 1918), 72. Review of *The Pretty Lady* by Arnold Bennett.

"The Retort Courteous." *Poetry*, 12 (September 1918), 341–44. Letter, with Van Wyck Brooks, replying to Harriet Monroe's criticism of Bourne's "Traps for the Unwary."

"Two Scandinavian Novelists." *Dial*, 65 (September 5, 1918), 167–68. Review of *The Holy City* by Selma Lagerlöf; and *Marie Grubbe* by Jens Peter Jacobsen.

"The Relegation of God." *Dial*, 65 (September 19, 1918), 215–16 (*WRB*, 219–22). Review of *Joan and Peter* by H. G. Wells.

"Dostoyevsky's Stories." *New Republic*, 16 (September 28, 1918), 267. Review of *The Gambler* by F. Dostoyevsky.

"The Morality of Sacrifice." *Dial*, 65 (October 19, 1918), 309–10. Review of *Three French Moralists* by Edmund Gosse.

"From an Older Time." *Dial*, 65 (November 2, 1918), 363–65 (*TRW*, 475–79). Review of *Lovers of Louisiana* by George Washington Cable.

"The Light Essay." *Dial*, 65 (November 16, 1918), 419–20 (*TRW*, 506–10). Review of *Walking Stick Papers* by Robert Cortes Holliday; and *The Merry-Go-Round* by Carl Van Vechten.

"A Mirror of the Middle West." *Dial*, 65 (November 30, 1918), 480–82 (*HLR*, 128–39; *THLR*, 285–93; *TRW*, 265–70). Review of *The Valley of Democracy* by Meredith Nicholson.

"Morals and Art From the West." *Dial*, 65 (December 14, 1918), 556–57 (*WRB*, 222–26). Review of *In the Heart of a Fool* by William Allen White; and *My Ántonia* by Willa Cather.

"An Examination of Eminences." *Dial*, 65 (December 28, 1918), 603–4 (*TRW*, 489–93). Review of *Eminent Victorians* by Lytton Strachey.

2. Posthumous publications

Untimely Papers. Edited with foreward by James Oppenheim. New York: B. W. Huebsch, 1919. Five essays from the *Seven Arts:* "The War and the Intellectuals," "Below the Battle," "The Collapse of American Strategy," "A War Diary," and "Twilight of Idols." Two fragments newly published: "Old Tyrannies" (*WRB*, 286–90; *TRW*, 169–73); "Unfinished Fragment on the State" (in corrected sequence as "The State," in *WI*, 65–104; similar sequence with textual corrections in *WRB*, 243–85, and this latter followed in *TRW*, 355–95).

"History of a Literary Radical." *Yale Review*, 8 (April 1919), 468–84 (*HLR*, 1-30; *THLR*, 21–42; *WI*, 184–97; *WRB*, 229–43; *TRW*, 423–34).

Translation. *Vagabonds of the Sea* by Maurice Larrouy. New York: E. P. Dutton, 1919.

"An Autobiographic Chapter." *Dial*, 68 (January 1920), 1–21 (as "Fragment of a Novel," in *HLR*, 300–343).

History of a Literary Radical and Other Essays. Edited with introduction by Van Wyck Brooks. New York: B. W. Huebsch, 1920. "The Uses of Infallibility," pp. 205–29, first published here (and in *THLR* 159–77; *TRW*, 494–505).

The History of a Literary Radical and Other Papers. Introduction by Van Wyck Brooks. New York: S. A. Russell, 1956. Though retaining the Brooks introduction to the 1920 *HLR*, this is a very different collection, omitting seven essays that Brooks had included, and adding twelve others.

War and the Intellectuals: Essays by Randolph S. Bourne, 1915-1919. Edited with introduction by Carl Resek. New York: Harper and Row, 1964.

The World of Randolph Bourne: An Anthology of Essays and Letters. Edited with introduction by Lillian Schlissel. New York: E. P. Dutton & Co., 1965.

The Radical Will: Randolph Bourne, Selected Writings, 1911-1918. Edited with introduction by Olaf Hansen, preface by Christopher Lasch. New York: Urizen Books, 1977. First publication from manuscripts in Columbia University's Bourne collection: "The Doctrine of the Rights of Man as Formulated by Thomas Paine," "The 'Scientific' Manager," "Practice vs. Product," "The Disillusionment," "The Artist in Wartime," "Suffrage and Josella," "Chivalry and Sin," "Pageantry and Social Art," "A Sociological Poet," "A Little Thing of Brunelleschi's," and "The Night Court."

3. Published letters

"Randolph Bourne: A Letter to Van Wyck Brooks." *Twice-a-Year*, no. 1 (Fall–Winter 1938), 50–55.

"Randolph Bourne: Some Pre-War Letters (1912–1914)." *Twice-a-Year*, no. 2 (Spring–Summer 1939), 79–102. Thirteen letters, not all complete.

"Randolph Bourne: Letters (1913–1914)." *Twice-a-Year*, nos. 5–6 (Fall–Winter 1940; Spring–Summer 1941), 79–88; and "Randolph Bourne: Diary for 1901," 89–98. Nine letters, not all complete.

"Randolph Bourne: Letters (1913–1916)." *Twice-a-Year*, no. 7 (Fall–Winter 1941), 76–90. Ten letters, whole or in part.

"Letters, 1912–1918." In *The World of Randolph Bourne*, edited by Lillian Schlissel, pp. 293–326. New York: E. P. Dutton & Co., 1965. Eighteen letters, and excerpts.

The Letters of Randolph Bourne: A Comprehensive Edition. Edited with commentary by Eric John Sandeen. Troy, N.Y.: Whitston Publishing Co., 1981. Over 200 letters, the source cited in this study.

4. Bibliographies

No one bibliography or checklist of Bourne's writings in print can presume to be complete—including this one—since some unsigned contributions may yet be identified and verified as his. Excepting only some letters to the editor, travel pieces, and miscellaneous contributions to his hometown newspaper, the Bloomfield (N.J.) *Citizen*, 1903–19, I have tried to include everything that can with some certainty be attributed to his hand. Though I believe this list is the most inclusive and reliable to date, the interested student of Bourne may want to check my listings against the following:

HANSEN, OLAF. ed. *The Radical Will.* New York: Urizen Books, 1977. Pp. 541–45. Listings by magazine contributions.

HARRIS MARK. "Randolph Bourne: A Study in Immiscibility." Ph.D. dissertation, University of Minnesota, 1956. "Bibliography," Pp. 238–62. Many omissions, but lists letters as well.

MOREAU, JOHN ADAM. "Randolph Bourne: A Biography." Ph.D. dissertation, University of Virginia, 1964. "Selected Bibliography," pp. 333–43. Unfortunately, not included in Moreau's published book, *Randolph Bourne: Legend and Reality.*

SCHLISSEL, LILLIAN. ed. *The World of Randolph Bourne.* New York: E. P. Dutton & Co., 1965. pp. 327–33. Listings by magazine contributions.

TRUE, MICHAEL T. "The Achievement of an American Literary Radical: A Bibliography of Randolph Silliman Bourne (1889–1918)." *Bulletin of the New York Public Library,* 69 (October 1965), 523–36. Chronological listing. Cites reprintings of Bourne's essays in other collections than his own.

SECONDARY SOURCES

1. Works wholly about Bourne

BRODERICK, VINCENT. "Randolph Bourne." History Department thesis, Princeton University, 1941. Marks the beginning of scholarly inquiry by a later generation than that of Bourne's contemporaries and of a generation also confronting the issue of war. Insists, however, that

Bourne be understood in the context of his own times, and seeks to cut through the veil of mythology around him. A first-rate pioneering essay.

FILLER, LOUIS. *Randolph Bourne*. Washington, D.C.: American Council on Public Affairs, 1943. Introduction by Max Lerner. The first published full-length study; emphasizes Bourne's political dissent.

MOREAU, JOHN ADAM. *Randolph Bourne—Legend and Reality.* Washington, D.C.: Public Affairs Press, 1966. Most thorough biography to date, dispassionately objective in sifting facts from legend, but finally labeling Bourne "a casualty of his time."

PAUL, SHERMAN. *Randolph Bourne.* University of Minnesota Pamphlets on American Writers. Minneapolis: University of Minnesota, 1966. Brief (46 pages) but excellent, succinct setting of Bourne in an American literary tradition with Thoreau, Whitman, Mark Twain.

2. Books with sections or chapters on Bourne

BROOKS, VAN WYCK. "Introduction." In *History of a Literary Radical and other Essays.* New York: B. W. Huebsch, 1920. Pp. ix–xxxv. Reprinted in Brooks, *Emerson and Others* (New York: E. P. Dutton, 1927), and in *The History of a Literary Radical and Other Papers* (New York: S. A. Russell, 1956). The definitive portrait for Bourne's contemporaries, elegiac and mythmaking.

________"The Younger Generation of 1915." In *The Confident Years: 1885–1915.* New York: E. P. Dutton & Co., 1952. Pp. 491–512. Bourne as a spokesman for youth and a "federation of cultures."

________"Randolph Bourne." In *Fenollosa and His Circle: With Other Essays in Biography.* New York: E. P. Dutton & Co., 1962. Pp. 259–321. A much less passionate estimate than the 1920 essay.

DREISER, THEODORE. "Appearance and Reality." In *The American Spectator Year Book.* New York: Frederick A. Stokes Co., 1934. Pp. 204–9. Impressionistic reminiscence and tribute to "a major mind."

FRANK, WALDO. *Our America.* New York: Boni & Liveright, 1919. Tribute to the liberating influence of Brooks and Bourne.

HANSEN, OLAF. "Affinity and Ambivalence." In *Randolph Bourne: The Radical Will: Selected Writings, 1911–1918.* Edited by Hansen, preface by Christopher Lasch. New York: Urizen Books, 1977. Pp. 17–62. This, with four additional prefatory commentaries ("Youth and Life: In Search of a Radical Metaphor," Pp. 65–71; "Education & Politics," Pp. 179–83; "Politics, State & Society," Pp. 225–31; and "Portraits, Criticisms and the Art of Reviewing," Pp. 415–20) makes for another small book. Wide-ranging, stresses Bourne's power for critical analysis as it is combined with skillful evocation of metaphor and symbol, deriving as much from his experience as from books.

LASCH, CHRISTOPHER. "Randolph Bourne and the Experimental Life." In

The New Radicalism in America, 1889–1963: The Intellectual as a Social Type. New York: Vintage Books, Random House, 1967. Pp. 69–103. Bourne's radicalism not political so much as cultural.

LERNER, MAX. "Randolph Bourne and Two Generations." In *Ideas for the Ice Age*. New York: Viking Press, 1941. Pp. 116–42. First published in *Twice-a-Year*, nos. 5–6 (Fall–Winter 1940; Spring–Summer 1941), 54–78. A good summation of Bourne's intellectual development, focusing finally on the war essays and "The State," less to test their validity for Bourne's generation than for the dilemmas of 1941.

RESEK, CARL. "Introduction." In *Randolph S. Bourne: War and the Intellectuals*. New York: Harper Torchbook, Harper and Row, 1964. Pp. vii–xv. Challenges some of the legend but sees it as "an essential part of the intellectual history of the nineteen twenties."

ROSENFELD, PAUL. "Randolph Bourne." In *Port of New York: Essays on Fourteen American Moderns*. New York: Harcourt, Brace, 1924. Pp. 211–36. First published in the *Dial*, 75 (December 1923). By a friend and associate, a tribute to Bourne's talismanic role as "artist-fighter" and martyr.

3. Books giving significant attention to Bourne within a wider frame of

AARON, DANIEL. *Writers on the Left*. New York: Harcourt, Brace & World, 1961. Bourne as one of four radicals (with Max Eastman, Floyd Dell, John Reed), and his "resurrection" in the late 1930s.

GILBERT, JAMES BURKHART. *Writers and Partisans: A History of Literary Radicalism in America*. New York: John Wiley & Sons, 1968. Bourne effectively joined an awareness of politics to the idea of cultural revival. Links 1910s with the 1930s.

KAZIN, ALFRED. *On Native Grounds*. New York: Harcourt, Brace, 1942. "Bourne must always seem less a writer than an incarnation of his time." Many references throughout.

MAY, HENRY F. *The End of American Innocence: The First Years of Our Own Time, 1912–1917*. New York: Alfred A. Knopf, 1959. Essential for an understanding of the intellectual and cultural milieu within which Bourne thrived, acting and reacting. Bourne assigned a prominent role.

SPILLER, ROBERT E. "The Battle of the Books." In *The Literary History of the United States*, edited by Spiller et al., II,1135–56. New York: Macmillan, 1948. The literary radicals versus the neo-humanists.

TRACHTENBERG, ALAN. "Introduction: The Genteel Tradition and Its Critics." In *Critics of Culture: Literature and Society in the Early Twentieth Century*, edited by Trachtenberg, Pp. 3–13. New York: John Wiley & Sons, 1976. While generalizing about the group of critics represented in this anthology, Bourne among them, one of the best definitions of the role Bourne helped develop—that of the independent literary-social critic.

VITELLI, JAMES R. *Van Wyck Brooks*. Twayne Publishers, 1969. For the influence of Bourne on Brooks, their relationship with the *Seven Arts*.

WASSERSTROM, WILLIAM. *The Time of the Dial*. Syracuse: Syracuse University Press, 1963. Bourne judged the chief inspiration of the reconstructed *Dial* under Scofield Thayer.

WERTHEIM, ARTHUR FRANK. *The New York Little Renaissance: Iconoclasm, Modernism, and Nationalism in American Culture, 1908–1917*. New York: New York University Press, 1976. Survey of the literary and artistic scene, covering the cultural nationalists of the *Seven Arts* and the *New Republic*. Concludes that Bourne still remains "the legendary prewar crusader" created by his friends.

4. Memoirs, Fiction, Verse

BROOKS, VAN WYCK. *An Autobiography*. New York: E. P. Dutton & Co., 1965.

CHAMBERLAIN, JOHN. *Farewell to Reform*. New York: Liveright, 1932.

DELL, FLOYD. *Homecoming*. New York: Farrar & Rinehart, 1933.

DEUTSCH, BABBETTE. *A Brittle Heaven*. New York: Greenberg Publishers, 1926. "Mark Gideon," character in this novel, seems derived from Bourne.

DOS PASSOS, JOHN. "Randolph Bourne." In *U.S.A.* New York: Random House, Modern Library, 1937.

EASTMAN, MAX. *Love and Revolution: My Journey Through an Epoch*. New York: Random House, 1964.

FRANK, WALDO. *Memoirs of Waldo Frank*. Edited by Alan Trachtenberg, with introduction by Lewis Mumford. Amherst: University of Massachusetts Press 1973.

FREEMAN, JOSEPH. *An American Testament: A Narrative of Rebels and Romantics*. New York: Farrar and Rinehart, 1936.

GREGORY, HORACE. "Salvos For Randolph Bourne." In *Selected Poems of Horace Gregory*. New York: Viking Press, 1951.

OPPENHEIM, JAMES. "Randolph Bourne: Died December 22 [*sic*], 1918." *Dial*, 66 (January 11, 1919), 7. Same title, but a different set of verses in the *Liberator*, 1 (February 1919), 14–15. Only part of the *Dial* poem was used as preface to Brooks's *History of a Literary Radical (1920)*. The title poem is included in Oppenheim's *The Solitary* (New York: B. W. Huebsch, 1919).

5. Articles

BERINGAUSE, A. F. "The Double Martyrdom of Randolph Bourne." *Journal of the History of Ideas*, 18 (October 1957), 594–603.

BOURKE, PAUL F. "The Status of Politics 1909–1919: *The New Republic*, Randolph Bourne and Van Wyck Brooks." *Journal of American Studies*, 8 (August 1974), 171–202.

CANTOR, MILTON. "The Radical Confrontation with Foreign Policy: War and Revolution, 1914–1920." In *Dissent: Explorations in the History of American Radicalism*, edited by Alfred F. Young. DeKalb: Northern Illinois University Press, 1968.

CHATFIELD, CHARLES. "World War I and the Liberal Pacifist in the U.S." *American Historical Review*, 75 (December 1970), 1920–37.

CURTIS, TOM. "Bourne, [Dwight] Macdonald, [Noam] Chomsky, and the Rhetoric of Resistance." *The Antioch Review*, 29 (Summer 1969), 245–52.

DOWELL, PETER W. "Van Wyck Brooks and the Progressive Frame of Mind." *Midcontinent American Studies Journal*, 11 (Spring 1970), 30–44.

FILLER, LOUIS. "Randolph Bourne: Reality and Myth." *The Humanist*, 10 (September–October 1950), 198–202.

GLEASON, PHILIP. "The Melting Pot: Symbol of Fusion or Confusion." *American Quarterly*, 16 (Spring 1964), 20–46.

LASKI, HAROLD. "The Liberalism of Randolph Bourne." *Freeman, 1* (May 19, 1920), 237.

LEVINE, DANIEL. "Randolph Bourne, John Dewey and the Legacy of Liberalism." *The Antioch Review*, 29 (Summer 1969), 234–44.

MACDONALD, DWIGHT. "War and the Intellectuals: Act II." *Partisan Review*, 6 (Spring 1939), 3–20.

________"Randolph Bourne." *Politics*, 1 (March 1944), 35–36.

MONROE, HARRIET. "Mr. Bourne on Traps." *Poetry*, 12 (May 1918), 91–94.

MUMFORD, LEWIS. "The Image of Randolph Bourne." *New Republic*, 64 (September 24, 1930), 151–52.

OPPENHEIM, JAMES. "The Story of the Seven Arts." *American Mercury*, 20 (June 1930), 156–64.

SILLEN, SAMUEL. "The Challenge of Randolph Bourne." *Masses and Mainstream*, 6 (December 1953), 24–32.

TEALL, DOROTHY. "Bourne into Myth." *Bookman*, 75 (October 1932), 590–99.

Index

WITHDRAWN